EDWARD ARDIZZONE

sitting on the garden wall,
thinking and thinking, whom
should she see trudging along
the road but a small boy of
about her own age? He was
carrying a bundle and a stick.

Frontispiece: The arrival of Ardizzone's child hero Little Tim
from *Tim and Lucy go to Sea* (1938 item 7, reduced)

EDWARD ARDIZZONE

A Bibliographic Commentary

By BRIAN ALDERSON

PRIVATE LIBRARIES ASSOCIATION

THE BRITISH LIBRARY

OAK KNOLL PRESS

2003

ISBN 1 900002 47 6 (PLA); ISBN 0 7123 4759 3 (BL)
ISBN 1 58456 103 3 (OKP)

A CIP catalogue record for this book is available
from the British Library and the Library of Congress

Designed, typeset and indexed by Paul W. Nash

Published by the Private Libraries Association,
Ravelston, South View Road, Pinner,
Middlesex HA5 3YD, England

The British Library, 96 Euston Road,
London NW1 2DB, England

Oak Knoll Press, 310 Delaware Street,
New Castle, Delaware 19720, U.S.A.

Printed in Great Britain by Butler and Tanner
1003795597

Dedicated to
CHRISTIANNA
(aka Lucy Brown)
with love and gratitude

Half-title: Title-page vignette from *The London Magazine* (1954 item C26)
Overleaf: Title-page vignette from *Home from Sea* ([1970] item 150)

CONTENTS

PREFACE

O N T H E sixteenth of October 1970, journeying with the century, Edward Ardizzone celebrated his seventieth birthday. To mark the occasion David Chambers and I had planned to publish in *The Private Library* a brief descriptive listing of his work as a book illustrator. I was much helped in this by visits to the artist himself (whose hospitality extended to liberal pourings of Johnnie Walker Black Label and, at lunch, a Chilean cabernet which he'd recently discovered); but, possibly because of this hospitality, and, more probably, because of my disorderly methods of proceeding, the *Hand-list* of his work for the period 1929 to 1970 did not appear until the Spring 1972 number of the journal.

Despite what I now see to be its shortcomings, the *Hand-list* was kindly received and David and I discussed publishing a supplement to cover Ted's subsequent illustrations. This however was delayed, first by the artist's continued productivity (he was working on *Ardizzone's English Fairy Tales* almost up to his death on the eighth of November 1979), and second by a decision to expand the treatment of his work and to publish a complete study as part of the Private Library Association's 'members' book' sequence. What could be better timing for such a publication than the year marking the centenary of the artist's birth, and what could be more appropriate than my once again failing to meet my deadline? I hope that fellow members of the P.L.A. will forgive the delay in completing this second survey.

The additions, expansions and corrections that I have incorporated in this extended treatment of Ted's graphic work are explained in the following Introduction, which seeks also to offer a (surely redundant) appraisal of his undemonstrative, loveable art. Tracking down details of both the printed *oeuvre* and its original artwork has inevitably proved diffi-cult – bibliographical techniques applied to modern book illustration are not much further advanced than when I wrote about them in 1972 – but I have been helped immeasurably by Christianna Clemence, the artist's daughter. She has allowed me further access to the family collection of

Ted's own copies of his books and, indeed, has provided me with lodgings for much of the time that I worked on the material in London. And with a selflessness bordering on the saintly she has transferred the crabbed handwriting which is my chosen medium of expression to disks from which the present pages have been set. David Chambers has worked closely with both of us as an adviser on the planning of the book and Paul Nash, as its designer and compiler of the index, has seen the whole project through to fulfilment. Both these gallant gentlemen have proved a benign influence, always ready to calm their harassed author in times of crisis and despair.

Thanks are also due to the many friends, collectors, booksellers, librarians listed below, or noted under individual items, who have given me assistance in pursuing material and in attempting to frame an adequate descriptive structure for the catalogue of works. Geoff Green has shown an almost paternal interest in my efforts to hunt out the more obscure Ardizzoniana and has been indefatigable in sending me not merely references but photocopies from the ephemera and periodicals in his own collection. Similarly, Nial and Margaret Devitt have gone beyond their professional role as booksellers to advise me of refinements needed in the present book and to commend to me oddities that I would never have otherwise found. Their own three specialist Ardizzone catalogues almost amount to a preliminary study for what is here. And Nicholas Ardizzone, the artist's younger son, has not only allowed me to delve among work in his own collection, but has been (however unintentionally) a great help through his own bibliographical endeavours. His doctoral thesis at the Imperial War Museum documents in detail his father's work as an Official War Artist, while his catalogue of Ardizzone prints, compiled and published almost in parallel with the present book, has disburdened me of the need to devote a section here to that very tricky subject. I do however give a note on page 253 below to indicate the role of print-making in Ardizzone's career as a graphic artist and to mention points where I have duplicated a Nicholas Ardizzone reference.

To these, and to the following, my deepest gratitude is due, but, lacking as I do the ruthless tenacity of 'the born bibliographer', I must claim responsibility for the errors and omissions that will continue to be found: Patrick Ashton, Iain Bain, Geoffrey and Geraldine Beare, Ian Beck, John Bell, Ulla Bergstrand, Quentin Blake, the late Barry Bloomfield, Mike Bott, Laura Cecil, Margaret Clark, Vera Coleman, the late James Davis, Pat Garrett, Greg Gillert, Anne Harvey, Jean Hedger,

Jim Helliwell, the late Grace Hogarth, Antony Kamm, Peter Newbolt, Rosemary Poole, Margarita Reeve, Hidekazu Sato, Pat Schaefer, Terry Sole, Judy Taylor, Margaret Weedon, Colin White, and also Marie Frederiksen, Anne Kristin Lande and Cecilia Östlund, librarians at the Children's Book Institutes of, respectively, Denmark, Norway and Sweden; Dee Jones, Curator of the de Grummond Collection of the University of Southern Mississippi; Dr. Martin Maw and the Delegates of the Oxford University Press for access to the Press's archive; Dr Sally White, Principal Curator of the Worthing Museum & Art Gallery; Tim Wilson, Keeper of Western Art, Ashmolean Museum, Oxford and the staffs of the British Library, the London Library and the National Art Library, Victoria & Albert Museum.

Finally I must thank, first, Chris Casson (although I have not been able to substantiate his allegations of a Chinese edition of *Baggage to the Enemy* and an Algerian one of *Mrs Malone*) and second, my wife Valerie, whose help on investigative forays has been invaluable, and whose demeanour towards Ardizzoniana scattered throughout the house has shown a forbearance hoped for by all private librarians.

A NOTE ON THE ILLUSTRATIONS

The illustrations in this bibliography have mostly been taken from material (including photocopies) in my own collection of Ardizzone's work. The exceptions are as follows: colour plates I and III and the illustration on page [140] were supplied by Nicholas Ardizzone; colour plate II came from the Victoria and Albert Museum Picture Library; images on pages [71] and [233] came from Christianna Clemence; those on pages [75] and [113] came from the Ashmolean Museum; and those on pages 94 and 101 from Geoff Green. I am most grateful to those named for allowing me to reproduce items in their hands, and to Edward Ardizzone's estate for permission to reproduce copyright material. Special thanks are due to R. Guy Powell for generously funding the colour reproduction of the frontispiece to the volume.

Saturday
rain.

Wind and then

INTRODUCTION

SITTING on the floor in the studio at Elgin Avenue, sorting out
ephemeral works on such matters as old tweed jackets and Blumenthal's bubbly, I had a worm's eye view of the Master at work. He sat
at his drawing-board in the bay window, serenely penning his illustrations
to fit his text-plan for that 'doom-laden book' *Tim's Last Voyage*.

The significance of the two levels remains with me now. While in those
far-off days I had a sight more hair than the 'old, learned, respectable bald
heads' who figured in Yeats's poem about the exegesis of Catullus, my
shuffling and coughing in ink was not much different from theirs then and
is even more pronounced and asthmatic now. To so many people who
knew him, Ted Ardizzone was the equable, companionable figure, benignly
presiding over many of the works listed here – unflustered by, but by no
means uncaring about, setbacks whether on the Pas de Calais in 1940 or
upstream on the Thames in a damp boat some time later. And his work
reflects such a temperament ('Arcadian' said Quentin Blake at the opening
of the 'Running Away to Sea' exhibition at Camberwell in 1999). Why
should such genial and life-enhancing artistry be subject to the measure-
ments and tabulations of which this volume is largely composed?

Searching for a more objective answer to that question than a simple
'because I wanted to do it', the word 'helpfulness' comes to mind. For fifty
years this great illustrator toiled away at his drawing-board or over the
lithographic stones, or in his by no means sketchy sketch-books – drawing for
the fun of drawing, drawing to keep the reflexes working properly, drawing to meet the demands of a wide range of requests and commissions. Thus
it seems that it may be helpful to everyone who loves, admires, reveres his
work to have a fairly systematic tally of its quantity and of its variety. And
perhaps too it may be helpful to the artist himself – or his substantial shade
– to delineate in some detail that large part of his life that was devoted to
book illustration and to show something of the techniques and strategies
that he called upon to keep the worst of the weather outside the boat.

At a rough count (but excluding dozens, if not hundreds, of drawings
done for periodicals) the individual drawings in line or colour listed here

11

Opposite: Page from *The Saturday Book* (1951 item A12, margins reduced)

amount to over five thousand. The most prodigious effort was the very first commission: the 153 pen drawings for *In a Glass Darkly*; the most prolific period was the decade from 1958–1967 when he illustrated or contributed to more than eighty books; and the range of subjects which he tackled and the target audiences for his work were wider and more diverse than is generally acknowledged. 'Little Tim' or the war drawings, or pubs (an illustrator of genius for 'drunks and men leaning against bars' said David Garnett in 1944) were the foundations of his success and are still perhaps most remarked upon, but of the fifty-odd books that he illustrated primarily for adult readers the most numerous are the sixteen for (mostly classic) fiction, and the most joyous are his celebrations, along with Maurice Gorham and G. W. Stonier, of a London scene now submerged under fumes and monstrosities.

As for the children's books – aside from the picture stories where he illustrates his own narrative, the overwhelming number are the pen-drawn accompaniments for fictions or for collections of short stories, most notably by his friends Eleanor Farjeon and James Reeves; but these subsist alongside a dozen or so classic texts and a run of sensitively illustrated collections of poetry. (I have indulged myself by expanding on these matters with two *pièces justificatives* on *Peacock Pie* and *Peter Pan* in Appendices III and IV.) Nor should 'Little Tim' be seen as the be-all and end-all of his picture books. Paul and Nicholas and Johnny and Diana and Peter the Wanderer may be lesser relatives of Tim, but the books in which they appear are no less successful, while Ardizzone's skills as a picture-book craftsman are found in collaborations over a couple of dozen texts by other writers, ranging in complexity from the demy quarto *Titus in Trouble* with James Reeves to the little oblong octavo *Muffletumps* with Jan Wahl.

Some of this huge output has been regularly reprinted. As I write, the planned re-origination of the 'Tim' series direct from Ardizzone's artwork is well advanced, although he would surely wish that the reproduction of his pen drawings from other continuing titles such as *Minnow on the Say* or *Stig of the Dump* or the Trollope novels might be carried out with equal care. But it is reasonable to assume that much else has gone for good and, indeed, that the circumstances for successfully reviving the drawings done on the stone, as distinct from paper, must hinge on digital technology as well as on perceptions of a suitable market.

As the owners of private libraries and the enthusiasts for book illustration will recognise however, 'the market' is a fickle thing of little relevance to the value of Ardizzone's *oeuvre* seen in its entirety. 'One does an awful lot of bad work' he murmured to me, while I was sitting on the floor, echoing something of his dismissive, but amused, remark about himself in his article on 'Paying the Artist' in *The Author* in 1967: 'Old hacks will work at speed, dashing off two or three drawings a day, based on old clichés, in order to make the job a viable one. I must confess I am something of an old hack myself. The result of course … is deplorable'. But that very admission emphasises a fact which has never been far from my thoughts in compiling this catalogue: that it is not so much a record of artistic achievement (although it is that) as of sustained professionalism in a craft. Ardizzone loved illustrating, but he illustrated to live, and the mingled succession revealed here of commissions and creative inventions gives an insight not just into the demands made on a professional illustrator but also into the far from deplorable dedication that he brought to every job. He always insisted on careful readings of the text to be illustrated, believing that illustrators were artists whose 'creative imagination tends to be stimulated by ideas and stories rather than by things seen' (*Ark* 11; p. 278 below) but the genius lies in determining what pictures will best enhance the author's work, what viewpoint will best serve what is being portrayed and how the finished scene will be placed on the page. His eye for such matters was unerring.

The consistency with which Ardizzone achieved his graphic interpretations, whether in full-dress full-pages, or spot drawings, or vignettes, or – delectably – pictorial initials, stemmed from self-knowledge as well as constant practice. Like so many of his admired predecessors, from Hogarth to Caldecott, he was a realist. That is not to say that he avoided the mysterious – some of his greatest books, including his first, revelled in it – but his handling of the mysterious, the incredible, or the fantastic gained strength from his rooting it in a mundane world. (Maurice Sendak's description of a drawing in *The Dragon* with the page-boy eating his lunch juxtaposed against the dragon 'placidly devouring the bald, middle-aged Prince' sums the matter up to perfection – see item 125 below.) Ardizzone has himself written about the value to the illustrator of knowing the look of everyday things almost instinctively and his passion for sketching (a *sine qua non* for the born illustrator) ensured the spontaneity with which he could develop a pictorial interpretation. The multiplicity of his 'little paintings' in line that are his instantly recognisable trade-mark testifies to the pleasure he took in conveying the reality of his author's scenes and characters.

That 'truth to life' seems to me of consequence in assessing Ardizzone's significance within his period too. Most illustrators cannot help but be creatures of their time, especially those like Ardizzone for whom a kind of journalism (the *Radio Times* work, the war drawings, the London scenes, the commercial jobs) is allied to book work developed around contemporary themes. In his children's book illustrations in particular, both for his own stories and for commissioned work, he reflects the ethos of a particularly fruitful period. The span of material from 1945 onwards in the following list is almost a history-in-little of the optimism, the willingness to experiment, and the respect for standards of production that prevailed during the last years of civilised, traditional publishing. It is a matter for regret that, under new dispensations, the validity of that ethos is often overlooked or denied.

The following formal listing of Ardizzone's graphic work is intended primarily to provide a chronological account of his career as an illustrator with descriptions of both books and more ephemeral printed matter at the point of their first (discoverable) appearance. It is not a bibliography in the full technical sense of that word, but rather a more advanced form of the *Hand-list* which was published in *The Private Library* in 1972. The composition of entries for the published books in the first section has been somewhat expanded and is described in the following notes. The degressive principle has been applied to the eight subsequent sections where descriptive information gradually declines into summary comments.

1) *Numeration:* The main sequence retains the numbering of the 1972 *Hand-list* and continues it down to the final entries. On the few occasions when an item has been moved it has been interpolated elsewhere using a decimal point and with an appropriate cross-reference. The attempt in the *Hand-list* to assign subsidiary numbers to later editions (as distinct from reprints, foreign editions, etc.) now seems misguided and has been adandoned. References to these subsidiary entries are made to the dated subheading, if necessary with a page reference. One or two projected, unpublished or reprinted titles have been inserted into the chronological sequence, but without numbers.

Much more material has been added to subsequent categories and the very few 1972 supplementary numbers have therefore been abandoned in favour of new and separate chronological listings for sections A: contributions to books; B: book jackets; and C: commercial brochures and ephemera. The final four sections (D: periodicals and advertising; E: war drawings; F: prints, posters and bookplates; and G: 'adoptions') are all brief and more discursive but have also been given a broadly chronological form. Descriptions in all these sections are neither so detailed nor so consistently-treated as in the main list.

2) *Date:* Since the main sections are arranged chronologically a note of the date follows the list number for ease of reference. Works published in the same year are given in alphabetical order by title or, in section C (for the most part), by type of publication.

3) *Title-page:* Given in a standardized rather than 'facsimile' form but with some attention paid to the manner of its layout. The title, as given, in capitals, is followed by the subtitle and author, as given, with an indication of whether 'by' is included or not. Acknowledgement of the illustrator is given as '[Credit]' when the usual term 'Illustrated by Edward Ardizzone' is used, otherwise it is given in the publisher's wording (or not given at all where it does not appear). Place, publisher and date follow and where any of these is taken from the verso of the title-leaf or the colophon it is given in square brackets. Refinements in the publisher's address have sometimes been retained. Illustrations within the t.p. entry are also indicated.

4) *Format, size, collation:* Traditional designations of format are given, followed by page-sizes in both millimetres and inches, height first (all other dimension are given in millimetres alone). All books have been collated, but in most cases no formula is given since the signatures are regularly-gathered full or half sheets. Where something less usual occurs this is shown either in the format statement or with a full collation.

5) *Pagination:* All leaves are indicated, with the pagination usually regularised to roman numerals for prelims and arabic for the main text. Unpaginated pages are set in square brackets, and I have not been too finicky about detailing unnumbered or numbered pages which occur intermittently. On a number of occasions it will be found that pastedowns and free endpapers have (confusingly) been included by the publisher in the pagination or in part of the printed gathering.

6) *Contents sequence:* Following the pagination statement, and placed in parentheses, is a listing of the main elements of the book which includes, in italics, direct statements of imprints, authorial notes, colophons etc. Blank, or otherwise-insignificant pages are not noted.

7) *Production details:* Unlike the authors of unadorned texts, who hope chiefly for accuracy and legibility, book illustrators are much more heavily dependent on publishers' production departments and on printers for the successful reproduction of their work. For this reason I have attempted to give an indication, as follows, of the quantity, variety and physical production of E.A.'s illustrations.

a) Paper: Decisions about paper for trade-books will normally fall to publishers' production departments and points to be taken into consideration will include such matters as the machinery to be used for printing the book, the varying prices for stock, and its likely homogeneity through the print-run.

The results of these decisions have had marked consequences in the production of work by Ardizzone and his contemporaries. The fifty years from 1930 to 1980 saw multiple changes in the economics and the technology of papermaking, with various restrictions imposed during the Second World War and its aftermath. Working often in fine line and in watercolour, with much of his work printed separately in Britain and in the U.S.A., Ardizzone could be vulnerable to circumstances over which he had little control beyond his opportunity to comment on proofs.

I have therefore felt it necessary to include in the following descriptions a general note on the paper used in first (and sometimes subsequent) editions. My professional competence in preparing these notes is, I fear, negligible and, in discussing a possible approach with several members of publishers' productions teams, I have come to realize that the only sure way of providing exact information would be to consult the production records for each book. Such a course presents near-insuperable difficulties and, in consequence, I have attempted an amateurish compromise with the aim of providing readers with a rough indication of the vital physical qualities of the paper being used, the nature of its surface and its colour. The following are the chief terms that I have adopted:

Antique wove: A general term for a fairly bulky paper with a softish surface, having had little in the way of machine finish. Unless otherwise stated it may be assumed to have a pleasant off-white colour and, given care in the press work, it gives a good reproduction of line blocks.

Antique laid: Similar to wove, but because it is machined to give the appearance of a hand-made paper, with wire-lines and chain-lines impressed from a roller, its surface will tend to be harder with a contrast between the upper and lower sides.

Cartridge: Here used as a shortened form for what are mostly 'offset cartridge' papers, a large and indeterminate group, used in preference to antiques because their harder, well-sized surfaces are better adapted to taking half-tone blocks and colour-work printed lithographically. I have tried to describe both the colour and the surface quality of the cartridges encountered here – offering, as a personal view, the opinion that the harder and whiter the paper the less suited it is for reproducing Ardizzone's line and colour work.

M.f. (machine-finished): A smoother, less bulky off-white paper than antique, but less highly finished than cartridge (and usually cheaper too). Subject to browning at edges exposed to light.

Newsprint: Cheap papers containing a fair percentage of wood-pulp in their make-up, used here from time to time in cheap reprints or paperbacks. They tend to a greyish or brownish colour, subject to further browning, and largely unsatisfactory for reproduction of fine line work.

Coated: In one or two instances mention is made of papers (sometimes called art papers) with a mineral coating, and usually dead white in colour, suitable for reproducing half-tone blocks, especially in colour sequences.

Colour: Subjective judgements have been made throughout to try to distinguish paper shades, varying from dead white through plain white to the often more hospitable off-white, creamy, cream, and yellowish finishes.

b) Number and nature of illustrations: The original form of the illustrations is the main element here, but it is inextricably related to the manner in which the illustrations are to be printed:

Pen drawings: These would conventionally be converted by photography into line-blocks of a size required by the page-layout (E.A.

tended to prefer a small reduction of his originals to 'tighten up' the drawing). With the growth of lithographic printing however the drawings might be photographed down on the plate for a process which could lead to some loss of definition.

Watercolours (or colour wash drawings): These would be prepared by the artist as compositions in line and colour to be photographically separated to print as four intermingled colours: yellow, cyan, magenta and black (sometimes one or more additional colours would be laid down, but these are not always easy to distinguish and, in most cases here, a 4-colour printing may be assumed).

Colour with Kodatrace: A constant problem for illustrations printed as above is the breaking up of the black line in the fourth printing and E.A. attempted to solve this by drawing the line separately on a transparent sheet. His account of his method is given in Appendix II. He also sought to overcome the difficulty in some instances by abandoning black outlines in favour of red.

Line separations: Where colour was to be printed in simple blocks the artist would prepare his own separations for the block-maker or photographer. These would be composed as monochrome designs, on separate transparent sheets registered over the foundation drawing in line. They are usually referred to as overlays in the following descriptions.

Lithographs: E.A. was a highly skilled lithographer who prepared both single prints and monochrome and multi-colour book illustrations on the stone (or on grained plates), separating the colours for the latter himself. For normal trade books however the lithographic originals would be photographed for printing by offset.

All entries seek to give details of the form of E.A.'s originals, whose subsequent printing followed one of the above paths. The number of illustrations for each form of composition is given and also their placing in the book and their character (frontispieces, full-page drawings, vignettes etc.).

c) Bindings: Man-made fabric is distinguished from varieties of cloth by use of the generic term 'linson'; colour names have been given without recourse to formulae on colour-charts. Paperbacks are described as having 'wrappers' and information on the treatment of endpapers is usually incorporated in this section rather than with the illustrations.

d) Dust Jackets: The neglect of jacket-designs in bibliographical descriptions is regrettable, especially where illustrative work is in question. Not only is information printed on jackets that does not appear within the book (this may extend to the illustrator's name) but very often the jacket will have additional illustrations which have been intentionally designed for it, and which are thus part of the artist's total contribution. The printing of jackets is not always easy to describe, since publishers' designers often have the white paper printed with an overall colour which may then be overlaid with further colours or 'cut through' to allow the white paper to show. My account will not always give lengthy full descriptions of these matters.

8) *Subsequent printings:* An attempt is made here, in many entries, to give a brief history of the illustrated texts following their first publication. A primarily chronological approach is adopted, first for English language editions and then for translations, although much of the material is not systematically recorded. Hence this element of the bibliography must be regarded as more serendipitous than authoritative. I must express special gratitude to Ardizzone's agent, Laura Cecil, who has been very helpful in sending me details of some of the translations:

a) American/British editions: Where a first edition is published in England or the U.S.A. I append publishing details of follow-up editions published on the opposite side of the Atlantic[1]. Sometimes I have been able to note the appearance of these editions as publishers'

1. As is apparent in the listing, E.A. worked directly with several U.S. publishers and, in some instances, books that he illustrated for them never found their way to England. The most frequent name to occur though is that of Henry Z. Walck, who (as noted under item 30) took over the O.U.P. children's list in the U.S.A. in 1957. By way of publicity he eventually issued a catalogue-booklet *Profiles of Some Authors and Illustrators Published by Walck; with a Bibliography in the Form of a Graded List* (copy seen dated 1966–1967).

bind-ups of the original printed sheets. Where a U.S. or British edition follows a reprint of the first edition it will appear below that reprint.

b) Reprints: Straight reprints (sometimes referred to as new editions by their publishers) are noted with their frequency where I have been able to establish it – sometimes from imprint statements rather than copies examined.

c) New editions: I have tried to be strict in defining new editions as publications where a re-setting of text or a re-working of illustrative matter has created a distinctly different book from its predecessor, even if this is not noted in the publisher's imprint.

e) Paperbacks: Sometimes a paperback will figure as a new edition. Mostly though, they and their reprints will be run-ons or photographically-reduced versions of the original text settings.

f) Translations: Where I have (not without difficulty) gleaned information about the existence of these I have tried to give date, language, title, translator's name and publication details, but translations into non-Roman scripts are designated by their language alone, with no attempt at transliteration.

g) Original artwork, sketchbooks and manuscripts: Where the artist's original artwork (or part of it) is known to be present in a public collection, or where information has been gleaned about its sale, this will usually be recorded under the rubric MS. DRAWINGS. Here too, or sometimes in the annotations, a note may be added about the presence of draft material in E.A.'s sketchbooks. These are mostly to be found in the print-room of the Department of Western Art in the Ashmolean Museum, Oxford, but, by and large, the artist used them for general sketching, a regular keeping-in of his hand, rather than for anything so formal as a story-board or suchlike. Readers consulting the sketchbooks should know that the presence on most of the leaves of an intrusive (and sometimes disfiguring) 'atelier mark' consisting of the artist's initials was not stamped in by him, or by the Ashmolean authorities and is unlikely to have met with his approval. Manuscripts of texts, sometimes including sketches or finished artwork, are noted under the rubric MANUSCRIPT.

h) Varia: Ephemeral printed items, ceramics, sound recordings, films etc. relating to or derived from the book under discussion are briefly described, as far as possible in chronological order.

9) *Annotations:* Where present, general notes are given in italics at the end of the entry. They aim to add information that may help to explain a book's status or to provide comments that may be helpful, critical or even anecdotal. Where mention of pre-decimalization prices occurs, these are uniformly given as £.s.d. rather than with the slashes that were often used by publishers and others.

10) *Print runs:* Only rarely, apart from in limited editions, is the size of a print-run given in the book itself. As with paper specifications, one needs access to a multiplicity of publishers' files to establish quantities ordered. Such information would be of some interest in the case of obscure publications like *The Modern Prometheus* (item 36) or of some of the books published in the difficult period around the war, but even here we are dealing with 'standard' trade books for which a general figure of 3,000–5,000 copies probably applies. It is important to bear in mind however, that almost the whole of Ardizzone's oeuvre was published during the heyday of commercial and public libraries and that a large proportion of the printing of first editions, both for adults and children saw service among the borrowers and was eventually honourably discharged into oblivion. And even in the case of titles printed in longer runs (Oxford's 'Tim' books were usually first published in runs of 10,000 or more) a proportion of the sheet-stock would be bound up for distribution in the U.S.A. or Australia, where, again, major customers would be the bulk-purchasing librarians. My assumption is that a knowledge of the figures is chiefly treasured by dealers and collectors in quest of evidence for gradations of rarity, but experience teaches that mysterious forces operate on this debatable ground and that no clear reason can be assigned for the scarcity of certain titles compared to works of a similar calibre which probably enjoyed a similar print-run.

ABBREVIATIONS

ad(s).	advertisement(s)	illus.	illustrated, illustration(s)
a.e.g.	all edges gilt	m.f.	machine-finished
c.	*circa*	ms.	manuscript
cat.	catalogue	NAP	(see p. 253)
coll.	collection	n.d.	no date
dec.	decorated, decoration(s)	p(p).	pages(s)
d.j.	dust-jacket	pr.	printed
ed(s).	edited, editions(s)	t.p.	title-page
ephem.	ephemeron, ephemera	trs.	translator, translated
f(f).	folio(s) or leaves	vig(s).	vignette(s)
frontis.	frontispiece	vol(s).	volume(s)

Risking accusations of *lèse majesté*, I have frequently shortened Edward Ardizzone's name to E.A. He forgave me for it in 1972 and I hope he would still do so now.

Head-piece from *In a Glass Darkly* (1929 item 1)

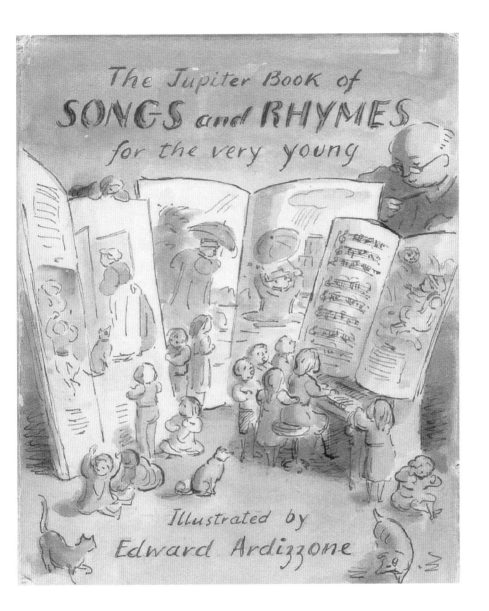

Colour plate I: Cover design for the unpublished
Jupiter Book of Songs and Rhymes (1964 see p. 139, reduced)

Overleaf: Colour plate II: Unpublished spread from
Little Tim and the Brave Sea Captain (1936 item 4, reduced)

When off duty Tim woul[...]
dancing a hornpipe or [...]
Wave", which pleased them [...]

...tertain the sailors by ...inging a "Life on the ocean" ...uch. They called him "Sunny Boy".

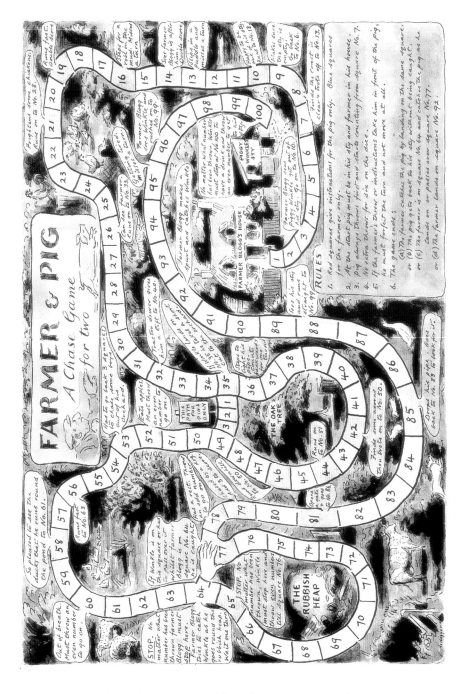

Colour plate III: Unpublished game *Farmer and Pig*
([1951?] see p. 227, reduced)

BIBLIOGRAPHIC
COMMENTARY

Overleaf: vignette from *Naughty Children* (1962 item 95)

THE ILLUSTRATED BOOKS

I. **1929** IN A GLASS DARKLY [by] J. Sheridan Le Fanu. With numerous illustrations by E.A. [vig.] London: Peter Davies, 1929.

Large crown 8°. 217 × 137 mm. (8½ × 5¼ in.). Pp. [6] vii–[viii] [3] 4–382 [2] ([i] half-title; [ii] frontis.; [iii] t.p.; [iv] imprint: *Joseph Sheridan Le Fanu. Born 1814, died 1873. In a Glass Darkly was first published in three volumes in 1872; the several tales having previously appeared in various periodicals. The present edition was published in November, 1929. Pr. in G.B. ... by W. Lewis M.A. at the Cambridge University Press*; [v]–vii *Contents*; [1] section-title: *Green Tea*; [3]–382 text, with further section-titles on pp. [47], [101], [145] and [291]). § Stiffish antique wove paper, hospitable to the line blocks. 153 pen drawings: frontis. and 5 full-page section-titles hand-lettered by E.A.; t.p. vig. and 146 in text including many chapter-head and tailpieces. § Black cloth boards, gilt lettering with publisher's monogram on spine. D.j. thickish cream laid paper, pen drawings and hand-lettering by E.A. throughout on front and spine; letterpress ad. on rear. Later issues can be found in purplish buckram with black lettering and the title at the head of the spine and the publisher's surname at foot, both with Oxford rules above and below, and in orange cloth, ditto (see below). M. & D. Reeve, *Cat. 40*, list a copy in pink cloth.

1988 SELECTED REPRINT: including five illus. by E.A., extracted and adapted from the above for *The Illustrated J. S. Le Fanu: Ghost Stories and Mysteries* ... ed. Michael Cox. Wellingborough: Equation [i.e. Thorsons].

MS. DRAWINGS: apparently scattered, but two were exhibited at the Michael Parkin Gallery, November 1991.

Sales, at 12s.6d. net, probably did not come up to expectation, and in 1931 the book was transferred to Peter Davies's 'Covent Garden Library'. Trimmed to a smaller page-size (205 × 130 mm) this is the issue in yellow cloth, selling at 5s. net and with a new three-colour jacket of art deco design. The front flap of the jacket describes the

Overleaf: Title-page and frontispiece from
In a Glass Darkly (1929 item I)

J. SHERIDAN LE FANU

IN A GLASS DARKLY

With Numerous Illustrations
by
EDWARD ARDIZZONE

LONDON
PETER DAVIES
1929

Library as incorporating 'the latest successes, both in modern literature and classical reprints, which have appeared from the house of Peter Davies'. These included John Collier's edition of The Scandal and Credulities of John Aubrey *with engravings by Helen Kapp, and Jane Austen's* Pride and Prejudice, *illustrated by Vera Willoughby. (I am grateful to Bromlea Books for sending me a colour photocopy of the d.j. for this issue).*

The 'several tales' are Green Tea, The Familiar, Mr. Justice Harbottle, The Room in the Dragon Volant *and* Carmilla.

In his study of Ardizzone, Gabriel White refers to and includes an illustration from a portfolio of illustrations which the artist prepared in the 1920s, for Richard Head's The English Rogue, Described in the Life of Meriton Latroon, *first published in 1665. The illustrations never found a publisher and E.A.'s first appearance in print was (along with Gabriel White) as a contributor to the 1929* Christmas Tree Annual, *listed below as item A1. In* a Glass Darkly *was thus his first appearance as illustrator of a complete book, and he gives a brief account of what it meant to him in* The Young Ardizzone *(item 151 below), where he records that he 'lived and dreamt that book for three whole months' producing for £75 some drawings that he thought 'the best I have done'. The book certainly establishes that remarkable blend of freedom and precision that characterises much of his work — sketches exactly keyed to the spirit of the author's words and the book's character. The pen drawing is denser here, with more emphatic outlines than in later books, with interest focused on figures rather than scenes or objects.*

2. 1930 THE LIBRARY [by] George Crabbe. With Drawings in Black and White by E. J. I. Ardizzone. [vig.] London at the De La More Press, [1930]. (The Saint George Series).

Crown 8° in fours. 187 × 125 mm. (7⅜ × 5 in.). Pp. [4] 5–31 [1] ([1] *The Saint George series published by Alexander Moring Ltd., The De La More Press, 2a Cork Street, Bond Street, London W.1.* [series device]; [3] t.p.; [4] imprint: *Made and pr. in G.B.*; 31 colophon: *George Crabbe was born at Aldborough on 24th December, 1754, and died in February, 1832. The Library was first published in 1781 largely through the efforts of Edmund Burke. First published in the Saint George Series in 1930. Notes ...*). § Parchment-finished wove paper, fore-edges of [A]1–2 and B1–2 untrimmed. 12 pen drawings: t.p. vig. and 11 in text. § Mottled buff paper boards, black letterpress titling with the drawing from p. 7 on front. Plain endpapers. No d.j. Price 3s. net.

CHEAPER ISSUE: as above, but without the t.p. vig. and endpapers. Fore-edges and upper edges of sigs. [A] and B, and C3–4 and D3–4 untrimmed, also upper edges of C1–2 and D1–2. Price 2s. net.

Colin White (section F below) notes that the drawing on p. 7 was used for two bookplates and adapted for a third (see p. [252] below).

— 1931 THE RAKE'S PROGRESS.

Five drawings in pen and watercolour, sizes varying between 152 × 172 mm and 190 × 158 mm, signed *E. Ardizzone '31*, are at the Tate Gallery. They portray in sequence: 'At the Brasserie'; 'The Meeting'; 'The Arrival'; 'The Bedroom'; and 'The Departure'. *Although never intended for conversion into a reproductive medium, these watercolours are included here as works which early on establish E.A.'s liking for narrative images, which manifests itself as much in single pictures and prints as in illustrations. As may be guessed, the title to the suite acknowledges a debt to Hogarth's penchant for narrative pictures, although his critique of contemporary manners is here given comic force.*

3. 1935 THE MEDITERRANEAN an Anthology. Compiled by Paul Bloomfield & Decorated by E.A. [device] London, Toronto, Melbourne and Sydney: Cassell and Company, Ltd., [1935].

Small crown 8°. 184 × 120 mm. (7¼ × 4¾ in.). Pp. [4] 5–247 [1] + 1 inset between pp. [2] and [3] ([i] half-title; inset leaf: dec. title on recto, verso blank; [3] t.p.; [4] imprint: *First Published 1935. Pr. in G.B. by Hazell, Watson & Viney, Ltd., London and Aylesbury*; 5–8 Introduction; 9–12 *Contents*; 13–14 *Acknowledgements*; [15] section-title: *The Mediterranean in General*; 17–244 text, with further section-titles on pp. [23], [33], [47], [57], [93], [113], [129], [147], [155], [177], [211] and [229]; 245–247 *Authors ... quoted*). § Antique wove paper, the inset leaf on a smooth cartridge. 14 illustrations: line and watercolour pictorial title-page printed in 3-colour half-tone, and 13 pen-drawn section-titles, all hand-lettered by E.A. § Drab brocade boards, blue titling on spine after E.A. D.j. with repeat of pictorial t.p. on front and an additional colour-drawing on spine, all hand-lettered by E.A.

4. 1936 LITTLE TIM AND THE BRAVE SEA CAPTAIN by E.A. [full colour vig.] – *To Philip from his father* – London, New York, Toronto: Oxford University Press. Copyright 1936, by Oxford University Press[2], New York, Inc. Lithographed in the U.S.A. [all hand-lettered by E.A.].

Foolscap folio in eights. 330 × 220 mm. (13 × 8¾ in.). Ff. [32] (f. [1] t.p. and dedication, as above; ff. [2–32] text hand-lettered by Grace Hogarth). § Thickish off-white cartridge paper. T.p. vig. and 40 drawings in line and watercolour, printed offset litho. § Paper boards with 2 full-colour drawings and hand-lettering by E.A. on front, rear a plain grey-brown wash, spine unlettered and printed bright red; U.S. copies in quarter grey linen with the same boards. D.j. white paper with overall printing in line and wash as cover; plain, unprinted flaps; U.S. copies with blurb on the inner front and ads on the inner back. Plain cream end-papers.

1936 SECOND PRINTING: November 1936 (also pr. in U.S.A.).

1940 THIRD PRINTING: (also pr. in U.S.A.), modified as follows: small foolscap folio in eights. 303 × 227 mm. Pp. [32] (text and illus. as above, but now printed on both sides of the leaf). A thinner paper stock has been used and the inking of the colours is too pale, giving more prominence to the line-work. Binding as above but probably with a plain grey linen spine for all copies. D.j. as above, but with the front flap carrying a 20-line encomium taken from Anne Eaton's review in the *New York Times*, followed by the note *Out of print for the last few years, this book has always been immensely popular.* The price is given as $2.00, covered in the British issue with a brown 'lion' sticker marked 8s.6d. net. Rear flap blank.

1944 PAPERBACK EDITION: small demy 8°. A single gathering of 16 leaves. 216 × 140 mm. Pp. [1] 2–32. Text and illus. follow the sequence of the folio ed., but the hand-lettering is now replaced by a setting in Gill Sans. White art paper. The illus. photographically reduced and printed as four-colour half-tones. White thin card covers with overall line and wash design similar to above. The rear cover carries the imprint: *Engraved and printed by Henry Stone & Son. Ltd., Banbury.*

2. This was, in fact, an error. As the 1935 contract makes clear, the copyright belonged to, and remained with, E.A.

1955 SECOND EDITION: London – New York – Toronto: Oxford University Press. *Completely redrawn and with additional text* [re-copyrighted to E.A.]. Crown 4°. Pp. [48]. Printed by W. S. Cowell Ltd., at the Butter Market, Ipswich. T.p. hand-lettered by E.A. 50 illustrations: t.p. vig. and 21 drawings in line, on Kodatrace, and watercolour, reproduced by four-colour litho; 28 pen drawings. *This new edition (arguably the third) is the fourth book to follow the production formula introduced with* Tim to the Rescue *in 1949 (see item 30 below). Most of the illus. replicate the subjects of the first ed., with some now being in monochrome. The additional text and drawings have been introduced chiefly to pace the story through the now standard 48 pages, but Tim has been given the more youthful and less self-assured appearance that characterises the post-war sequence. This edition was reprinted six times to 1967.*

1977 PAPERBACK EDITION: Harmondsworth: Penguin Books (Picture Puffin series). 192 × 155 mm.

1982 REPRINT: of the 1955 crown 4° edition. London: Kestrel Books, published simultaneously with a further Puffin ed. Printed in Milan by New Interlitho.

1999 FOURTH EDITION: London, New York (and 6 others): Scholastic Press. Printed by Proost, Belgium. Follows the 1955 ed. in all respects, apart from a differently coloured binding and d.j., but the illustrations have all been re-originated from E.A.'s artwork, as part of a project to 're-master' the Tim series; see below items 7, 30, 34, 39, 55, 100, 120, 141, 157 and 172.

2000 U.S. EDITION: New York: Lothrop, Lee and Shepard.

TRANSLATIONS:
1962 [German] *Der Kleine Tim und der Tapfere Kapitän*. Trs. Tilde Michels. Munich: Lentz.
1962 [Danish] *Lille Tim og den Tapre Kaptajn*. Trs. Inge and Klaus Rifbjerg. Copenhagen: Gyldendal. Pr. in England (not seen).
1964 [Norwegian] 'Vesle Tim og den Modige Skipperen'. Anonymous translation in an anthology, *Barndomslandet*. Oslo: Gyldendal.
1976 [Swedish] *Lille Tim på det Stora Havet*. Trs. by Margareta Ströstedt. [Stockholm]: Rabén & Sjögren. Printed in England as a Swedish run-on of the Picture Puffin, noted above as being published in Britain in 1977.

Above and opposite: The metamorphoses of Little Tim. Top: from the
first edition of *Little Tim and the Brave Sea Captain* (1936 item 4).
Bottom: from *Tim to the Rescue* (1949 item 30). Both slightly reduced.

From the second edition of *Little Tim and the Brave Sea Captain*
(1953 item 4; reduced)

1977 [Norwegian] Trs. Jo Tenfjord, bound in with *Tim til Sjøs* (item 30 below).

1983 [German] *Tim Fährt zur See*. Trs. Angelika Feilhauer. Ravensburg: Lesen und Freizeit Verlag. The jacket design adapted from E.A. by Gerald Ahrens.

1999 [Dutch] *Tim en de Dappere Zeekapitein*. Trs. not acknowledged. Mechelen: Bakermat.

2000 [French] *Tim fait Naufrage*. Trs. not acknowledged. Paris: Autrement Jeunesse.

2001 [Japanese] Trs. Teiji Seta. Tokyo: Fukuinkan Shoten.

VARIA:

[*c.* 1950] *Vulcanised rubber statuette*: of Little Tim, approx. 750 mm high and appropriately coloured, was used by O.U.P. to assist sales (now to be found in the O.U.P. archive).

1964 *Gramophone record:* 45 rpm. The story read by David Davis. Delysé Recording Co. (DEL 127). One of five records of 'Little Tim Stories' told by 'David' of Children's Hour fame and numbered DEL 127–131.

[*c.* 1975] *Audio-visual adaptations:* Weston CT, Weston Woods. The book became part of a fashionable movement to convert picture-books into 'iconographic motion pictures', whereby images or parts of images were moved in front of a static camera to synchronise with an audio recording of the story. The same company also issued the work as a filmstrip with cassette recording or with a booklet of the text that could be read aloud by teachers or librarians as the strip was run. The 'motion picture' version received an award as a notable film from the American Library Association. A copy was also available in Afrikaans.

1987   *Tape cassette:* one of *Six Seaworthy Adventures* read by Michael Williams. Puffin Cover to Cover series.

MANUSCRIPT: the book was prepared for printing from E.A.'s original ms. which is now in the Dept. of Prints and Drawings at the Victoria and Albert Museum (press mark 94.F.33). 39 ff. of cartridge paper (except for f. [1]), misnumbered recently in an attempt to match the foliation of the published volume (the correct foliation has been used here, within square brackets). 350 × 245 mm, removed from, and now remounted on stubs in, the original sketch-book from L. Cornelissen & Son, Gt. Queen St. Price 1s.6d. Bound in mottled brown paper boards, with glazed linen spine, the inner front board signed by E.A. with his Elgin Avenue address. The first two ff. have drawings on their rectos; all following leaves are affixed to give double-page spreads with E.A.'s original ms. text covered by the pasted-on lettering by Grace Hogarth. A half-sheet inserted between ff. [8] and [9] has the printed version of the book's f. 8 on its verso and E.A.'s ms. text for the second paragraph ('He was so sad that …') unillustrated on the recto. Here follows a description of significant points:

[1]   Design for front cover.

[2]   Leaf of thick, smooth white card with E.A.'s lettering and design for the t.p.

[3–4]   Text commences (with loss of paste-over lettering) with printer's note on colours in right-hand margin.

[5–6]   Some lettering by E.A. revealed. 'That's a P & O' has the (accepted) change to 'Cunarder' written above.

[20–21]   Large spread with the following text has been omitted: 'When off duty Tim would entertain the sailors by dancing a horn-pipe or singing a "Life on the Ocean Wave", which pleased them very much. They called him "Sunny Boy"'. As with ff. [24–25] below, the spread has been dropped in order to contain the story within the book's 32 leaves and not (in 1936) because of any fears over the (rather splendid) portrait of a negro sailor in a brown suit. See colour plate II.

[24–25] Two pictures omitted: a ship tossing on a green sea and the cook offering tit-bits. The text is reorganised to fit on the following spread.

[38] Picture showing Tim and the Captain expatiating to Tim's parents in front of the fireplace has been omitted and the text carried over to make the concluding leaf of the book.

In photographing the ms. the original size has been reduced by approximately one twelfth. The colour reproduction is very fair, although, broadly speaking, somewhat 'warmer' than the watercolours.

Published to considerable acclaim in both Britain and the United States, Little Tim and the Brave Sea Captain *brought welcome recognition to the artist so near to the start of his career. Its two immediate successors (items 5 and 7 below) show that he had found a method of pictorial storytelling that happily balanced the new and the traditional, and there is every reason to think that, but for the coming of war, he would rapidly have developed and diversified his ideas. Glimmerings of both* Nicholas and the Fast-Moving Diesel *and* Nurse Matilda *are present in his correspondence with his publisher at this time.*

One tradition that played its part in Little Tim *and* Lucy Brown *was that of making up stories to be told and illustrated in the family.* Lucy Brown, *for the artist's eldest child, Christianna, was the first to be worked up as a picture book, but* Little Tim, *similarly devised for its dedicatee, Philip, was the manuscript that was submitted to Oxford University Press in 1935, as* Tim the Sailor.

The Press, in the persons of its two London children's books editors, Herbert Ely and C. J. L'Estrange (who wrote together as 'Herbert Strang' and were known as 'the Heavenly Twins'), and its American editor, Grace Allen, were enthusiastic from the start and the manuscript was taken to New York by Allen in order to investigate the possibility of its being printed by the newish process of offset lithography. Mrs. Hogarth, as Grace Allen became, has given an account of her adventures with the book in 'The Artist and his Editor' (see Sources p. 284) and elsewhere but the full complexity of its production can only be seen in records preserved in the Press's archive.

The central difficulty was to achieve an accurate printing of a large and novel picture book at a cost sufficient to ensure profitable sales at a cover price of no more than 7s.6d. in Britain and $2.00 in the U.S.A. To this end – and here the *record differs from Mrs. Hogarth's recollection – it would be necessary to print on one side of the sheet only in order to bulk out the book. Printing on both sides would produce so slim an article that sales might be drastically inhibited.*

Eventually the sums were made to come out. The book was printed by Messrs. Duenwald of New York City using the 'Crayon Process' of offset lithography and the artist was persuaded to take reduced royalty payments of 5% on the first 5,000 copies sold, 10% on the second 5,000 and 12.5% thereafter. He received his copies round about 22 September 1936 when he wrote to the Press expressing disappointment over the 'blotting-paper effect' in the colour-printing, reducing the freshness of his watercolours. Grace Hogarth has made the point that the printers encountered difficulties over getting the ink to dry in New York's summer humidity. There may also have been problems with paper shrinkage which may account in part for the loss of register in the early printings of the three folio books.

5. 1937 LUCY BROWN AND MR. GRIMES by Edward Ardizzone [placed between two vignetted line and watercolour drawings] – *To Christianna from her father* – London, New York, Toronto: Oxford University Press. Printed in Great Britain, [1937].

Foolscap folio, following closely the design of the previous item, but printed by W. S. Cowell, Ltd., London and Ipswich. § 43 drawings in line and watercolour, including the two t.p. vigs. § The binding and d.j. carry two additional full colour drawings with the spine printed bright green.

1970 SECOND EDITION: London, Sydney, Toronto: The Bodley Head. Crown 4°. 255 × 188 mm. Pp. [4] 5–48 ([2] *A new version of an old story which was written for my daughter Christianna. This new version is for my grand-daughter JOANNA* [all hand-lettered by E.A.]; [3] t.p. with large central pen-drawn vig., the title and the author's name hand-lettered by E.A.; [4] imprint: *Pr. and bound in G.B. by William Clowes & Sons Ltd., Beccles*; 5–48 text). White cartridge paper. 51 illustrations: 24 in line and watercolour, 27 pen-drawings including t.p. vig. Many follow the original drawings in their substance but at least 13 could be said to be new or re-drawn with alterations. Binding and d.j. follow the style established with *Tim in Danger* (item 30).

1971 U.S. EDITION: New York: Henry Z. Walck, Inc.

TRANSLATION: 1976 [Japanese] Tokyo: Fukuinkan Shoten[?]. Notable for its inclusion of a prefatory letter in English in E.A.'s script, creakily written and probably despatched for translation, but printed in facsimile: *Dear children: this book was made for my little daughter many many years ago. She was a pretty little girl rather like Lucy Brown and on fine days she would take her scooter and scoot about in a recreation ground close to our London home. The recreation ground was like the one I have drawn in the book. She loved the story and when she had grown up and had a daughter of her own her daughter loved it, so I hope you will like it too.*

MANUSCRIPT: in a letter to Lena Young de Grummond of the University of Southern Mississippi, dated 17 Feb. 1966, E.A. notes that he had sold the original ms. of *Lucy Brown* to the University of California at Los Angeles for £250 (copies of the book now sell for more than twice that price!). The following description is based chiefly on notes kindly sent to me by the late James Davis, formerly of U.C.L.A. Library Special Collections: 32 ff., approx. 350 × 200 mm containing the t.p. and E.A.'s holograph ms. of the story (with some corrections in his hand) and all his watercolour drawings. The t.p. with its two illus. is already pasted up for photographing, the text illus. are those reproduced in the printed book, but the 'improved' script has not yet been pasted over that by the artist. The artwork for the cover is also present.

Unlike Little Tim, Lucy Brown *has had to confront editorial vicissitudes. The dedicatee of the first edition reports that the story as originally invented by her father ended with Mr Grimes's demise and a grand funeral (hence Lucy's shopping expedition for black clothes). Although much enjoyed by E.A.'s young audience this did not suit the publisher and a happy ending was substituted.*

 Lacking the derring-do of the two picture books that flanked it, Lucy Brown *did not have the same commercial success in either Britain or the U.S.A., where the first edition was imported and sold by Oxford University Press. Indeed, copies remained in stock until about 1950, although a fillip may have been given to sales in 1946 when the book was chosen for the National Book League's exhibition of illustrated books 1935–1945, noted below at item 14. Some time after this however, librarianly concerns over stories in which little girls are picked up by elderly gentlemen led to the shunning of this work in the Ardizzone canon and the very late arrival of the second edition of 1970 came about only after the author was prevailed upon to convert Mr Grimes into 'an old family friend'. This occurred under the editorial guidance of Judy Taylor at the Bodley Head and the resultant revised edition preceded two new titles in the 'Tim' series to come from that house (see items 157 and 172). The books followed the standard quarto style, but the present volume has here been described in fuller detail as being the first of the Bodley Head group.*

6. 1937 TOM, DICK AND HARRIET by A. Neil Lyons. [Credit] The Cresset Press Ltd. 11 Fitzroy Square, London W.1. 1937.

Crown 8°. 198 × 130 mm. (7¾ × 5 in.). Pp. [10] 11–254 [2] ([1] half-title; [4] frontis.; [5] t.p.; [6] imprint: *First published 1937 Printed in Guernsey, C.I., British Isles, by the Star and Gazette Ltd.*; [7] dedication: *To Joe and Sammy*; [9–10] *Contents*; 11–[255] text). § Antique wove paper. 51 pen drawings: frontis., 29 chapter-heads or spot-drawings at initials, 11 tailpieces and 10 in text. § Green cloth boards, gilt lettering on black panels on front and spine. D.j. grey with black and red letterpress titling, reductions of E.A.'s frontis. on front and the drawing on p. 28 on spine. Ads. on the rear are for two eminent illustrated books: J. B. S. Haldane's *My Friend Mr. Leakey*, illus. by Leonard Rosoman, and E. L. Grant-Watson's *More Enigmas of Natural History* 'with numerous wood-engravings by Barbara Greg'.

Albert Neil Lyons (1880–1940) was a minor writer of the period with leftish leanings. Although divided into chapters, his present book, apparently his last, is not a novel, but a series of anecdotes emanating from the storyteller's connections in a London pub: 'The Dog and Bacon'. As such it can be seen as a forerunner for E.A. of his commissions to illustrate H. E. Bates and of his explorations of 'the locals'.

7. 1938 TIM AND LUCY GO TO SEA by E.A. [large vig. drawing in line and watercolour] London – New York – Toronto: Oxford University Press, [1938].

Foolscap folio, following closely the design of items 4 and 5 above, and again printed by Cowell's. § 36 drawings in line and watercolour (see the frontispiece to this volume), including that on the t.p. § The binding and d.j. carry 2 additional full-colour drawings with the spine printed yellow.

[1944] PAPERBACK EDITION: in all respects a companion to the 1944 card covered ed. of *Little Tim* (item 4 above), and apparently reprinted in 1947.

1958 THIRD EDITION: London, New York, Toronto: Oxford University Press. Crown 4°. Pp. [48]. Printed by W. S. Cowell Ltd. 45 illustrations: t.p. vig. and 21 drawings in line, on Kodatrace, and watercolour reproduced by 4-colour litho; 21 pen drawings. *The sixth book to follow the production formula introduced with* Tim to the Rescue *in 1949 (item 30). No indication is given in the book that the work had been previously published but the front flap of the jacket notes that it is* an early Tim book which has now been largely rewritten and entirely redrawn. *In fact, only minimal changes have taken place, similar to those made for the 1955 ed. of item 4 above, including the slightly changed portrayal of both Tim and Lucy. The book was reprinted five times to 1975.*

1958 U.S. ISSUE: New York, Henry Z. Walck, Inc. English sheets.

1999 FOURTH EDITION: London etc.: Scholastic Press. Second title in the projected reprinting of the Tim series (see item 4 above).

TRANSLATIONS:
1958 [Swedish] Trs. Britt G. Hallqvist. Stockholm: Sven-Erik Bergh.
1999 [Dutch] *Tim en Sofie op Zee.* Trs. not acknowledged. Mechelen: Bakermat.
2000 [French] *Tim, Lucie et les Mutins.* Trs. not acknowledged. Paris: Autrement Jeunesse.
2001 [Japanese] Trs. Chihiro Nakagawa. Tokyo: Fukuinkan Shoten.

8. 1939 GREAT EXPECTATIONS by Charles Dickens [vig.] [Credit] New York for the members of the Heritage Club, [1939].

Medium 8°. 227 × 146 mm. (9 × 5¾ in.). Pp. [10] 11–457 [7] + 8 insets ([3] half-title; inset frontis. between pp. [4] and [5]; [5] t.p.; [6] imprint: *Manufactured in the United States of America. The special contents of this edition are copyright 1939 by the Heritage Club*; [7] *Table of Chapters*; [9] *List of Color Plates*; 11–457 text; [459] colophon: *The illustrations for this edition of* Great Expectations *were made by E.A. the English artist. The volume is in companion* [sic] *with the other volumes of the novels of Charles Dickens made*

'In the afternoons my mother … would read to us. Her favourite reading was from Dickens …' from *The Young Ardizzone* ([1970] item 151)

for this series). § Antique wove paper 'especially made for this book by the International Paper Company', the 8 insets on a thicker offset paper. 67 illustrations: frontis. and 7 full-page lithographs by E.A. printed in five colours, each with a letterpress legend printed black, all within a triple-rule frame printed grey. The plates inserted to face pp. 64, 108, 180, 258, 304, 382, 416. Also t.p. vig. duplicating the headpiece on p. 58 and printed reddish brown, and 59 pen-drawn vignetted chapter headpieces. According to the Heritage Press's news-sheet *Sandglass* (no. VII, 15 [1939]): 'Mr. Ardizzone [whose three picture books are praised] … has made eight *actual lithographs in colors* to serve as the color-plates. He has drawn them on the stones himself … at the shop of The Curwen Press in London'. § Series binding in grey linen boards with design in maroon, gilt titling oval on spine above two sketches in maroon of characters from the book. These were by the designer, Clarence Pearson Hornung, who provided similar portrayals for other titles. Top edge stained maroon. Slip-case.

[1962] SECOND EDITION: Great Expectations By Charles Dickens. New York: The Heritage Press. Medium 8°. 227 × 146 mm. Collation: [1]¹⁶ [2–15]³². Pp. [4] 10 [2] 11–457 [1] + 8 insets ([i] half-title; inset frontis. between pp. [ii] and [iii]; [iii] t.p.; [iv] imprint: as given for the first ed.; 1–10 *How This Book Came to Be:* intro. signed John T. Winterich; the leaf between pp. 10 and 11 contains the *Table of Contents,* with blank verso; 11-457 text). Antique wove paper, the 8 insets on a thicker stock. Frontis. and 7 insets as above. The subjects of these illus. all correspond to those of the 1939 ed., with the same titling and framing, but all have been redrawn, with minor alterations, and all have been given darker and more dramatic colouring. Four proofs in possession of the family carry a legend below the lower frame edge 'Printed in England' and a stock of these and their companions was presumably shipped to the U.S.A. for insertion, the original 1939 plates doubtless having been destroyed when the Curwen Press was bombed in 1940. Also four artist's proofs for this ed. signed by E.A. and with his colour guide for the printer dabbed-in in watercolour were exhibited at Wolseley Fine Arts in February 2000 (see Sources p. 282). These may be associated with what looks to be a small issue of signed proofs put out by the Curwen Press for purposes best known to themselves. A 'complete set' was sold at Sotheby's on 5 December 1986, lot 420, and another sheet has been seen in a private collection (510 × 635 mm) with the eight plates printed down, each signed by the artist. Heritage Press's edition of the novel has continued to be reprinted (later issues carry a second half-title on p. [v] instead of the 'Table of Contents') and, presumably, later printings of the illus. were undertaken in the U.S.A. Changed make-up of the book has led to the plates of this ed. facing pp. 66, 114, 178, 258, 306, 382 and 418. The series binding continued to be used, with slip-case.

1979 'COLLECTORS' EDITION': Essentially a reprint of the second edition, issued by the Easton Press, Norwalk, CT, but with only seven plates, the frontispiece being replaced by a portrait of Dickens. Advertised as 'bound in genuine leather', a.e.g. The Easton Press appears to have been established to continue marketing Heritage Press titles (the Press having migrated to Norwalk around 1970). They publicised the 'Collectors' Edition' as being issued 'by advance reservation exclusively to subscribers to the … collection of *The 100 Greatest Books Ever Written*'. Two further titles illus. by E.A. were included (items 62.1 and 153 below), and see also a similarly vulgar production of *Barchester Towers* (item 38).

In 1929 (just before the Great Crash) enthusiasm in America for collecting press books and first editions was at its height. At this point the publishing entrepreneur, George Macy, decided to set up the Limited Editions Club to issue handsomely-produced books to a membership of 1500 collectors. Although the first book – Gulliver's Travels *– was published on the very day of the Crash, the Club proved successful and encouraged Macy to think of additional methods for exploiting public taste in the United States for fancy publications.*

This led him, in 1935, to set up the Heritage Press for publishing 'semi-luxe' illustrated books in unlimited editions – a scheme which engendered the Heritage Club which operated as a general book club, with a newsletter, to spread and sustain sales of Heritage Press books. (Some of the earliest examples of these works, published 1935–1936, bore the English imprint of the Nonesuch Press alongside the Heritage imprint, for Macy had taken over Nonesuch from Francis Meynell in July 1936.)

One source of copy for Heritage Press books was the material that was originally commissioned for Limited Editions Club books, which could be presented in a less extravagant form to the wider readership, and E.A.'s involvement in such projects after the war is detailed at items 42, 50 and 152 below. The Dickens series however was planned only as a Heritage publication (in 1937 Macy was simultaneously involved with the huge endeavour of producing the great Nonesuch Dickens). Great Expectations *was an early title to appear in the Heritage series (probably the first) and the making of a fresh set of illustrations for it after the war betokens first its success and second the continuance of the project to which a number of notable British illustrators contributed (including Barnett Freedman for* Oliver Twist *(1939) and Stephen Spurrier for* Nicholas Nickleby *(1940)).*

The Blumenthal design for the book-block and binding was adhered to throughout, although with the Short Stories *of 1971 (item 153 below) we find the Heritage edition being preceded by a more pompous affair done for Limited Editions.*

9. 1939 THE LOCAL. Lithographs by E.A. Text by Maurice Gorham. Cassell & Co. Ltd., La Belle Sauvage, London, [1939].

Large medium 8°. 230 × 155 mm. (9⅛ × 6 in.). Collation: [A]⁸ B–D⁸ E². Pp. [6] vii–xvi [2] 3–51 [1] + frontis. and 14 insets ([i] half-title; [iii] t.p.; [iv] imprint: *Printed in England at the Curwen Press, Plaistow, E.13. F.1039 First published 1939*; [v]–xvi *Preface*; [1] fly-title; 3–30 text; 31 *Postscript*; 33–50

Glossary of terms commonly used in connection with London pubs). § Creamy, thickish offset cartridge paper. Frontis., one double-spread and 13 full-page lithographs by E.A. printed in 4 colours, each with a title-legend in E.A.'s hand, printed black. The frontis. is attached to a stub hooked into f. [A]7; the next 7 plates are inserted to face pp. 4, 6, 8, 10, 12, 14 and 16; the final 7 plates are on conjugate leaves facing pp. 18/30, 20/28, 22/26, with the double-spread between pp. 24/25. § Grey paper boards, letterpress titling in red on front, red and black on spine, with a pen drawing and legend in black by E.A. on front: *Christmas Eve at the Warrington* (another version of the Lounge scene facing p. 8). Glassine wrapper to which are affixed front and rear flaps of paper with letterpress blurb and ads.

MS. DRAWINGS: a sketch-book numbered 43, dating from 1939–1940, in a private collection in the U.S.A. includes several preparatory sketches of scenes for the book.

E.A. had known Maurice Gorham as a childhood friend but only met up with him again later, during his first one-man show at the Bloomsbury Gallery. Gorham was then art-editor of Radio Times *and forthwith began to commission drawings (see item D1 below). The two men also enjoyed the conviviality of pub life (E.A. is here described as a bitter-drinker for preference) and this is the first of their joint investigations of pubs and popular goings-on. In a successor, post-war volume (item 26 below) Gorham notes that the unsold copies of the present book, together with the unbound sheets and plates 'went up together in the burning of Cassell's premises in Belle Sauvage Yard.'*

The preparation and printing of the lithographs was one instance of E.A.'s happy and fruitful collaborative work with the Curwen Press. Round about 1936 he had met Oliver Simon, who recorded in his autobiography Printer and Playground *(1956) 'how unappreciated [E.A.'s] work was' at that time, and 'how hard he found the struggle for recognition or even to earn a bare living until he achieved the status of one of our leading artist-professional illustrators'. As a result the Press commissioned the* News-Letter *drawings, noted below at item C1, and also printed E.A.'s autolithography for* Great Expectations *(above) and for the print 'The Bus Stop' in their Contemporary Lithographs series (NAP 82). Pat Gilmour in* Artists at Curwen *(1977) notes that E.A. 'fondly remembered' Wally Gapp, the press-man in charge of lithographic transfers, and was himself fondly remembered 'as a great charmer with his snuff, his partiality to a pint, and his propensity for eating fish and chips' on his homeward walk (all the way?) from Plaistow.*

10. 1939 MIMFF the Story of a Boy who was not Afraid. By H. J. Kaeser [Credit] London, New York, Toronto: Oxford University Press, [1939].

Demy 8° with ff. E1 and H1 mis-signed 'E2' and 'H2'. 215 × 135 mm. (8½ × 5¼ in.). Pp. [11] 12–192 including frontis. and 7 plates ([1] half-title; [4] frontis.; [5] t.p.; [6] imprint: *Translated by Kathleen Williamson. Pr. in G.B. at the University Press, Oxford, by John Johnson*; [11]–192 text and unpaginated plates). § Antique wove paper throughout. 18 illustrations: frontis. and 7 ff. watercolours by E.A. all printed as 4-colour half-tones by offset litho on conjugate leaves, all but the frontis. with letterpress legends and chapter denotations (the plates on pp. [17], [70], [87], [122], [139], [160] and [173] of text do not correspond exactly with the passages illustrated) plus 10 pen-drawings as chapter heads. § Blue cloth boards, gilt-lettered on front and spine. D.j. wrap-round watercolour, partially hand-lettered on the front by E.A., printed offset litho.

REPRINTED: by O.U.P. in 1947, 1951, 1956 and 1960; the plates at some point printed on a smoother stock and the signatures corrected.

Although written in German the book was first published in a Swedish edition, Mimm Pojken som Aldrig var Rädd *(Lund: Gleerups, 1937). The first edition in German appeared in Stockholm as* Mimpf der Junge, der Auszog, das Fürchten zu Lernen *(Fritzes Bokförlags, 1941), and the second, illustrated by Lilly Renner, in Aarau, Switzerland in 1942. In 1952 an edition in German with E.A.'s illustrations was published in Amsterdam, followed in 1953 by a further edition at Ravensburg published by Maier Verlag. Three sequels are described at items 27, 41 and 64 below.*

Hildegard Johanna Kaeser is the subject of a thesis, written in German by Inger Lundmark (Stockholm University, 1971). Born in Germany, as Hildegard Zander, in 1904, of Jewish descent she worked in children's book publishing in Berlin where she married Walter Kaeser. They left Germany in 1933, ending up in Sweden in 1935 (naturalised 1946), but Kaeser's writing, which included novels, was always in German. After some personal difficulties, her husband died of heart-failure in 1965 and Kaeser then took her own life.[3]

3. I am grateful to Ulla Bergstrand and Lena Törnqvist of the Swedish Barnboks-institutet for providing me with information about the complex publishing history of Kaeser's works.

11. 1939 MY UNCLE SILAS [vig.] Stories by H. E. Bates Drawings by E.A. London, Jonathan Cape, [1939].

Crown 4° in eights. 248 × 183 mm. (9¾ × 7¼ in.). Pp. [6] 7–190 [2] ([1] half-title; [4] frontis.; [5] t.p.; [6] imprint: *First published 1939. Pr. in G.B. by the Camelot Press Ltd., Southampton and London. Paper made by John Dickinson & Co. Ltd. Bound by A. W. Bain & Co. Ltd.*; 9–12 *Preface*; [13] section-title: *The Lily*; 14–190 text; [191] tailpiece illus.). § Antique wove paper. 47 pen drawings: frontis.; t.p. vig.; 13 vigs. for 14 section-titles; 2 full-page drawings for each section, that on p. [133] a repeat of the frontis.; 3 tailpieces below text; 2 tailpieces on separate pages. § Green linen boards, blocked in black on front (a reduced version of the frontis.), gilt-lettered spine. D.j. with letterpress titling and the drawing on p. [43] reproduced on a pink ground. § *Ref:* Eads A35.

Vignette from *My Uncle Silas* (1939 item 11, reduced)

1947 NEW EDITION: reduced to crown 8° format, 183 × 115 mm. All illustrations present, but slightly reorganised in placing, reduced in size and printed on a softer, yellower antique paper giving a muddier reproduction of the drawings. Binding and d.j. of similar design to the above. The typesetting was also used in a Reprint Society ed. *by arrangement with Jonathan Cape*, 1947, bound in the green buckram of the series with maroon leather label. It had a pale buff d.j. titled in green letterpress with a greatly reduced version of the drawing on p. [43] on front. The inner flap reads *This book is an 'extra' choice and one of a limited edition,* a point elaborated in the laid-in prospectus which explains that, because of paper rationing, 'members will be restricted to one copy each. Half this edition will be available to over-seas members …'.

1958 PAPERBACK EDITION: Harmondsworth: Penguin Books no 1265. Small crown 8°. Cover illus. from p. [108] in full colour.

The d.j. blurb on the first edition mistakenly says that there are 27 (rather than 28) full-page drawings by E.A. The artist's contribution is recognised by the author in his preface where he hopes that in any future volume 'I shall again be lucky enough to have the collaboration of Mr. E.A. whose crabbed and crusty pictures are so absolutely and perfectly in the spirit of every page they illustrate.'

— 1939–1940 RICHARD THE THIRD by William Shakespeare. New York: The Limited Editions Club.

References have occasionally been made to E.A. having published illustrations for this volume in the Limited Editions Shakespeare (most notably in Dr. Nicholas Ardizzone's dissertation noted above on p. 8). E.A. did indeed prepare a set of illustrations, having been commissioned by Macy in 1938 when Frank Brangwyn found the work to be beyond him. But, as the 'commentary' laid into copies of the play as eventually published reveals: 'E.A. … who is at the present moment an Official War Artist … made a series of beautiful water-colours for us. These were reproduced in Paris by lithography and through stencils. They were finished on the seventh of June [1940]. On the fifteenth of June, Mr. Fernand Mourlot, the lithographer, wrote us a letter from Bordeaux. He had got out of Paris before the Germans got in and had actually, in an excess of remarkable loyalty, carried with him to Bordeaux several packing cases containing the reproductions of E.A.'s water-colours. On June 16, according to his advice, he was able to ship them from Bordeaux … [but] they never reached us. We can only conclude that they are at the bottom of the sea.' Richard III was nevertheless published (with surprising speed) in 1940, with illustrations by Fritz Eichenberg.

12. 1940 THE BATTLE OF FRANCE [by] André Maurois, Translated from the French by F. R. Ludman. London: John Lane The Bodley Head, 1940.

Large post 8°. 210 × 133 mm. (8¼ × 5¼ in.). Pp. [14] 15–210 [6] + frontis. and 7 insets ([3] half-title; [4] *by the same author* …; [inset frontis. leaf]; [5] t.p.; [6] imprint: *First published 1940. Pr. in G.B. by Stephen Austin and Sons, Ltd., Hertford for* …; [9] *Illustrations* … ¶ *All the above are reproduced from the original drawings by E.A., official War Office Artist. Crown Copyright reserved*; [11–12] *Foreword* by A.M., dated *London, July 1940*; [13] section-title; 15–210 text; [211–212] ads.). § Antique wove paper; the insets on thicker, smooth cartridge paper of similar tone. Frontis. and 7 plates, facing pp. 24, 32, 52, 86, 134, 174, 180, printed in sepia half-tone from watercolours by E.A., each with a letterpress title. § Rose-red cloth boards, lettered in blue on spine. D.j. front and spine overprinted red with titling reversed white, reading on front: 'André Maurois' Battle of France with drawings by E.A.' below a sepia illustration additional to the plates; rear of d.j. and jacket-flaps letterpress printed in black and red.

1940 BOOK CLUB EDITION: probably reprinted from standing type for the Right Book Club, 121 Charing Cross Road. Blue cloth boards. (Not seen: Bookmark *Cat.* May 1988, item 34).

The foreword by Maurois points out that this 'strangely built book' consists of two separate elements. Part I 'is made up of sketches of the B.E.F. [British Expeditionary Force] which were published in Paris each week from the beginning of November [1939]' – the period of the 'conspiracy of optimism'. Part II is 'a diary of the Thirty Days' War' ending in June 1940.

E.A.'s artwork is more properly recognised at the foot of the list of illustrations than on the title-page, since the eight pictures were chosen from his 'official' drawings made while he was with the B.E.F. in France and were not prepared specifically for this book. As such they have also been reproduced elsewhere: three, for instance, in Army *(1942 see item E4 below).*

The 'Right' Book Club, as it punningly called itself to begin with, came into being after the formation by Victor Gollancz of the vigorously proselytizing Left Book Club in 1936. Despite a five-man Selection Committee and some 45 patrons (including peers of the realm, privy councillors, generals, admirals, and an air-vice-marshal) the Club had a low profile compared with its fractious rival and seems to have been run like any 'reprint club', publishing general literature

47

rather than politically contentious works. From its address it appears to have been housed in Foyle's Bookshop at this time, having moved there from Soho Square.

13. 1940 THE ROAD TO BORDEAUX by C. Denis Freeman and Douglas Cooper [Credit]. London: The Cresset Press, 1940.

Small crown 8°. 184 × 120 mm. (7¼ × 4¾ in.). Pp. [10] 3–408 ([i] half-title; [iii] t.p.; [iv] imprint: *Pr. in G.B. by The Shenval Press*; [v] full-page dedication and apologia: *To Those Whom We Left Behind*; [2] full-page illus.; 3–408 text). § Creamy antique laid paper. 6 full-page pen-drawings on the versos of section-titles, i.e. pp. [2], [26], [132], [180], [300] and [360]. § Cream canvas boards, spine lettered in red. D.j. with grey-bordered panel at front within which is the drawing on p. [181] 'Panic', with a pale green overlay. Endpaper maps of France repeated front and rear.

SECOND–FOURTH IMPRESSIONS: 1940 and 1941 (twice), all lacking the 'Panic' block which was perhaps lost during the printing of the first impression d.j. Some bindings of the earlier impressions are in a parti-coloured pink/cream sand-grain cloth; the fourth has a reduced leaf-size (175 × 112 mm) and is in blue cloth with dark blue lettering.

1942 BOOK CLUB EDITION: Readers Union Ltd. and The Cresset Press. 185 × 118 mm. 345 pp., the drawings now placed within the chapters.

14. 1941 BAGGAGE TO THE ENEMY by E.A. [vig.] London: John Murray, Albemarle Street, 1941.

Small crown 8°. 183 × 120 mm. (7¼ × 4¾ in.). Pp. [6] 121 [1] ([i] half-title; [ii] frontis.; [iii] t.p.; [iv] imprint: *Printed at the Curwen Press, Plaistow ...*; [v] contents and note: *The illustrations are all by E.A.; copyright in them is reserved to the Crown*; 1–121 text). § Thickish off-white antique wove paper. 108 pen drawings: frontis. and 16 full-page to face chapter openings; t.p. vig.; 90 vigs. and spot-drawings in text, 6 of which serve as chapter tail-pieces. 81 of these have legends below set in italics (for an example see p. 251), as also do the full-page drawings except – significantly – for that illustrating *Some of the dead were lying on the step of the small bandstand*

Opposite: Bodies in the Station Square at Amiens, page from *Baggage to the Enemy* (1941 item 14)

(p. [94]). § Red cloth boards (E.A.'s copy is dated 'November, 1941'), gilt lettering on spine. D.j. plum-red wash on pale buff laid paper with line-blocks front and rear repeating the drawings on p. 33 and the t.p. These are printed on patches cut through to the unprinted paper and have 2-colour overlays in yellow and blue; black lettering on front by E.A., typographic spine. Many copies noted are bound in blue cloth, and E.A. has what may be an untrimmed proof (195 × 130 mm) put up in blue paper boards, dated January 1942. This may be a trial for:

1942 BOOK CLUB REPRINT: printed from standing type for The Right Book Club (see item 12 above). 180 × 120 mm. Blue cloth boards; orange/red d.j. lettered in white with one unsigned line-drawing on front, not by E.A.

MS. DRAWINGS: Imperial War Museum.

In November 1946 the recently-founded National Book League held an exhibition of 'British Book Illustration 1935–1945' and it speaks much for their judgment that Baggage to the Enemy *(along with* Lucy Brown*) was among the fifty chosen books. It is, arguably, one of E.A.'s finest, and although some of the drawings repeat subjects which were given full-page treatment in item 12, their smaller scale and unpretentious draughtsmanship add to rather than detract from their impact. The very English brand of wit, understatement and precision in these small drawings of the last of France in 1940 is itself a commentary on the holocaust that lies just beyond the final page of the book.*

From the point of view of style the book marks a significant stage in E.A.'s transition from the heavy pen sketches of his earlier books to the lighter, often very delicate vignettes which characterise much of his later work.

15. 1946 PEACOCK PIE a book of rhymes by Walter de la Mare with drawings by E.A. [vig.] London: Faber & Faber Ltd., 1946.

Medium 8°. 225 × 148 mm. (8⅞ × 6 in.). Collation: [A]⁸ B–F⁸ G⁶. Pp. [4] 5–107 [1] ([1] half-title; [3] t.p.; [4] imprint: *First published 1913 … This new edition* [Credit], *first published 1946. Pr. … by Latimer, Trend & Co. Limited, Mount Pleasant, Plymouth. All rights reserved.*; 9–107 text). § T.p. vig. and 75 pen-drawings in text, so arranged that in almost all instances they alternate as head- or tailpieces to the poems. The paper is unusual. It appears to be a creamy cartridge but with the wire side markedly yellower than the felt side, the colour of alternate page openings thus changes in a slightly disconcerting manner. § Yellow cloth boards, the front with the image from the d.j. blocked in blue, the spine lettered in blue and red. D.j. cream, with a large pink wash front panel within a quadruple black ruled frame, typographic lettering on front and spine in black and blue, and with a central line-block from a drawing by E.A. not among the illustrations in the book.

REPRINTED: November 1946.

'"I'm tired of books," said Jack,' from *Peacock Pie* (1946 item 15)

1953 REPRINT IN LARGER FORMAT: crown 4° in eights. 248 × 180 mm. Same pagination and illus. on antique wove paper. Green paper boards, decorations and titling in 2 colours, line-block on rear cover as that on p. 46. D.j. as binding, but ads. on rear. An exact reprint (apparently stereotyped) of the first ed., with partially reset imprint. The paper retains – but consistently – the warm creaminess of the earlier printing. Reprinted 1955 and 1962.

1958 PAPERBACK EDITION: small crown 8°. 184 × 122 mm. Pp. [6] 7–121 [7 blanks]. A complete text, slightly rearranged and omitting the drawings on pp. 45 and 104 of the first ed. Reprinted with various cover designs 1963, 1967, 1970, 1974, and 1980.

'Tom he piped low ....' from *Peacock Pie* (1946 item 15)

1969 REVISED AND ENLARGED DEFINITIVE EDITION: as the 1953 reprint, but [4] 5–115 [1] pp., with ten additional poems being printed which had only formerly appeared in the ed. of 1924 illus. by C. Lovat Fraser. To help accommodate these the tailpiece on p. 45 is omitted, and many illustrations are now less happily reproduced, partly because of wear to the blocks and partly because of the hard-surfaced, dead-white cartridge paper used. (*Gruesome chalk-white stuff* says Nial Devitt in *Ardizzone 1* no. 78.) Paper boards designed as the foregoing, but printed in 4 colours, with a grey-blue wash over most of the board. Laminated d.j. as binding. Reprinted 1970, 1975 and (as a strengthened paperback, 210 × 145 mm) 1988.

2001 PAPERBACK EDITION: Faber Children's Classics series. A new setting of the foregoing, 196 × 125 mm.

TRANSLATION: 1977 [Japanese] Tokyo: Tuttle Mori. 225 × 150 mm. 74 illus. by E.A., printed sepia throughout, as is the text. 'Vellum' paper boards with fine full-colour designs by a Japanese artist front and rear.

Peacock Pie *was first published in 1913 and is probably de la Mare's most widely-known and best-loved work. Such have been its many transformations that a full synopsis is here given in an appendix on pp. 268–272. The poet himself would seem to have regarded E.A.'s illustrations as the masterpieces that they are, writing to his illustrator in 1946 that the drawings had given him 'the most various pleasure ... I love your light – and therefore your dark – whether candleshine or sun, & the rhythmical beauty of your trees and the wateriness of your water. If this is not too extreme a back-handed compliment to the fireman, I think you have entered into the* intention *& spirit of the rhymes with extraordinary insight and, as I say, I am most grateful ...'.*

   The illustrations were probably commissioned by Richard de la Mare, the director concerned with production at Faber & Faber, when E.A. was briefly in London on leave in the summer of 1944. He carried the text with him to Italy when he returned to duty and his diary records on 1 October 'Spend the morning doing rather a horrid little drawing for Dick' and then on 5 November 'Just completed a tremendous month's work here, twenty-two paintings, of which I am destroying five as not up to standard, three Xmas cards and sixteen drawings for Peacock Pie *done in my spare time after dark ...'. See also the note at C5 below and the reproduction on p. 272.*

16. 1946 THE POEMS OF FRANÇOIS VILLON Translated by H. B. McCaskie [Credit]. London: The Cresset Press, [1946].

Demy 8°. 217 × 135 mm. (8⅝ × 5⅜ in.). Collation: [A]⁸ B–O⁸ P¹⁰. Pp. [6] 7–243 [1] + frontis. and 11 insets ([1] half-title; [3] t.p.; [4] imprint: *First published 1946 by The Cresset Press Ltd., 11 Fitzroy Square, London, W1. pr. by The Shenval Press, London and Hertford*; [7]–19 *Introduction* by H. B. McCaskie; [21]–46 *The Legacy. Le Lais* with French text on rectos in italic faced by the English translation on versos in roman throughout; [47]–195 *The Testament. Le Testament*; [197]–243 *Various Poems. Poesies Diverses*). § Wove paper watermarked 'Basingwerk Parchment' for text, a thicker lithographic stock for illustrations. Frontis. and 11 full-page lithographs in grey and sepia with a third colour varying between pale blue, lemon yellow, peach and pale green. All plates untrimmed at the bottom, leaving instructions to binder on placement. § Creamy yellow linen boards, gilt-lettered front and spine. D.j. pale peach incorporating on front an adaptation of the design appearing between pp. 170–171 with the green tint now peach. Titling on front by E.A., letterpress titling and ads. on spine and rear.

17. 1947 HEY NONNY YES Passions and Conceits from Shakespeare. Assembled by Hallam Fordham [Credit] Produced by S. John Woods for the Saturn Press, [1947].

12°. 140 × 105 mm. (5⅜ × 4¼ in.). Unsigned gatherings collating [1]⁴ [2]⁸ [3–8]⁴. Pp. [72] + 8 insets lithographed on both sides of the leaf ([1] half-title; [3] t.p.; [4] imprint: *First published in 1947 by The Saturn Press 128 Baker Street, London W1 Pr. in G.B. Letterpress by Fredk. W. Kahn Ltd., London EC1 Lithographs by Graphic Reproductions Ltd., London WC2*; [5] dedication: *for B.F.G.*; [7–8] *Introduction*; [9–64] text of 473 numbered quotations, '*not unlike literary fragments*' (intro.); [65–72] *Index*, identifying sources). § Antique wove paper, the plates on a thicker matching stock. 16 full-page lithographs by E.A., probably printed from two pairs of plates, one printing mauve and yellow, the other grey and peach, all with handwritten legends by E.A. including the number of the quote illustrated. § Cream paper boards with lithographs front and rear and titling on front by E.A. using the mauve/yellow plates; letterpress titling on spine. The d.j. replicates this but using the grey/peach plates.

'The illustrations to the book are designed as an occasional commentary to the text, and show the finality and perpetual aptness of this Language by suggesting its use in familiar setting ...' (introduction) hence giving E.A. licence to illustrate the Bard with a succession of his favourite drinkers, lovers and fierce ladies. The chalk lithographs are sadly wanting in definition in many of the reproductions.

18. 1947 NICHOLAS AND THE FAST MOVING DIESEL. Transferred to 23.1.

19. 1947 THE PILGRIM'S PROGRESS From This World to That Which is to Come Delivered Under the Similitude of a Dream by John Bunyan [Credit]. [vig.] London: Faber and Faber Limited, [1947].

Large crown 8°. 203 × 122 mm. (8 × 4¾ in.). Pp. [4] 5–320 ([1] half-title; [3] t.p.; [4] imprint: *First published in 1947 … pr. in G.B. by R. MacLehose and Company Limited, The University Press, Glasgow …*; 5–11 *The Author's Apology for his Book*; [13] section-title: *The Pilgrim's Progress The First Part*; 15–[167] text of part I; [169] section-title: *The Pilgrim's Progress The Second Part*; 171–178 *The Author's way of sending forth his Second Part of the Pilgrim*; 179–320 text of part II). § Cream wove paper watermarked 'Basingwerk Parchment'. 119 pen-drawings: 3 vigs. for t.p. and section-titles; 21 drawings centred across text, 34 spot drawings in margins, 4 pairs of drawings occupying a full page in part I; 25, 21 and 3 of the same in part II; tailpiece vig. to part I. § Rose-red buckram boards blocked in blue on front with an enlarged version of the spot drawing on p. 134, blue panel and gilt titling on spine. D.j. largely coated yellow, with a large drawing, hand-lettered by E.A., printed black and repeated front and rear, letterpress titling on spine and below the block on front.

REPRINTS: three impressions to 1957. These were printed on a thicker, whiter cartridge paper and the d.j. was redesigned: cream paper, upper and lower panels wrapped round in dark red, the centre panel rear and front with a repeated new drawing of Pilgrim setting forth, and the spine with a new drawing of Pilgrim reading.

The Giant's rage.

Giant Despair from the Bagster edition compared with E.A.'s version of the same incident

In Creation of a Picture Book *and in other places, E.A. has paid tribute to the influence of an edition of* The Pilgrim's Progress *which he had as a child. First published by Bagster around 1845, this version was illustrated with many marginal wood engravings, and was printed over the years in various formats. E.A.'s copy,*

which survives, is a 'miniature' edition of around 1893. The pictures obviously influenced his own spot drawings; can one also see the artist himself helping to hew down Doubting Castle on p. [289]? In a letter to the artist, dated 19 October, 1947, Edward Bawden praises 'the conversational ease of the drawings; it is as though you knew by heart the grim, ogre-infested countryside through which winds the road to Paradise ...'. Some of the drawings gave rise to fuller pictorial treatment in pen and watercolour, three examples being exhibited at the Scottish Arts Council display in 1979 (cat. nos. 41–43). In a sale at Sotheby's on 5 December 1986, a pen and wash drawing was sold (lot 422) showing Timorous and Mistrust running downhill as on p. 49 of the book.

20. 1947 THREE BROTHERS AND A LADY by Margaret Black [Credit]. The Acorn Press, [1947].

Crown 4°. 245 × 180 mm. (9¾ × 7 in.) . Pp. [4] 5–62 [2] ([1] half-title; [2] imprint: *First published in 1947 by the Acorn Press, 48 Victoria Street, Westminster, London SW1. Set in Monotype Plantin and pr. in G.B. by Sanders Phillips & Co. Ltd.*; [3] t.p.; [4] 'frontispiece'; 5–[63] text). § Creamy smooth cartridge paper. 39 pen drawings reproduced in line with blocks in 2 colours: t.p. vig.; full-page 'frontispiece'; 10 serving as chapter-heads, 8 as tailpieces, and 19 of various sizes and dispositions in text. The blocks (unscreened) vary in colour according to the side of the sheet on which they are printed. In the first four gatherings pink is teamed with either green or khaki; in the second four it is teamed with grey or yellow. § Paper boards with six pen-drawn portraits of characters in the story and hand-written captions by E.A., and with 2-colour overlays in pink and green; letterpress titling on front and spine; rear blank. D.j. as binding but with ad. for *Acorn Press Publications* on rear.

PRINTING BLOCKS: two boxes containing the line-blocks and zincos, with proof pulls of the latter are in the Lilly Library of the University of Indiana at Bloomington.

The Acorn Press was established in 1927 to publish limited editions of village histories and poetry. In 1945 it came into the hands of the emigré wood-engraver Hellmuth Weissenborn. He and his wife Lesley employed the imprint chiefly for publishing Hellmuth's work, and Three Brothers *is one of the few books brought into the list 'from outside'. Writing as Lesley Macdonald, Mrs Weissenborn published a brief recollection of the production of this book – in three-colour lithography(?) – in the German magazine* Illustration *(no. 63, 1979, pp. 58–61). At some point the stock was either sold to, or distributed by, Abelard Schuman and, in the later 1960s, John Calder.*

Initial from *Desbarollda* (1947 item 21)

21. 1947 THE TRUE AND PATHETIC HISTORY OF DES-BAROLLDA THE WALTZING MOUSE by Noel Langley [colour vig.] With Illustrations by E.A. Lindsay Drummond, 2 Guilford Place, London W.C.1., [1947]

Crown 8°. 187 × 130 mm. (7⅜ × 5 in.). Pp. [8] 1–63 [1] ([i] half-title; [ii] *Books by the same author* …; [iii] t.p.; [iv] *First published in 1947*; [v] dedic-ation: *To the Rev. Quinton Morris This work is inscribed by his sincere and affectionate friend The Author. Kingston, Surrey*; [vii] 'frontispiece'; 1–63 text; [64] imprint: *This edition first published by Lindsay Drummond … set in 12 on 14 pt. Baskerville. Pr. and bound in G.B. by McCorquodale & Co. Ltd. London, S.E.1. on paper made by John Dickinson Co. Ltd. …*). § Thin, buffish antique wove paper. 31 drawings in ink and watercolour, plus a decorative initial in black above the imprint on p. [64] reduced from the design on p. 39: t.p. vig.; 5 full-page drawings (the first serving as a delayed frontispiece); decorated pictorial initials for each of the fifteen chapters, 8 tailpieces, and 2 drawings in the text. The watercolours appear to have been separated photographically to give a black line and three colours, printed flat from a grained plate, so that the printings in pale pink, grey and yellow have the effect of hand-colouring. (Loss of register in gathering [4] indicates that the book was printed on 4½ sheets). § Grey paper boards, the front with a repeat of the decorated initial on p. [64]; red linen spine. D.j. wrap-round pen-drawn design hand-lettered by, and with the signature, 'E. Ardizzone'; overlays in the three colours of the text illus.

MS. DRAWINGS: untraced, but 18 of the watercolour drawings were sold at Sotheby's on 2 December 1988, lot 416.

22. 1948 CAMBERWELL SCHOOL OF ARTS AND CRAFTS. London County Council. [vig. printed sepia] 1898 Jubilee 1948 [by Leonard Daniels].

Non-standard format. 252 × 175 mm. (9⅞ × 6⅞ in.). A single gathering of 10 leaves. Pp. [2] 3–18 [2] ([1] t.p.; [2] *Dedicated to the past and present students and staff*; 3–18 text, with, on p. 18, authorship accreditation *Leonard Daniels. Principal,* and imprint: *This booklet, which was designed and printed in the ... Camberwell School ... was issued to celebrate the fiftieth anniversary of the founding of the School*; [19] vig. tailpiece, printed sepia, as is the 'publisher': *Graham Savage, Education Officer, The County Hall, S.E.1.*). § Eight pen drawings, the t.p. and final vignette and a tailpiece on p. 14 printed sepia; half-page drawings labelled: *Entrance Hall; Life Class; Pottery; Modelling; Typography*, printed black. § The leaves stapled within grey paper boards, letterpress titling in sepia on front, grey linen spine, double endpapers of a wove cartridge paper matching the shade of the text paper. Another state has a gathering of 12 leaves, the outer conjugates blank, stapled within grey paper covers. No endpapers.

A brief account of the School finishes on p. 14 and is followed by a slightly pugnacious policy statement by the principal: 'Book illustration, a blood relation of painting, but sometimes estranged and a little touchy about its own independence, ought to be reunited with the family. And [verb. sap.] Experimentation may be an activity peculiarly attractive to youth, but in art, as in science, it is of little account at an uninformed and inexperienced level'. E.A.'s contribution is nowhere acknowledged.

23. 1948 CHARLES DICKENS BIRTHDAY BOOK Compiled by Enid Dickens Hawksley with Drawings by E.A. [vig.] London: Faber and Faber Limited, 24 Russell Square, [1948].

Large crown 8°. 210 × 147 mm. (8⅜ × 5⅞ in.). Pp. [288] ([3] half-title; [4] frontis.; [5] t.p.; [6] imprint: *First published in 1948 ... Pr. in G.B. by R. and R. Clark Ltd. Edinburgh ...*; [7] dedication: *To my Grandchildren*; [9–10] *A few interesting anecdotes about my grandfather ...*; [11–287] text, consisting of a calendar with each month given a title-page, made up of a heading and an illustration to an appropriate quotation, and then followed by page-openings framed for, usually, three successive dates, the versos supply varied quotations, the rectos have their boxes left blank for the insertion of birthdays). § Antique wove paper. 14 pen drawings: frontis., t.p. vig. and 12 monthly titles. § Canvas boards with a design and lettering (originating as autolithography) by E.A. in three colours front and rear, spine ditto, hand-lettered by E.A. D.j. as binding.

MS. DRAWINGS: all catalogued for sale by a bookseller in 2002.

The quotation for October 16, E.A.'s birthday, is from The Pickwick Papers: *'Wery good, my dear,' replied Sam. 'Let me have nine penn'orth o' brandy and water luke, and the inkstand, will you, Miss?'*

23.1. 1948 NICHOLAS AND THE FAST MOVING DIESEL [by] E.A. [large colour vig.] *To Nicholas from his Father* London: Eyre & Spottiswoode, [1948] [all hand-lettered by E.A.]

Foolscap folio. 330 × 227 mm. (13 × 9 in.). Unsigned gatherings collating [1]⁴ [2]² [3]₁ [4]⁴ [5–6]² [7]⁴. Pp. [3] 35 ([i–ii] blank; [iii] t.p. and dedication; 1–35 text, with imprint on final page: *Pr. in G.B. by W.S. Cowell Ltd., London and Ipswich*). § Creamy antique wove paper. T.p. vig. and 40 lithographs in text of varying sizes from corner-piece vignettes to near double-page spreads, prepared in line, litho ink and crayon for reproduction in four colours. Text hand-written by E.A. in a cursive script (with 'medecine' at the top of p. 5) printed in the dark grey of the fourth colour. The blurb states of the pictures: 'These have been drawn directly on the stone by the famous artist who is perhaps best known to children by his *Captain Grimes and Lucy* [!]'. § Paper boards with overall lemon-yellow wash apart from a large central illustration on front using the three additional colours, title, etc. above and below this in dark grey lettering by E.A., as is the publisher's imprint on rear. D.j. as binding. The edition is undated and although ascribed to 1947 by several authorities it was published in November 1948. As noted above, the pagination begins, unusually, on the verso of the title-leaf, with the even page-numbers on the rectos.

1958 ANTHOLOGISED EDITION: in *A Golden Land* ed. by James Reeves, pp. 312–322 (see item A17 below) with 4 pen drawings based upon images in the first ed. and small adjustments to text.

1959 SECOND EDITION: London etc. Oxford University Press. Crown 4°. Pp. [48]. Pr. by W.S. Cowell Ltd. T.p. hand-lettered by E.A. 46 illustrations: 21 drawings in line, on Kodatrace, and watercolour; 25 pen drawings. All the original subjects are repeated, but redrawn, and several new compositions added. The make-up and binding follow the style of the 'Tim' series established with *Tim to the Rescue* (item 30 below). Reprinted in 1959 and 1966.

1959 U.S. EDITION: New York.: Henry Z. Walck, Inc. Pr. in U.S.A.

1980 THIRD EDITION: London, etc. The Bodley Head. In effect a reprint of the second edition in slightly narrower format from a new publisher, put up in laminated pictorial boards with no d.j.

TRANSLATION: 1959 [Swedish] *Niklas och Expresståget*. Trs. Britt G. Hallqvist. Stockholm: Bergh.

MANUSCRIPT: The illustrated ms. on which the printed book is based was sold at Sotheby's on 2 December 1988, lot 415 (illus. with 2 colour plates in the catalogue): 'comprising cover design, pictorial title, and 35 pages of text with 38 ink and watercolour illustrations ... bound up in dummy form, a few revisions to the text in ink and markings in pencil, one small tipped in illustration no longer present, original wrappers, printer's stamp on covers dated 2 Oct. 1946'. This ms. is exactly the same size as the printed book and, judging from the illus. of two page-openings, was used to trace the text and the images on to the stone, where, of course, they had to be in reverse. The ms. was sold to Abbott & Holder who failed to sell it on complete and broke it up into separate units. One of these, the illustration on p. 9, was in the Wolseley Fine Arts centenary exhibition in February 2000 (cat. no. 12.).

Thoughts about this story date back at least to 1938 when E.A. wrote to Grace Allen about 'the germ of an idea for a new book – a small one about trains, with a title "Tom and his Train" or something like that'. The ten-year wait led to something larger and, in its first edition, done for a publisher with less formal procedures than O.U.P. Nicholas stands out among E.A.'s picture books as a work almost entirely his own. The hand-lettering, the disposition of the illustrations on the large pages, and the auto-lithographic composition give it a spontaneity not found in the previous folio volumes. Nicholas and his friend Peter Perkins are clearly forerunners (if not doubles) of Tim and Ginger, while the Diesel is a rather startling participant. It bears some resemblance to an idealised American locomotive but very little to the twelve- and sixteen-cylinder prototypes that were beginning to see service in Britain from 1945 onwards.

24. 1948 THE OTTERBURY INCIDENT [by] C. Day Lewis [Credit] London: Putnam & Company Ltd. 42 Great Russell Street, W.C.1., [1948].

Crown 8°. 203 × 135 mm. (8 × 5½ in.). Pp. [10] 148 [2] ([i] half-title; [ii] *Books for Boys and Girls by the Same Author (Published by Basil Blackwell)* …; [iv] frontis.: *The Battle in Abbey Lane;* [v] t.p.; [vi] imprint: *First published September 1948. Pr. and bound in England by Hazell, Watson & Viney, Ltd* … [and] The Otterbury Incident *is an adaptation of the French film* Nous les Gosses, *which can be seen in England under the title* Us Kids *and I am greatly indebted to the Academy Cinema, Ltd., and to Messrs. Pathéscope for their kind permission to use the plot of that delightful film as the starting point of my story. C.D.L.;* [viii] dedication: *To Jonathan Fenby and Richard Osborne;* 1–148 text). § Creamy antique wove paper. 23 pen drawings: frontis., 6 full-page and 16 in text, all with italic letterpress legends. § Red cloth boards, gilt titling on spine. D.j. a wrap-round four-colour pen and wash drawing based on the illustration on p. 133, hand-lettered throughout by E.A.

REPRINTED: 1958, 1963.

1949 U.S. EDITION: New York.: The Viking Press Inc. First issued with 'Copyright 1948 by the Viking Press Inc.' in the imprint with the publishing date September 1949, and bound in green glazed cloth boards with the illus. from p. 13 blocked on the front. At some point the copyright line was deleted in ink and replaced with the printed correction 'Copyright 1948 by C. Day Lewis'. Copy noted thus in heavy fawn cloth boards.

1950 SCHOOL EDITION: London: Heinemann Educational Books. (The Windmill Series). Reprinted many times before and after a reset ed. of 1967.

1961 PAPERBACK EDITION: Harmondsworth: Penguin Books. (Puffin Books no. 163). Reprinted many times, with variant settings of the t.p.

1966 NEW HARDBACK EDITION: London: The Bodley Head. Reprinted 1970, 1975, 1982.

1969 U.S. EDITION: Cleveland & New York.: The World Publishing Co. In lemon-yellow linen boards with a version of the drawing from the rear of the d.j. blocked in blue.

TRANSLATIONS:
1948 [Norwegian] *Uløkka i Otterbury*. Trs. Lise Houm. Oslo: Aschehoug. 1952 [Serbian] Trs. Slobodan Galogazha. Belgrade. In wrappers.

At the time of the book's first publication at the end of 1948 Messrs. Putnam advertised that the original drawings were available for display by booksellers

25. 1948 PAUL THE HERO OF THE FIRE [by] E.A. [large colour vig.] by E.A. [West Drayton]: A Porpoise Book, [1948].

Large foolscap 4°, the first and last leaves pastedowns. 220 × 180 mm. (8¾ × 7 in.). Pp. [3] 2–40 [2] ([i] dedication etc.: *To Antony White from his Uncle* [device in blue] *Porpoise Books are edited by Grace Hogarth and published in Great Britain by Penguin Books Ltd. and in the United States of America by Houghton Mifflin Co. Boston, Massachusetts*; [1] t.p.; 2–40 text, with imprint on p. 2 *Made and Pr. in England by Van Leer, 1948*). § Creamy antique wove paper. Large t.p. vig. and 42 drawings (including 'facsimiles' of a letter by Paul and a newspaper report), variably placed throughout the text, all the watercolours with the black line separately drawn, initially on a transparency (which shrank) and subsequently on the glass negatives; printed in 6-colour offset litho. § Paper over thin boards washed bright yellow with a large 4-colour illus. front centre, titled in a combination of typography and cursive lettering by E.A.; typographic spine; rear blank. D.j. as cover but with letterpress ads. for Porpoise Books on rear. End-papers a full-colour spread repeated front and rear.

1948 U.S. ISSUE: Boston, as noted on p. [i] above.

1958 ANTHOLOGISED EDITION: in *A Golden Land* ed. James Reeves, pp. 24–35 (see item A17 below)with six pen drawings mostly related to images in the book version.

1962 JAPANESE 'WORKBOOK' EDITION: Tokyo: Eirinsha, *Copyright 1962 by E.A. English Language textbook with Japanese annotations* [by Mikio Komura] … 181 × 125 mm. Pp. 39 [1]. T.p. vig., 19 toned drawings, all being monochrome illus. based (along with the text) on the 1948 ed. and reworked presumably by a Japanese draughtsman. Orange paper wrappers, the front with composite group of illus. from the book on a yellow over-lay. An eight-page supplement of English/Japanese 'review exercises' laid in.

1962 SECOND EDITION: with the dedication *A new version of an old story for my grandson Dominic.* London: Constable & Co. Ltd. Crown 4°. 254 × 186 mm. Modelled on the design of the post-war 'Tim' books (see item 30 be-low) but [32] pp. Pr. by A. & M. Weston Ltd., South Wigston, Leics. 34 illus.: t.p. vig. and 22 further pen drawings (including the 2 'facsimiles'), 11 in line and watercolour (see p. 65). Red linson boards, blocked centre front with a design after part of the t.p. vig. in black; black lettering on spine by E.A. for title. D.j. three horizontal panels with pictorial design hand-lettered by E.A. on front, the central watercolour repeated on rear.

1963 U.S. ISSUE: New York.: Henry Z. Walck, Inc. The English sheets in grey linen boards blocked on front in green with the drawing from p. [5]. D.j. as above, printed in England with Walck copy.

1969 PAPERBACK EDITION: Harmondsworth: Penguin Books. (Picture Puffin series). Large crown 8°. 197 × 145 mm, 32 pp.

1974 FIFTH IMPRESSION: London: Kestrel Books. The Leicester printer is now E. Hannibel & Co. (Litho) Ltd. Front board plain. The second–fourth impressions were published by Constable, which transferred its children's book list to Longman (Kestrel) in 1974.

First (1948) and second (1958 from *A Golden Land*) version of the closing drawing from *Paul the Hero of the Fire* (item 25, both slightly reduced)

Final version (1962, from the second edition) of the closing drawing from
Paul the Hero of the Fire (item 25, slightly reduced)

TRANSLATION: 1962 [Swedish] *Paul i Rök och Eld*. Trs. unknown. Stockholm: Bergh.

VARIA: a single-fold leaflet (120 × 140 mm) was put out by Constable in
1962 to publicise their new edition. It included two of E.A.'s colour illus.
and 2 drawings from the book.

The chequered history of the commissioning and printing of Paul *and of the Porpoise
series is given in* Lost Causes *edited by Steve Hare as the Penguin Collectors'
Society 'Miscellany 13' (1998) and it includes much of the surviving correspondence of Grace Hogarth and E.A. on the subject. Three other titles were published
with the same specification as here:* The Flying Postman *by V. H. Drummond,
Andersen's* The Ugly Duckling *illus. Will Nickless, and* Aladdin, *illus. John
Harwood. At least four other projected titles were abandoned.*

*On the publication of the 1969 paperback edition Kaye Webb asked E.A. for a
brief contribution to the 'Young Puffin Page' of* Puffin Post, *the magazine of the
Puffin Club (vol. 3, no. 1, 1969, p. 11). He wrote about his recollection of a fire and
introduced a competition for under-eights and his article was headed by a pen-sketch
'I and some of my grandchildren' drawn for the occasion.*

26. 1949 BACK TO THE LOCAL by Maurice Gorham. Illustrations by E.A. [vig.] London: Percival Marshall, [1949].

Demy 8°. 215 × 138 mm. (8½ × 5¼ in.). Pp. viii, 126 [2] ([i] half-title; [ii] frontis.; [iii] t.p.; [iv] imprint: *First published 1949 by Percival Marshall & Company Limited, 25 Great Queen Street, London W.C.2. Set and printed ... by Tonbridge Printers Ltd., Peach Hall Works, Tonbridge, in Bembo twelve point*; v–vi *Foreword*; 1–122 text; 123–126 *Index of pubs mentioned*). § Antique wove paper. 21 pen drawings: frontis. t.p. vig., 18 full-page and one double-page, captioned in cursive script by E.A. § Red cloth boards, gilt-lettered on spine, followed by a later remainder binding of pale blue linson lettered in black. D.j. pale orange incorporating the frontis. illus. on front; letterpress titling.

MS. DRAWINGS: seven drawings in a single frame were exhibited for sale in the New Grafton Gallery show in 1981.

Described by the author as following 'the same scheme' as The Local *(item 9) but nevertheless being 'a different book'. Thirteen of E.A.'s subjects from* The Local *have been retained, including the frontispiece, and their new treatment points to some of the transformations that the pub scene has undergone between 1939 and 1949. The drawing of 'Domino Players' has been replaced by 'Darts at the Alfred' and there are five other fresh subjects including a comfortable 'Drunk' and a depressive 'Bombed Pub'.*

It is possible to view Back to the Local *alongside the two other post-war books by Gorham (items 32 and 33 below) and that by Stonier (item 47) as doubly valedictory. They celebrate a London and a quality of life that will soon be beyond anyone's recollection and they provided E.A. with opportunities for deploying his powers of graphic journalism that would rarely come again. His delighted engagement with the scenes and characters in these books led him to compose pictures and integral decorations of resplendent wit.*

27. 1949 MIMFF IN CHARGE [by] H. J. Kaeser [Credit]. Oxford University Press, 1949.

Demy 8°. 215 × 135 mm. (8½ × 5½ in.). Pp. [8] 9–206 [2] + 8 insets ([1] half-title; [3] t.p.; [4] imprint etc.: [publisher's slug] *Translated by David Ascoli. Pr. in G.B. by W. & J. Mackay & Co. Ltd. Chatham 639*; [5] *Contents*;

Opposite: Page from *Back to the Local* (1949 item 26), with a pen-drawing sensitively reproducing the 1939 colour lithograph

The Cornet Player

[7] *List of illustrations*; 9–206 text, with the insets facing pp. 37, 48, 97, 112, 145, 160, 177 and 192). § Off-white cartridge paper. 8 full-page illustrations in line and watercolour with letterpress legends and instructions for placing. § Bright green linen boards, gilt-lettered spine. D.j. a wrap-round line and watercolour drawing, hand-lettered on front and spine by E.A. Full-colour pictorial endpapers repeated front and rear.

A sequel to item 10 above. Translated from the German, but not published in Germany until 1954 as Mimpf hat die Antwortung *illus. by E.A. (Ravensburg: Maier).*

28. 1949 SOMEBODY'S ROCKING MY DREAMBOAT
by Noel Langley and Hazel Pynegar [device]. London: Arthur Barker Ltd., 30 Museum Street, [1949].

Small crown 8°. 182 × 117 mm. (7⅜ × 4⅝ in.). Pp. [4] 5–223 [1] ([1] half-title; [3] t.p.; [4] dedication: *To YOU, dear, probably* and imprint: *Made and pr. in G.B. by Morrison and Gibb Ltd., London and Edinburgh*; [7] section-title*: Part I: Embarkation*; 9–223 text; [224] *Coda*). § Greyish antique wove paper. 3 full-page pen drawings as section-titles on pp. [7], [100] and [183]. § Bright blue linen, spine lettered in white. D.j. watercolour by E.A. with his lettering, printed in 4 colours on front; letterpress spine and rear.

Although the d.j. watercolour is signed by Ardizzone, the artist is nowhere formally acknowledged. The book was published in June 1949.

29. 1949 THE TALE OF ALI BABA & THE FORTY THIEVES
Being Literally Translated from the Arabic into French by J.C. Mardrus; and then Translated into Modern English by E. Powys Mathers [oval coloured vig.]. [Credit]. New York: The Limited Editions Club, 1949.

Imperial 8° in fours. 305 × 200 mm. (12 × 7⅞ in.) Pp. [6] v–vii [3] 50 [2] ([i] half-title: *The Evergreen Tales; or Tales for the Ageless* and title; [ii] frontis.; [iii] t.p.; [iv] imprint: *Pr. in G.B. at the Curwen Press, London E.13*; v–vii *Introduction*; [ix] fly-title; [x] second frontis., spreading across to form a headpiece on p. 1; 1–[51] text; [52] colophon: *This legendary tale … is included in the series of the Evergreen Tales of which Jean Hersholt is General Editor … the drawings were made direct on stone by E.A., the typography is by Ernest Ingham and the letterpress text and lithographic illustrations were printed at the Curwen Press … The edition consists of twenty-five hundred copies … and this copy is signed by [E.A. ms. signature]).* § Creamy antique wove paper. 15 pen-drawn lithographs in six colours: 2 frontispieces as above; t.p. vig.; 8 full-page illustrations, 3 in text and 1 tailpiece. One pen-drawn vig. in monochrome at head of introduction. § Lemon yellow linen boards with an oval framed illustration by E.A. in blue on front; blue typographic titling on spine. No d.j. Endpapers: a spread in full colour duplicated front and rear.

The book is one of three 'Evergreen Tales' issued as a set in a red slip-case. The other two titles (without printer's imprint and presumably printed in the U.S.) are Perrault's The Sleeping Beauty *translated by Percy Muir, illustrated by Sylvain Sauvage (unsigned), and Andersen's* The Ugly Duckling *translated by Jean Hersholt and illustrated by Everett Gee Jackson (signed by both parties). Neither has quite the lavish design of* Ali Baba. *At least one copy of that book alone was put up in quarter blue linen with decorated paper sides and a printed label* (hors série) *by the Curwen Press.*

30. 1949 TIM TO THE RESCUE [colour vig.]. By E.A. London, New York, Toronto: Oxford University Press, [1949] [all hand-lettered by E.A.].

Crown 4° in eights. 253 × 188 mm. (10 × 7½ in.). Pp. [48] ([1] t.p.; [2] imprint: [OUP slug] *Geoffrey Cumberlege, Publisher to the University. First published 1949. Pr. in G.B. by W.S. Cowell Ltd., Ipswich and London;* [3]– 48 text, the openings printed alternately in colour (from p. [3]) and black and white (from pp. 4–5), hand-lettered throughout by an unknown hand). § Off-white cartridge paper. 46 illustrations: 21 watercolours, with black line and ms. text on Kodatrace: t.p. vig. and 20 variously disposed within or across the spreads; 25 pen drawings, similarly varied. § Paper boards with grey wash over blank rear board and part of front board; yellow spine and panelling to front interrupted by red on white titling, and with a central coloured vig. by E.A. similar to that on t.p. D.j. as binding with price (8s.6d.) on front flap and ads. for E.A.'s previous picture books on rear flap, noting the folio *Lucy Brown* and the two paper-wrapped 'Tim' books at 2s. each.

REPRINTED: many times.

1957 U.S. ISSUES AND REPRINTS: New York: Henry Z. Walck. In November 1957 Walck graduated from being the 'American branch' to the 'successor' to Oxford Books for Boys and Girls in the U.S.A. Printing was, at this stage, still done mainly in England but from the early 1960s it was more and more done in the U.S.A. from film. The publisher's bindings were of full cloth, usually with an image from the book blocked on the front board. Heavily reinforced, side-sewn library bindings are also frequently found, apparently designed to prevent the books being held open without resort to force.

1981 PAPERBACK EDITION: Harmondsworth: Penguin Books. (Picture Puffin series). Foolscap 4°. 228 × 170 mm. Pp. [48].

1989 U.S. 'EDUCATIONAL ADAPTATION': in *Castles of Sand,* Needham, MA. etc. Silver Burdett & Ginn (World of Reading series), pp. 102–114. The text is accompanied by 5 of E.A.'s watercolours reproduced in lurid shades of blue, green and yellow, and is followed by a page of questions and a chart headed *Writing to Learn.*

2000 SECOND EDITION: London: Scholastic Press, as the first ed. but reoriginated from the original artwork (see item 4 above).

2000 U.S. ISSUE: New York.: Lothrop Lee & Shephard.

TRANSLATIONS:
1949 [Swedish] *Tim till Sjöss.* Trs. Britt G. Hallqvist. Stockholm: Bergh.
1974 [Afrikaans] *Tim se Heldedaad.* Trs. Freda Linde. Durban: Qualitas.
1977 [Norwegian] *Tim til Sjös.* Trs. Jo Tenfjord. Stabbeck: Bokklubers Barn. A book-club edition bound with a trs. of item 4 above.
1979 [Japanese]. Tokyo: Fukuinkan Shoten.
2000 [French] *Tim Sauve Ginger.* Trs. not acknowledged. Paris: Autrement Jeunesse.
2000 [Japanese]. Trs. Chihiro Nakagawa. Tokyo: Fukuinkan Shoten.

MS. DRAWINGS: One pen drawing is in the Kerlan Collection of the University of Minnesota.

Opposite: Illustration from *Tim to the Rescue* ([1949] item 30) and the original sketch for it (reduced)

Dear Wife
I am hoping you are as well as this finds me love from Joe
XXXXXXXX
SOAP

I am hoping that you are in the pink as this leaves me
13
Darling Bess
I am hoping you are as well as this finds me love from Joe
XXXXXX

Discussions about Tim to the Rescue, *the first post-war 'Tim' book, began in 1947 when Oxford University Press nurtured hopes of retaining the folio format but with openings in black and white alternating with those in colour. The financing proved intractable though, and eventually this quarto design was devised and the author was prevailed upon to accept a 5% royalty on the first 20,000 copies sold. (He did succeed in having his advance raised from £75 to £200.) At the behest of O.U.P.'s American department he also changed the ship's black cook into a white one.*

As the first of the quarto 'Tim' books this became the model for additions to the series, for new editions of its three predecessors, and for other picture books not directly about Tim, many of which were printed by Cowell's. The present entry is therefore used as a main reference point for the items numbered below, where the descriptions are limited to salient differences. Tim to the Rescue, *however, is the last of E.A.'s own books to be given a hand-lettered text.*

Associated volumes: items 4 (1955), 5 (1970), 7 (1958), 23.1 (1959), 25 (1962), 34, 39, 55, 78, 100, 103, 120, 141, 157 and 172. As is only to be expected, the quality of printing in both the British and the U.S. editions tended to deteriorate in the reprints of all these volumes until the decision was made in 1999 to reoriginate the 'Tim' series as far as possible from E.A.'s original artwork. For a comment on the reprinting of the next six books in the 'Tim' series, which has a uniform history, see item 34.

In 1949 E.A. was attempting to overcome the problem of the breaking-up of his line drawing in the course of four-colour process-work. His use of 'Kodatrace', noted here in previous entries for new editions of the 'Tim' books, was designed to allow a separate black printing to be made from a pen drawing on transparent plastic, with the watercolour wash then subject to three-colour separation. He gave an account of this method in the Penrose Annual *(vol. 46, 1952, pp. 66–67), reprinted below in Appendix II. In order to guide himself in the preparation of his artwork, E.A. here established what became a customary method of design. This involved use of a blank publisher's dummy of 48 pages in which he would draft the story and lay out the accompanying pictures. One such dummy in Special Collections at U.C.L.A. is noted at item 103 below.*

30.1 1950 FIRST STAGES IN WELSH. Welsh Home Service …
[BBC] 20 Sept.–6 Dec. 1950.

Large post 8°. 210 × 132 mm. (8¼ × 5¼ in.). Pp. [1] 2–31 [1], a single gathering including wrappers (2 t.p.; 3–31 text in Welsh throughout, with various music settings and 12 photographs). § Coated paper. T.p. and 6 other pen drawings. § Wrap-round photographic wrappers.

31. 1951 THE COMEDIES by William Shakespeare. Transferred to 62.1.

32. 1951 LONDONERS by Maurice Gorham. Illustrations by E.A. [vig.] London: Percival Marshall, [1951].

Demy 8°. 215 × 140 mm. (8½ × 5½ in.). Pp. [8] 158 [2] ([i] half-title; [ii] frontis.; [iii] t.p.; [iv] imprint: *Copyright 1951 by Percival Marshall … Other books by Maurice Gorham, illus. by E.A. … Made and pr. in G.B. by The Holborn Press, Holborn Place, High Holborn, W.C.1. …*; [v] dedication: *To David Mathew in exile*; 1–158 text). § Off-white antique wove paper, with sigs. A, I and K on a whiter stock. Pen-drawn frontis., t.p. vig., with one double-page spread and 21 full-page illus. for the 22 chapters, all captioned in a cursive script by E.A. Variable quality in the impressions of the line-blocks. § Maroon cloth boards, gilt-lettered spine. D.j. pale yellow wash on front and spine, hand-lettered throughout by E.A., with frontispiece drawing reproduced on front, highlighted in white; rear blank white. A binding in 'mid-brown cloth [?linson] with spine blocked in black' (communicated) is that for a remainder issue.

MS. DRAWINGS: the complete run of drawings, minus those for the frontis. and t.p. vig., was sold at Sotheby's on 19 June 1987, lot no. 629, noting the presence of preliminary drawings (including one for the frontis.) on the backs of 3 sheets. E.A.'s sketchbook no. 4 (Ashmolean) contains several drafts for 'Brighton Pier' and 'Meeting the Train', on pp. 119 and 149. For a reproduction see overleaf.

Meeting the train

'Meeting the train' from *Londoners* ([1951] item 32, margins not indicated)

Sketch for 'Meeting the train' from Sketchbook 4 (margins not indicated)

SHOWMEN & SUCKERS

An excursion on the crazy fringe of the entertainment world

by

MAURICE GORHAM

Illustrated by

Edward Ardizzone

Percival Marshall
London

33. 1951 SHOWMEN & SUCKERS an Excursion on the Crazy Fringe of the Entertainment World by Maurice Gorham [Credit]. London: Percival Marshall, [1951] [all hand-lettered within a 'monumental' frame by E.A. (see opposite)].

Demy 8°. 215 × 136 mm. (8½ × 5⅜ in.). Pp. [4] v–ix [1] 262 ([i] half-title in form of a small vignette; [ii] *Also by Maurice Gorham* …; [iii] pictorial t.p. by E.A.; iv imprint: *Copyright 1951 by Percival Marshall. Made and pr. in G.B. by W.R. Royle & Son Ltd* …; v dedication: *To my sister Nora Bartels*; vii–ix *Table of Contents*; [1] chapter-title: *Chapter One. Showmen and Suckers are made for each other*; [2]–262 text). § Off-white cartridge paper. 34 pen drawings: 'monumental' t.p. drawn and lettered by E.A.; contents page headpiece; and for each chapter a headpiece, incorporating an historiated initial letter, a tailpiece and (bar one) an illustration in the text. § Red cloth boards, gilt-lettered spine, with a later remainder binding in bright green linson lettered in black. D.j. pink-washed paper with a wrap-round pen drawing and hand-lettering throughout by E.A., highlighted in white.

MS. DRAWINGS: Sketchbook 18 contains a run of drafts related to this book on pp. 9–19.

34. 1951 TIM AND CHARLOTTE [colour vig.] by E.A. London, New York, Toronto: Oxford University Press, [1951].

Crown 4°. Size, make-up and binding follow the design of item 30 above, with t.p. vig. and 20 drawings in watercolour with black line on Kodatrace, and 35 pen drawings. The dedication is *For my niece Charlotte*.

REPRINTED: seven times to 1989. The publishing pattern in England for *Tim and Charlotte* and the five following 'Tim' books can be summed up here. Each original title was reprinted by O.U.P. a variable number of times according to demand down to 1989, later reprints in the sequence being published jointly as hardbacks and paperbacks. In 1989 the six titles were republished as a group of paperbacks, reset and in a newly-designed uniform cover. The titles were also collected in the 1985 compendium described as item 180 below and are all included in the sequence of printings reoriginated with digital colour-separation for publication in 1999 and 2000 by Scholastic Press in Britain and Harper Collins (formerly Lothrop, Lee and Shepard) in the U.S.A. (see also item 4 above).

Opposite: Title-page of *Showmen & Suckers* (1951 item 33)

1951 U.S. ISSUES AND EDITIONS: New York as noted on t.p. above for English sheets, subsequently pr. in U.S.A. and published by Henry Z. Walck, Inc.

TRANSLATIONS:

1958 [Swedish] *Tim och Charlotte*. Trs. Britt G. Hallqvist. Stockholm: Bergh.

2000 [French] *Tim et Charlotte*. Trs. not acknowledged. Paris: Autrement Jeunesse.

2000 [Japanese] Trs. Chihiro Nakagawa. Tokyo: Fukuinkan Shoten.

VARIA:

1964 *Gramophone record:* 45 rpm (DEL 129). In series with that noted above at item 4 (p.33).

1979 *Ceramics:* The watercolour for the front cover was (gaudily) reproduced on one of the three plates manufactured by Royal Grafton to celebrate the International Year of the Child. See also item 100.

1987 *Tape cassette:* One of the *Six Seaworthy Adventures* as noted at item 4 above (p.34).

35. 1952 THE BLACKBIRD IN THE LILAC. Poems for Children [by] James Reeves [vig.] [Credit]. [London]: Geoffrey Cumberlege. Oxford University Press, 1952.

Demy 8°. 217 × 135 mm. (8½ × 5¼ in.). Pp. [8] ix–xi [4] 4–95 [1] irregular pagination ([i] half-title; [iii] t.p.; [iv] imprint: *First published 1952* [O.U.P. slug] *Pr. in G.B.*; [v] dedication: *To Gareth*; [vii] *James Reeves has also written The Wandering Moon* ...; ix *Contents*; [x] blank; xi contents continued; [1] section-title; [3]–95 text in 6 further sections; [96] imprint: *Printed ... at the University Press Oxford by Charles Batey Printer to the University*). § 32 pen drawings: t.p. vig.; 7 illustrated full-page section-titles on pp. [1], [5], [25], [41], [61], [77] and [93]; 21 headpieces and 3 tailpieces to poems. § Blue cloth boards, silver lettering on spine. D.j. a wrap-round design in sepia line and 2 (separated) colours, hand-lettered throughout by E.A.

REPRINTED: four times to 1972, then included in Reeves's *Complete Poems for Children* (1973, item 159 below).

DANCE

AND RHYME

Section title from *The Blackbird in the Lilac*
(1952 item 35, margins not indicated)

1959 U.S. EDITION: New York: E. P. Dutton & Co., Inc., pr. in the U.S.A. reducing the prelims to 4 ff. and with the d.j. (horribly) redesigned by Sam Levene.

MS. DRAWINGS: dispersed. Six are in the Kerlan collection of the University of Minnesota, and 9 were catalogued for sale by Sally Hunter Fine Art, June 1991. Another drawing, that for 'W', was shown at the little *Ardiz-zodities* exhibition at Harrogate in November 2000, demonstrating the 60% photographic reduction of the original drawing (140 × 150 mm) to print at 63 × 75 mm.

The arrival of E.A. as collaborator on this near-perfect book seems almost to have been accidental. Reeves's ms. was accepted by the Press in September 1952 and hopes were expressed on both sides that F.R. Emett would illustrate it. He was too busy and Marion Rivers-Moore was then contracted to do so. Early drafts of her work however were deemed not to have 'affinity' with the poetry and on 23 January 1952 a decision was made to approach Ronald Searle. Simultaneously though, contact had occurred with E.A., perhaps on a separate matter, and on 24 January he was signed up to do the job for a fee of £100. 'Affinity' could not have been more complete, and, in view of his immediate sympathy with the verse, and the mastery of form and the delicacy of feeling in his drawings, it is good to know that a royalty of 2½% came his way once 7,500 copies had been sold.

This was the book that began E.A.'s long association with James Reeves, who was himself so delighted with it that he had a personal Christmas card printed using the block on p. 5.

36. 1952 THE MODERN PROMETHEUS. The Hope for Humanity. The Tragic Conflict of Knowledge and Ignorance. By Zareh Nubar [Credit]. London: Forge Press, 1952.

Demy 8°. 215 × 140 mm. (8½ × 5½ in.). Pp. [8] 9–70 [2] ([1] half-title; [3] caption for frontis.; [4] frontis.; [5] t.p.; [6] dedication: *To Einstein, the modern Prometheus* …; [7] *Dawn* [a poem by Norman Hill]; 9–12 *Foreword*; 13–70 text; [71] final illus.; [72] caption for the latter). § Thin m.f. printing paper. 3 full-page pen drawings (backed by captions). § White card covers, the front titled in maroon letterpress and incorporating the design from p. [47] in pale blue, the verso in maroon; the rear has the drawing from p. [71] in pale blue with the imprint in maroon: *Published in 1952. Pr. in G.B. by West Brothers, Mitcham.*

Much of the text from p. 18 onwards is a series of juxtaposed quotations aiming to support the author's desire for 'scientists everywhere to work together towards that common end, the building of the Civitas Dei ...'. Forge Press issued its first titles in 1948 (Ross Nichols's Seasons at War *and Rochester's* Lyrics and Satires *ed. Ronald Duncan).*

37. 1952 THE WARDEN [by] Anthony Trollope with an Introduction by Ronald Knox. Illustrations by E.A. London, New York, Toronto: Geoffrey Cumberlege: Oxford University Press, 1952. (The Oxford Trollope).

Crown 8°. 202 × 125 mm. (8 × 5 in.). Pp. [8] vii–xxii, 290 [2]; 6 full-page text illus. with blank versos are included in the gatherings but not in the pagination ([i] half-title and series title: *The Oxford Trollope. Crown Edition. General Editors: Michael Sadleir & Frederick Page*; [ii] O.U.P. slug; [iii] *Anthony Trollope. Born ... 24 April 1815. Died ... 6 December 1882*; [iv] *The Barsetshire Novels ...*; [a]3 frontis. on verso, recto blank; [v] t.p.; [vi] The Warden *was first published in 1855 ... Pr. in G.B.*; vii–xix *Introduction*; xxi *Contents*; xxii *List of Illustrations*; 1–290 text; [291] imprint: *Pr. in G.B. at the University Press Oxford by Charles Batey Printer to the University*). § Creamy cartridge paper. 28 pen drawings: frontis. and 6 full-page, 9 chapter headpieces, 12 in text. All the full-page drawings and one headpiece are given letterpress legends. § Brown buckram boards, gilt-lettered spine. D.j. series design in brown and pale blue for the Oxford Trollope with the headpiece from p. 239 on front centre panel.

1980 WORLD'S CLASSICS EDITION: edited by David Skilton, includes 22 of E.A.'s illustrations, printed monochrome (muddily); the full-page drawings were omitted. Reprinted 5 times to 1985, with a cloth-backed ed. appearing in New York in 1989.

38. 1953 BARCHESTER TOWERS. Illustrations by E.A. Volume I [II] London etc. ..., 1953. (The Oxford Trollope).

The format, disposition of pages and physical details of this two-volume set follow the series design also used in *The Warden*, above. Vol. I has pp. [12] 282 [2] with a frontis. and 6 full-page chalk lithographs, printed sepia, as insets, and 16 pen drawings in the text, including 7 chapter headpieces printed black. Vol. II has pp. [8] 279 [1] with 7 insets, as above, and 9 pen drawings in text.

1980 WORLD'S CLASSICS EDITION: in series with *The Warden*, has the 2 vols. combined in one with 7 of the insets and 9 of the drawings in vol. I followed by one of the insets and 8 of the drawings in vol. II.

[1982] U.S. FRANKLIN LIBRARY EDITION: Franklin Center, PA. One volume. 217 × 145 mm. Pp. [12] 3–533 [1]. Red leatherette, gilt. Illus. by E.A. reproduced in black and white line. One of a subscription series of classics published to illuminate the bookshelves of the non-reading classes. No equivalent production of *The Warden* has been traced.

— 1953 THE GOSPELS AND ACTS.

An aborted project. A bifolium exists, sewn into grey wrappers with letter-press titling: *First trials for an edition of the Gospels and Acts* [Credit]. With a demy 4° leaf size (280 × 190 mm) the four pages consist of a full-page pen drawing of the crucifixion, a two-page setting from St. John's gospel with a half-page drawing, and a blank. No publisher is given. Drawings intended for this edition are in the Ashmolean Museum, Dept. of Western Art. The publisher was to have been the Cambridge University Press.

39. 1953 TIM IN DANGER [colour vig.] by E.A. London, New York, Toronto: Oxford University Press, [1953].

Crown 4°. Size, make-up and binding follow the design of item 30 above, with t.p. vig. and 20 drawings in watercolour with black line on Kodatrace, and 35 pen drawings. The dedication is *For my nephew Simon*.

REPRINTED: eight times to 1989.

1953 U.S. ISSUE: New York as noted on t.p. above. English sheets. Later pr. in the U.S.A. and published by Henry Z. Walck, 1966.

OTHER REPRINTS: as noted at item 34 above.

TRANSLATIONS:

1961 [Swedish] *Tim i Fara*. Trs. Maj Britt Paul-Pont. Stockholm: Bergh.

1979 [German] *Tim in Gefahr*. Trs. Michaela Bach. Munich: Lentz; with a paperback ed. Ravensburg: Maier, 1984.

2000 [Japanese] Trs. Chihiro Nakagawa. Tokyo: Fukuinkan Shoten.

2002 [Finnish] *Tim i Fara*. Trs. Ulf Hyltén-Cavallius. Helsingborg: Go·boken.

2002 [Norwegian] *Tim i Fare*. Trs. Marianne Danielsen. Stavanger: Sandvik.

[n.d.] [Afrikaans] *Tim in Gevaar*. Trs. F. L. Mandini. Durban: Qualitas.

39.1. 1954 CHRISTMAS EVE by C. Day Lewis [Credit] [vig.] London, 24 Russell Square, W.C.1: Faber and Faber, [1954]. (Ariel Poems: new series).

Small demy 8°, a single gathering. 215 × 138 mm. (8½ × 5½ in.) Pp. [8] including wrapper ([1] front wrapper; [3] t.p.; [4] full-page illus.; [5–6] poem; [7] tailpiece vig. and imprint: *First published in 1954 ... Pr. in G.B. by Jesse Broad & Co. Ltd., Manchester ...*). § Three illustrations: the 2 vigs are lithographed in black litho crayon and the full-page drawing is a chalk lithograph in six colours. § Paper wrappers with letterpress titling on front, ads. for the series on rear, printed on a pale orange surface colour. Issued in a pale blue paper envelope with letterpress titling in black on front with marked space for a postage-stamp.

The 'Ariel' series was begun in 1927 when the Curwen Press collaborated with Faber in creating booklets described as 'alternatives to Christmas cards comprising an unpublished work by a distinguished poet illustrated by a sympathetic artist' (Gilmour p. 17). An attempt was made to revive the series after the war and the above is one of the resultant set of eight titles published in 1954.

40. 1954 THE FANTASTIC TALE OF THE PLUCKY SAILOR AND THE POSTAGE STAMP by Stephen Corrin [Credit]. London: Faber and Faber Limited, [1954]. [letterpress within full-page 4-colour illus.]

Foolscap 4°. 210 × 155 mm. (8¼ × 6⅛ in.) Pp. [24] ([1] half-title; [3] t.p.; [4] imprint: *First published in 1954 ... Pr. in G.B. by Latimer Trend and Co.*

Ltd. Plymouth …; [5–24] text, printed throughout on lightly-grained blocks of colour, variously orange, blue and yellow). § White cartridge paper. T.p. illus. and 18 further 4-colour line separations in the text, 2 being fitted across the spread. § Paper boards incorporating the t.p. design within a black surround front and rear, spine lettered in black on orange. D.j. as binding.

41. 1954 MIMFF TAKES OVER [by] H. J. Kaeser [Credit]. [London]: Geoffrey Cumberlege. Oxford University Press, 1954.

Demy 8°. 215 × 135 mm. (8½ × 5¼ in.) Pp. [8] 1–183 [1] (p. [i] half-title; [ii] frontis.; [iii] t.p.; [iv] imprint: *First published 1954* [O.U.P. slug] *Made and pr. in G.B. by Morrison and Gibb Limited, London and Edinburgh. Translated by David Ascoli*; v *Contents*; vii *Illustrations*; 1–183 text). § White antique wove paper. Frontis. and 9 full-page pen drawings with letterpress legends; sketch of a bottle of 'darncing water' let into text on p. 120; scenic endpaper spread (in line and colour), repeated front and rear. § Red cloth, silver lettering on spine. D.j. wrap-round colour-wash drawing hand-lettered by E.A.

REPRINTED: 1956, 1960.

The third book about Mimff, never apparently published in its original German. See also items 10, 27 and 64.

42. 1954 THE NEWCOMES. Memoirs of a Most Respectable Family Edited by Arthur Pendennis Esq. [By] William Makepeace Thackeray, with an introduction by Angela Thirkell and with illustrations by E.A. [Vig.: Centenary Edition Volume I] [Vol. II] Printed for the members of The Limited Edition Club at the University Press, Cambridge, 1954.

Royal 8°. 240 × 165 mm. (9¾ × 6½ in.) Vol. I pp. [2] xxii 332 + 9 insets; vol. II pp. vi [2] 353–742 [2] + 12 insets (Vol. I: [i] half-title; inset frontis.; [iii] t.p.; [iv] imprint: *Pr. in G.B. at the University Press, Cambridge (Brooke Crutchley, University Printer)*; [v]–vi *Contents of Vol. I.*; [vii] *Illustrations*; [ix]–xxii *Introduction*; 1–352 text. Vol. II: [i] half-title; inset frontis.; [iii] t.p.; [iv] imprint, as vol. I; [v]–vi *Contents* …; [vii] *Illustrations*; 353–742

text; [743] colophon: *Fifteen hundred copies of this Centenary Edition …
have been printed …* [vig.] *The illustrations were drawn by E.A. and coloured
through stencils by Maud Johnson. This is copy … signed by the illustrator.* [25
presentation copies bear an embossed stamp 'out of series']). § Creamy
antique wove paper for text and plates. 61 illustrations: vol. I frontis. (a
composite group of scenes) + 8 inset pen drawings, coloured through stencils + 18 pen drawings in text; vol. II frontis. (repeat of that in vol. I) + 11
and 22 of the same + t.p. vig. adapted for vol. II. § Pictorial linen boards,
lithographed in duplicate, for each vol. by E.A.; black linen spines with
titling in gilt. Black slip-case with letterpress title label. The set was
designed at Cambridge by John Dreyfus.

Tail-piece from *The Newcomes* (1954 item 42) inspired by one of Dicky
Doyle's original illustrations for the book (see the *Hand-list* pp. [26–27])

[1955?] SECOND EDITION: [New York]: Pr. for the Heritage Press at the
University Press, Cambridge [England]. Royal 8°, in sixteens. 228 × 150
mm. xxii, 761 pp. on cream offset cartridge paper, with a frontis. (a composite group of scenes), 19 full-page line drawings with letterpress legends
and 40 drawings in text by E.A. Linen boards with a lithographed design in
three colours on front and spine by E.A. hand-lettered on front, with a

typographic title panel gilt on black on upper spine; 3-colour portrait of Colonel Newcome after that on the frontis. by E.A. on rear. Top edge stained rust-brown. No d.j. Slip-case. *The illus. repeat those of the limited ed. but in line only and omitting the t.p. vigs and the repeat frontis. For a note on Limited Editions and Heritage Club books see under item 8 above.*

VARIA: 1955 *The Illustrated Illustrator.* A series of excerpts from the letters written by E.A. commenting in words and sketches upon his progress on the illustrations for *The Newcomes.* Issued by the Limited Editions Club. A two-fold inset, overall size 298 × 610 mm, on art paper, folded once more for insertion in the club's *Monthly Letter* for January 1955. The 6 pp. reproduce passages from 10 letters sent by E.A. to George Macy, reporting progress and enlivening the already lively prose with 10 reproductions of epistolary pen drawings (see opposite). The final two letters dated 10 and 20 October 1954, indicate that discussions may be starting about the illustrations for *Henry Esmond* (item 50 below).

43. 1955 BLEAK HOUSE by Charles Dickens. Abridged by Percy S. Winter [Credit]. London: Oxford University Press, 1955. (The Sheldon Library).

Small crown 8°. 182 × 120 mm. (7¼ × 4¾ in.). Pp. [9] 10–352 ([1] t.p.; [2] imprint: *Pr. in G.B. at the University Press, Oxford by Charles Batey, Printer to the University*; [3] *Preface* by Stanley Wood; [8] frontis. to text: *The High Court of Chancery*; [9]–352 text). § Wood-free m.f. printing paper. 12 pen drawings: 6 full-page, 6 in text all with letterpress legends. § Cream linson boards blocked with Sheldon Library series patterning in apple green. The verso of the front free endpaper has a printed list of six titles in the Library.

44. 1955 DAVID COPPERFIELD by Charles Dickens. Abridged by Stanley Wood [Credit]. London: Oxford University Press, 1955 (The Sheldon Library).

Specification as for previous item, but pp. [4] 5–218 [2] with the University Press imprint on p. [219] and the binding pattern in brown. 12 pen drawings: 6 full-page, 6 in text, with legends.

MS. DRAWINGS: 11 of the drawings were sold at Sotheby's on 5 December 1986, lot 421, and presumably dispersed. 7 of them were separately listed in Chris Beetles's *Illustrators* catalogue for 1992, nos. 342–348.

130 Elgin Avenue
London W.9
14ᵗʰ Nov 1·3

DEAR George

I stand reproved. The work
begins at once, and lost time
will be made up.
    About the printing I have no
preference. Of the names you mention
I of course know them all equally
well & have worked happily with
them before.. I would therefore
rather leave the choice to you.

Yours
Ted

From *The Illustrated Illustrator* (1955 see item 42, reduced)

45. 1955 THE LITTLE BOOKROOM [vig.] Eleanor Farjeon's
Short Stories for Children Chosen by Herself [Credit]. [London]: Geoffrey
Cumberlege, Oxford University Press, 1955.

Demy 8°. 215 × 135 mm. (8½ × 5¼ in.). Pp. xii 302 [2] ([i] half-title; [iii]
t.p.; [iv] imprint: *First published 1955* [O.U.P. slug] *Pr. in G.B. by Richard
Clay and Company Ltd. Bungay, Suffolk*; [v] dedication: *These stories are
dedicated with love to Denys Blakelock who began to share my childhood in the
Little Bookroom sixty years after*; vii–x *Author's Note*, dated *Hampstead, May*

Annar-Mariar lived in a queer old alley in one of the queerest and oldest parts of London. Once this part had been a real village all by itself, looking down from its hill upon the fields and lanes that divided it from the town. Then gradually the town had climbed the hill, the fields were eaten up by houses, and the lanes suffered that change which turned them into streets. But the hill was so steep, and the ways were so twisty, that even the town couldn't swallow the village when it got to the top. It was too much trouble to

1955; xi–[xii] *Contents*; 1–302 text of 27 stories). § Antique wove paper. 37 pen drawings: t.p. vig.; 28 headpieces, incorporating initial letters for the stories and the *Author's Note*; 8 drawings in text. § Orange linen boards, gilt lettering on spine. D.j. a wrap-round bookroom scene in 3 colours hand-lettered throughout by E.A.

REPRINTED: five times to 1966.

1956 U.S. EDITION: New York: Oxford University Press. pr. in the U.S.A.

1972 PAPERBACK EDITION: London: Oxford University Press. Crown 8°, omitting the t.p. vig. and the 8 drawings in the text. Typographic wrapper with 3-colour illus. by Robin Jacques on front.

1977 PAPERBACK EDITION: Harmondsworth: Puffin Books, in association with Oxford University Press. Small crown 8°. The drawings and original cover design restored, but the wrappers later given a new design by Pauline Baynes (*c.* 1987).

1979 CHEAP EDITION: New Oxford Library. Crown 8°. Laminated paper boards with colour version of the illus. on p. 7.

TRANSLATIONS:
1956 [Swedish] *Glasfågeln: Sagor och Berättelser*. Trs. Lena Fries. Stockholm: Rabén och Sjögren (not seen).
1957 [Danish] *Glasfuglen: Eventyr og Historier*. Trs. Tove Ditlevsen. Copenhagen: Thorkild Beck (not seen).
1957 [Norwegian] *Anna-Maria og Påfuglen og Andre Eventyr og Fortellinger*. Trs. Ebba Haslund. Oslo: N. W. Damm & Søn. Ten stories only, with their complement of illus. by E.A., but the headpieces adapted in order to omit the dec. initials.

MS. DRAWINGS: One drawing in the Dromkeen Coll., Victoria, Australia[4] and 5 + d.j. artwork in the Kerlan Coll., University of Minnesota.

4. In 1966 the Children's Book Circle (a group of publishers' editors) established an award 'for distinguished service to children's books' and named it after Eleanor Farjeon. In 1976, for the first time, the Award was presented jointly to two Commonwealth recipients, Joyce and Court Oldmeadow who had established the great Dromkeen Collection at their house in Victoria, and – with a nice feeling for the appropriate – the Circle presented them with E.A.'s drawing for page 184 of *The Little Bookroom* as part of the award. See J. Prentice and B. Bird, *Dromkeen: a Journey into Children's Literature*. London: The Bodley Head, 1988, pp. 147–148.

Opposite: Page from *The Little Bookroom* (1955 item 45)

Presentation inscription from E.A. to Eleanor Farjeon
in a copy of *The Little Bookroom* (1955 item 45)

*This book won a great succès d'estime among contemporary critics and gained
for its author the Library Association's Carnegie Medal in 1956 and also the
Hans Christian Andersen prize of the International Board of Books for Youth.
It also evoked reciprocal admiration between the author and her illustrator. A
copy of the book sold by Robert Vaughan at the 23rd Antiquarian Book Fair in
1981 carried on its t.p. a pen drawing by E.A. of himself at his Elgin Avenue
drawing-board with the inscription 'To Eleanor with love & thanks for writing*

such a lovely book to illustrate, from Edward' (see opposite), while his own copy carries a five-stanza poem[5] in E.F.'s holograph on its front endpaper, with a letter saying of the drawings '… All childhood is there, all I feel about childhood in the dim recesses where that part of me still lives. Thank you with all my heart'.

The book was the first of seven by E.F. which E.A. was to illustrate, a tally exceeded only by his collaborations with James Reeves, and its opening drawing of the child in the bookroom has featured many times in the documentation and journalism associated with children's literature. Denys Blakelock, the dedicatee of The Little Bookroom, *was to write a monograph on E.F. (see item A23).*

46. 1955 MINNOW ON THE SAY [by] A. Philippa Pearce [vig.] [Credit]. [London]: Geoffrey Cumberlege, Oxford University Press, 1955.

Demy 8°. 215 × 135 mm. (8½ × 5¼ in.). Pp. [8] 241 [3] ([i] half-title; [iii] t.p.; [iv] imprint: *First published 1955* [O.U.P. slug] *Pr. in G.B. by Richard Clay and Company, Ltd., Bungay, Suffolk*; [v] *Contents*; [vii] dedication: *To Ernest and Gertrude Pearce at the King's Mill*; 1–241 text). § Antique wove paper. 27 pen drawings: t.p. vig. and 26 chapter headpieces. § Pale blue cloth boards, spine lettered in red. D.j. three horizontal wash panels, pink, pale blue, pink, with letterpress titling front and spine and an enlarged version of the headpiece on p. 112 centre front and a new vignette centre spine.

REPRINTED: as above, three times to 1966. In 1989 there was a further reprint in the same format with a 241-page text setting, described as 'a classic edition reissued' with d.j. illus. by Robert Goldsmith.

1958 U.S. EDITION: as *Minnow Leads to Treasure*. Cleveland: World Publishing Co.

1972 PAPERBACK EDITION: London: Oxford University Press. Crown 8°, 217 text pages. Typographic wrapper with illus. by Robin Jacques on front.

1974 CHEAP EDITION: Oxford: Oxford Children's Library. Crown 8°, 241 text pages. Blue linen boards, d.j. illus. by an unidentified artist.

5. The poem is reprinted in *Morning has Broken: a Biography of E.F.* by Anabel Farjeon. London: Julia MacRae, 1986, pp. 288–289.

1978 PAPERBACK EDITION: Harmondsworth: Puffin Books in association with Oxford University Press. Small crown 8°, with wrapper by Graham Humphreys, and, from the 1988 reprint, by Caroline Binch.

1998 PAPERBACK EDITION: Oxford: Oxford Children's Modern Classics. Demy 8°, with wrapper by Tim Clarey.

2000 NEW U.S. EDITION: with original title. New York: Greenwillow Books. 210 × 135 mm. Pp. [8] 246, following the setting of earlier editions, but with pp. 242–246 an afterword by Philippa Pearce dated 'Great Shefford: April 1999'. Pr. in G.B. Bound in the U.S.A. in paper boards with a photographic d.j. by Edwina Stevenson

2001 PAPERBACK EDITION: Oxford: Oxford Univeristy Press. 200 × 125 mm. Pp. [11] 2–259 [3]. Cover photograph by Alex Buckingham/Digital Vision.

TRANSLATIONS:

1958 [German] *Die Verse Fährte des Herrn Laberdan: die Geschichte einer Merkwürdigen Schatzsuche.* Trs. Ursula Bruns. Freiburg: Verlag Herder. The word 'Verse' (verses) is cancelled with a large X on the title-page to allow the title to have the alternative reading 'Die Fährte …' (the journeys), a pun suggesting the mystery of the treasure-hunt.

1987 [Swedish] *Skatt Sökare i Kanot.* Trs. Karin Nyman. Stockholm: Sjöstrand. A previous Swedish edition (1956) was not illustrated by E.A.

47. 1955 PICTURES ON THE PAVEMENT by G. W. Stonier, [vig.] [Credit, in E.A.'s script]. London: Michael Joseph, [1955].

Small royal 8° in sixteens. 230 × 148 mm. (9⅛ × 5⅞ in.). Pp. [8] 9–214 [2] ([1] half-title and dedication: *To my Pat*; [2] *By the same author* [6 titles]; [3] t.p.; [4] imprint: *First published … 1955. Set and pr. in G.B. by Unwin Brothers Ltd., at the Gresham Press, Woking, in Perpetua type, thirteen point leaded, on paper made by Henry Bruce at Currie in Scotland and bound by James Burn at Esher*; [5–6] *Contents*; [7] *Acknowledgement* [to the Proprietors of 'Punch' and 'The New Statesman' for the use of text and 10 illus.]; 9–[215] text of 48 'London Scenes'). § Antique wove paper. 56 pen drawings: t.p. vig., 44 chapter headpieces incorporating an historiated initial letter, 4

Endleaf/cover/dust-jacket design from
Pictures on the Pavement (1955 item 47, reduced)

Unused design for the dust-jacket of
The Suburban Child (1955 item 48, reduced)

drawings in text and 7 chapter tailpieces. § Grey-brown cloth boards, the front repeating the endpaper drawing in red, the spine lettered in red after E.A.'s script. D.j. a further repeat of the endpaper drawing on the front, hand-lettered by E.A. on front and spine with a peach-pink overlay as second colour. A tiny vignetted version of the drawing (22 × 30 mm) appears in colour at the head of the front jacket-flap. Endpapers: a drawing by E.A. of a street-artist (slightly resembling himself) on the front pastedown, meets its mirror image on the free endpaper, the two versions being repeated on the rear endpapers (see p. [93]).

PROOFS: A 'bound copy of artist's proofs and original sketches' is in the de Grummond Collection of the University of Southern Mississippi (communicated).

The Acknowledgement records that ten of E.A.'s drawings first appeared in Punch, *although some have been modified to meet the needs of the changed format. All but the second ('The Enchanted Park') have hand-lettered titling by E.A. incorporated in the design. The decorated initial 'A' for the 'Elegant Pub' piece was also adapted by E.A. to make a bookplate for his wife, Catherine.*

In his History of Punch *(London, 1957) R. G. G. Price writes of Stonier's 'curlicues' as 'one of the glories of the magazine at this time'. The illustrations (by 'Ardizonne') he sees as being 'outside of any of the* Punch *traditions'. See also the notes to item D4 below.*

48. 1955 THE SUBURBAN CHILD [by] James Kenward [vig.] [Credit]. Cambridge: At the University Press, 1955.

Crown 8°. 192 × 122 mm. (7⅞ × 4¾ in.). Pp. [8] 141 [3] ([v] half-title; [vi] imprint: *Published by the Syndics … Printed … at the University Press, Cambridge (Brooke Crutchley, University Printer)*; [vii] t.p.; [viii] frontis.: *Suburbia*; 1–[142] text). § Antique wove paper. 11 pen drawings: t.p. vignette, frontispiece and 9 full-page drawings with letterpress legends and pagination. § 'Vellum' paper boards, letterpress titling in black and orange on front and spine with repeat of the t.p. vignette on front in orange. D.j. pen-drawn variant of the illus. on p. 93 with lettering by E.A. on front and spine with overlays separated in 3 colours.

MS. DRAWINGS: A rejected (or abandoned) design for the d.j., unrelated to any of the illus. in the book, is in the collection of Geoff Green, 290 × 205 mm, line and colour wash with Chinese white for lettering (see opposite).

Chapters 41 and 42 consider 'the literature appreciated by the Suburban child' with perceptive judgements on Caldecott, Beatrix Potter and The Rainbow *comic. Two later 'classic sequences' –* Babar *and* Dr Dolittle *– are also noted and 'equal with these, but not yet well enough known to rank with them as classics, are the books illustrated by E.A. with their true-to-life impetuous children, their diverse flesh-and-blood grown-ups, and their warm yellow-green or threatening purple-blue seas …'.*

49. 1955 SUN SLOWER SUN FASTER [by] Meriol Trevor [Credit]. St. James's Place, London: Collins, 1955.

Crown 8°. 191 × 125 mm. (7½ × 4⅞ in.). Pp. [6] 7–287 [1] ([1] half-title; [2] vig. frontis.; [3] t.p.; [4] imprint: *Pr. in G.B. Collins Clear-Type Press: London and Glasgow*; [5] dedication: *For Briony & Roger Duncan*; 7 Contents; 9–10 *Illustrations*; 11–287 text). § Antique wove paper. Frontis. and 21 pen drawings with letterpress legends in text. § Blue cloth boards, gilt titling on spine. D.j. pen-drawn variant of the frontis. on front, unrelated drawing on spine with lettering on both by E.A. with overlays separated in 2 colours.

1957 U.S. EDITION: New York: Sheed and Ward.

The machining of the heavily cross-hatched drawings on the soft paper leaves much to be desired.

— c. 1955 HISTOIRE DE MANON LESCAUT by the Abbé Prévost [not published].

On pages 68–69 of John Lewis's *Handbook of Type and Illustration* (see Sources p. 285) a specimen setting of the French text of *Manon*, set in 12 point Caslon Old Face, is faced by a full-page line-drawing by E.A. with a legend in his cursive script. This is reproduced as an example, with explanation, of how to prepare a line-block and is reproduced photographically by the Dow Etch process. This drawing was copied and re-fashioned from a suite of lithographs for *Manon* prepared, possibly as an exercise, before the war. It is unlikely that an edition was ever contemplated. See NAP Suite I, pp. 36–43. Pages 70–72 of the *Handbook* contain an account by E.A. of his method of preparing a line drawing, accompanied by an example of his three stages of work (see opposite). These drawings were also used by Messrs. Faber as part of a flyer to advertise the *Handbook* (see M. & D. Reeve *Cat.* 48, no. 42).

Stage 1. The drawing is indicated rather hesitatingly in outline

Stage 2. Shadows are then suggested by a very deliberate even hatching.
One has then a complete little picture in light and shade only

Above and overleaf: E.A.'s three stages of drawing and accompanying
text from John Lewis's *Handbook of Type and Illustration* (1956).

Stage 3. The shadows are heightened and colour indicated by cross hatching. Also outlines are corrected and accentuated and details added. In fact, at this stage, one treats the drawing as if it were a little painting, adding tone here and there, until it is brought up to the necessary pitch

50. 1956 THE HISTORY OF HENRY ESMOND, ESQ. A Colonel in the Service of Her Majesty Q. Anne, Written by Himself. [By] William Makepeace Thackeray. With a new introduction by Laura Benét and illustrations by E.A. [vig. in sepia]. [New York]: Printed for members of the Limited Editions Club, 1956 [all set within 4 boxes within a double-rule frame].

Royal 8°. 246 × 166 mm. (9¾ × 6½ in.). Pp. [xi] xii–xxi [xxii], [3] 4–441 [5] ([iii] half-title; [v] t.p.; [vi] *The special contents of this edition are copyright, 1956, by The George Macy Companies, Inc.*; [vii]–viii *Contents*; [ix] *List of Illustrations*; [xi]–xv *Introduction* by Laura Benét; [xvii]–xxi *Preface* by 'Rachel Esmond Warrington'; [1] t.p. to Book I; [3]–441 text; [443] colophon: *Fifteen hundred copies of ... Henry Esmond have been printed for the members of the Limited Editions Club by the John B. Watkins Company in New York. The illustrations were drawn by E.A. and coloured by hand in the studio of Walter Fischer. This is ...*). § Creamy cartridge paper. 36 pen drawings, hand-coloured as noted above in three tints: blue, yellow, pink, 16 full-page, 16 in text organised on conjugate leaves for ease of colouring.

§ Orange-brown brocade-covered boards, oval brown morocco title label, top edge stained brown. Brown slip-case, paper over board with an oval title label printed green.

SECOND IMPRESSION: New York: The Heritage Press, [1956]. A photographic reprint in medium 8° format, the t.p. vig. printed black and the 32 illustrations now coloured with 2-colour overlays in varying combinations of tints. Quarter black cloth, gilt titling on spine, linen boards lithographed in 4 colours by E.A. with full-length portraits of Esmond on front and Beatrix on rear; top edge stained green. Green slip-case.

MS. DRAWINGS: 32 watercolours, but not the t.p. vig., are in the Dept. of Special Collections at the University of California at Los Angeles.

51. 1956 HUNTING WITH MR. JORROCKS from *Handley Cross* by R. A. Surtees Edited by Lionel Gough [Credit]. [London]: Geoffrey Cumberlege, Oxford University Press, 1956.

Large crown 8°. 202 × 130 mm. (8 × 5¼ in.). Pp. [8] 186 [2] + frontis. and 8 insets ([i] half-title; [ii] *Lionel Gough is also the Editor of Hunting Scenes From Surtees (Rupert Hart-Davis)*; inset frontis.; [iii] t.p.; [iv] imprint: [O.U.P. slug] Handley Cross *was first published in 1843* Hunting with Mr. Jorrocks *(an abridged version of* Handley Cross*) first published 1956.* Pr. in G.B. by *W.S. Cowell, Ltd., Ipswich and London. Bound by G. and J. Kitcat, Ltd., London;* [v] dedication: *To three of my friends at Craven Arms ... Lionel Gough;* vii *Contents;* 1–186 text with insets on stubs facing pp. 28, 60, 76, 106, 112, 144, 168, 184). § Smooth offset cartridge paper; same stock for text and plates. Pen drawings with colour separations reproduced by 4-colour litho. § Grey linen boards, title-panel in red and gilt on spine. D.j. a wrap-round design in line and watercolour and hand-lettering by E.A.

The text is excerpted from Chapters 7–58 of Handley Cross *(expanded ed. 1854) and admirably serves its stated purpose – however much reprobated today – of providing 'the best of short cuts to Mr. Jorrocks and his hounds'. While E.A.'s drawing is looser and less detailed than the hand-coloured wood engravings after Leech that illustrated the 1854 edition, he shares a like freshness in his use of colour (doubly remarkable, given the cumbersome process of colour separation) and a like kindliness in his spirit of caricature.*

99

52. 1956 PIGEONS AND PRINCESSES [by] James Reeves [Credit]. London, Melbourne, Toronto: Heinemann, [1956].

Demy 8°. 214 × 137 mm. (8½ × 5½ in.). Pp. [6] 113 [1] ([i] half-title; [ii] *Books by James Reeves …*; [iii] t.p.; [iv] imprint: *Pr. in G.B. by the Windmill Press Ltd. Kingswood, Surrey*; [v] headpiece by E.A. and *Contents*; 1–113 text). § Off-white smooth cartridge paper. 20 pen drawings: 5 headpieces and 15 in text. § Red cloth boards, gilt lettering on spine. D.j. overall olive-green wash, but with cut-outs front and spine allowing for hand-lettered titling by E.A. on a pink overlay, repeat of drawing on p. 55 on white on front, author's name in white on spine.

REPRINTED: four times to 1966.

1962 U.S. EDITION: New York: E. P. Dutton, in the compendium noted at item 97 below.

1976 PAPERBACK EDITION: London: Hamlyn Group (Beaver Books). Crown 8°. Drawings by E.A. reproduced front and rear of a redesigned cover.

TRANSLATION: 1959 [Swedish] *Lilla Måndag*. Trs. Ingegärd Martinell. Stockholm: Bergh.

53. 1956 ST. LUKE'S LIFE OF CHRIST Translated into Modern English by J. B. Phillips. With illustrations by E.A. [winged-bull vig.]. St. James's Place, London: Collins, [1956].

Demy 8°. 220 × 136 mm. (8⅝ × 5⅜ in.). Pp. [8] vii–viii, 115 [3] ([i] half-title; [iii] t.p.; [iv] imprint: *1956 Pr. in England. The Curwen Press, Plaistow, London E.13*; [v] *Note: These translations … are taken from J. B. Phillips's* The Gospels … *and* The Young Church in Action *both published by Geoffrey Bles Ltd.*; vii–viii *Translator's Note*; 1–115 text with running heads on rectos; [117] tailpiece vig.). § Creamy laid paper, no watermark. 24 pen drawings: t.p. vig., headpiece, 21 in text and final vig. § Black buckram boards. D.j. overall mauve wash cut through for the illus. on p. 100 on front and pp. 35 and 106 on rear, all with a green overlay.

An impression limited to 150 copies, signed by translator and illustrator, was issued simultaneously, printed on Arnold Signature paper, quarter bound in dark orange morocco with grey linen sides. Thick card slip-case covered with a blue and black Curwen patterned paper by Edward Bawden. Barry McKay Rare Books Cat. 57 (1999) records a copy of the standard ed. 'marked up for printing with ms. amendments to the colophon and pencil and ink markings throughout'. He speculates that this was in preparation for a new ed., subsequently abandoned (item 443).

Unused drawing for *A Stickful of Nonpareil* (1956 item 54, reduced)

54. 1956 A STICKFUL OF NONPAREIL [large vig.] Written by George Scurfield [Credit]. Cambridge: Privately printed at the University Press, 1956.

Small crown 4°. 223 × 160 mm. (9 × 6⅜ in.). Pp. [8] 57 [3] ([i] half-title; [iii] t.p.; [iv] imprint: *Pr. in G.B.*; [v] *Five hundred copies printed and bound at the University Press, Cambridge for presentation by the University Printer to his friends in printing and publishing Christmas 1956*; [viii] *Preface* by Brooke Crutchley, University Printer; 1–55 text; 56–[58] Names and nicknames of

46 employees of the Press, giving *the feel and flavour of what working at the Press must have been like sixty years ago*). § Smooth off-white cartridge paper. 16 pen drawings: t.p. vig.; 9 section headpieces: 6 in text with letterpress captions. § Dark green buckram, decorations on front and spine in gilt (not by E.A.). Endpapers a pale green floral-patterned stock from the 1890s. No d.j.

ABRIDGED REPRINT: in *Matrix: a Review for Printers and Bibliophiles. No. 13* (Winter 1993) pp. 151–157; with two of E.A.'s drawings, reprinted in browny-orange.

MS. DRAWINGS: with proof-pulls in the Lilly Library of the University of Indiana at Bloomington. One unused pen drawing for the book is in the private collection of Geoff Green (see p. 101).

In A Printer's Christmas Books *(London: St Bride Printing Library, 1975) Brooke Crutchley notes: 'There is an element of pastiche about the production, not wholly successful, though the endpapers are authentic, a stock having been found in the possession of a London supplier which exactly and unbelievably matched a sample taken from a novel of the nineties. Ardizzone's drawings [are] full of authentic atmosphere ...'.*

55. 1956 TIM ALL ALONE [colour vig.] by E.A. London, New York, Toronto: Oxford University Press, [1956].

Crown 4°. Size, make-up, binding follow the design of item 30 above, with t.p. vig. and 19 drawings in watercolour with black line Kodatrace and 27 pen drawings. The dedication is *For my cousin Victoria*.

REPRINTED: nine times to 1989, and the year 2000 reoriginations as noted at item 34 above.

1956 U.S. ISSUE: New York as noted on t.p. above; printings for Walck in 1963 and 1964 were done in England by Cowell's.

TRANSLATIONS:
1975 [Afrikaans] *Tim Stokalleen*. Trs. F. L. Mandini. Durban: Qualitas.
2001 [Japanese] Trs. Chihiro Nakagawa. Tokyo: Fukuinkan Shoten.

VARIA:

1980 *Audio-visual adaptation:* Weston, CT, Weston Woods. Filmstrip and cassette versions in series with those noted at item 4 above (p. 33), but no 'iconographic' version was made.

1987 *Tape cassette:* One of *Six Seaworthy Adventures* as noted at item 4 above (p. 34).

In 1956 the Library Association established its Kate Greenaway Medal for the most distinguished illustrated book for children published in the previous year. As things turned out no 1955 book was found suitable, but a year later the first Medal was awarded to E.A. for Tim All Alone. *Following the award an oval label announcing it was affixed at the foot of the d.j.*

56. 1957 DING DONG BELL a First Book of Nursery Rhymes. Devised by Percy Young and E.A. [vig.], London: Dennis Dobson, [1957].

Crown 4° in eights. 242 × 180 mm. (9⅝ × 7 in.). Pp. [4] 5–143 [1] ([1] half-title; [2] *Books by Percy Young*; [3] t.p.; [4] imprint: *First published in 1957 ... Pr. and bound by N.V. Grafische Industrie Haarlem – Holland*; 5–7 Contents; 8 *Epigraphs*; 9–11 *Preface* by P.M.Y.; 12 dedication: *For Elizabeth and James*; [13]–137 text with musical accompaniments; [138] tailpiece vig.; 139 *List of works consulted*; 141–143 *Index of first lines*). § Off-white cartridge paper (now discolouring to edges). 17 pen drawings: 8 full-page section-titles; 9 smaller drawings and vigs repeating in variable sequence 31 times throughout the text. A vig. of a child piping is used on the t.p. and as the tailpiece on p. [138] and on four other occasions. § Pale blue paper boards, with 4 vigs. of children, each within an arch frame and each repeated four times as a pattern on front and rear boards; dark blue linen spine with gilt titling. D.j. a pen and wash drawing with hand-lettering by E.A. on front and spine, letterpress ad. on rear. The book's sub-title is given as *a first book of nursery songs.*

The eighty rhymes are arranged in eight subject groups – Animals, Birds & Insects, etc. – with full-page titles by E.A. in which he manages to include visual references to several items within the section. The selection of traditional rhymes (with five or so being from designated authors) and the notes on the musical versions and the technique for playing them show a fine appreciation of the songs as 'the beginning of poetic and musical experience', and P. M. Young, in his preface, associates E.A. in the venture.

57. 1957 LOTTIE by John Symonds [large vig. drawing] [Credit]. Books for Boys and Girls. London: The Bodley Head, [1957].

Small foolscap 4°. 202 × 154 mm. (8 × 6 in.). Pp. [4] 34 [2] ([i] half-title; [ii] dedication: *For Renata*; [iii] t.p.; [iv] imprint: *First published 1957 … Pr. in G.B. by W & J. Mackay & Co. Ltd., Chatham …*; 1–[35] text). § Off-white m.f. printing paper. 13 pen drawings: t.p. vig., 7 large chapter-heads (approx. 145 × 154 mm) and 5 similar in text. § Paper boards, large central panel a pen drawing, after the t.p. vig., with 2-colour separation by E.A. on front, repeated on rear, plain pink spine. D.j. as binding.

Vicissitudes in the life of a talking doll in partnership with a foundling dog. This first encounter with the Bodley Head children's department was not wholly to the artist's satisfaction. See item 72 below.

58. 1957 PREFABULOUS ANIMILES by James Reeves and E.A. [London]: Heinemann, [1957] [notice-board titling, hand-lettered by E.A., surrounded by pen drawings of Doze, Bisk, Catipoce and other animiles].

Demy 8°. 210 × 135 mm. (8¼ × 5⅜ in.). Pp. [8] 56 ([i] half-title; [ii] *Books by J.R. with illus. by E.A. …*; [iii] t.p.; [iv] imprint: *Published in 1957 … Pr. and bound in G.B. by Jarrold and Sons Limited Norwich*; [v] dedication: *To Janet Adam Smith*; [vi] *Acknowledgements are due to the Editor of the* New Statesman and Nation *in which some of these verses and drawings first appeared*; [vii] *Contents*; 1–56 text). § Off-white cartridge paper. 42 pen drawings illustrating 13 sets of verses: title-page, as above and 13 of the drawings running across the page-opening, sometimes framing the verses. § Blue linson boards. D.j. front a slightly enlarged reproduction of the t.p. drawing, hand-lettered by E.A., with 2-colour separation, blue and pink, added; letterpress spine and rear ads.

1960 U.S. EDITION: New York: E. P. Dutton & Co. Inc. published as a companion volume to item 35 above.

From 1973 the text was included in Reeves' Complete Poems for Children *(see item 159 below).*

59. 1957 THE SCHOOL IN OUR VILLAGE by Joan M. Goldman [vig.] [Credit]. London: B. T. Batsford Ltd., [1957].

Demy 8°. 215 × 135 mm. (8½ × 5⅜ in.). Pp. [4] 5–136 ([1] half-title; [3] t.p.; [4] imprint: *First published 1957. Pr. and bound in G.B. by Jarrold and Sons Ltd., London and Norwich* ...; 5 *Contents*; [6] *By the same author* ...; [7] *Abridged excerpts from this book have appeared in* The Times Educational Supplement *and the* Evesham Journal; 9–136 text). § Thickish smooth cream cartridge paper. T.p. vig. and 26 chapter-head drawings with pictorial initials. § Pale blue linson boards with matching blue endpapers, top edge stained blue. D.j. pink with repeats of tp. vig. on front and chapter-head drawing on p. 16 on rear.

MS. DRAWINGS: the t.p. vig. and 12 drawings are in the Kerlan Coll. of the University of Minnesota.

An account of a one-teacher village school, slightly akin to Sybil Marshall's later Experiment in Education *(Cambridge, 1963) detailing an almost-vanished way of educational life. In the chapter 'Story time' Joan Goldman notes 'There are, of course, chosen stories that do have a genuine all-age appeal. My choices differ greatly from one another ...' and she includes 'Catskin', the Brer Rabbit tales, 'the lovely Père Castor stories', and Edward Ardizzone's 'Tim' books.*

60. 1957 SUGAR FOR THE HORSE by H. E. Bates [vig.] [Credit]. London: Michael Joseph, [1957].

Crown 8°. 202 × 130 mm. (8 × 5 in.). Pp. [6] 7–119 [1] ([1] half-title; [3] t.p.; [4] imprint: *First published ... 1957. Set and pr. in G.B. by Unwin Brothers Ltd. at the Gresham Press, Woking, in Imprint type, 11 point, leaded, on paper made by Henry Bruce at Currie, Midlothian, and bound by James Burn at Esher, Surrey*; [5] *Contents*; 7–[120] text). § Antique wove paper. 25 pen drawings: t.p. vig. repeated on final tailpiece and one head-piece and one drawing in text for each of 12 chapters. § Blue linen with maroon panel and gilt titling on spine. D.j. pink with repeats of the drawings on pp. 91 and 31 front and rear. (See also p. 309). § *Ref:* Eads A85.

'Twelve further stories about the old countryman with the gargantuan appetite and thirst ...' (blurb) who first appeared in My Uncle Silas *(item 11 above).*

61. 1957 THE WANDERING MOON [by] James Reeves [Credit]. Melbourne, London, Toronto: Heinemann, [1957].

Crown 8°. 195 × 130 mm. (7¾ × 5 in.). Pp. [6] 73 [1] ([i] half-title and dedication: *To Julia*; [ii] frontis.; [iii] t.p.; [iv] *Books by James Reeves ... and* imprint: *First published 1950; Reprinted 1951; New edition 1957. Pr. in G.B. by Butler & Tanner Ltd. Frome and London*; [v–vi] *Contents*; 1–[74] text). § White cartridge paper. 13 pen drawings: frontis. + 6 head- and 6 tailpieces for the 49 poems. § Blue linson boards. D.j. wrap-round printed mid-blue, line drawing on front cut through for titling etc. by E.A. on front and spine, with a yellow separation; ad. on rear.

REPRINTED: four times to 1968, then included in Reeves's *Complete Poems for Children* (1973), later reprinted as *The Wandering Moon and Other Poems* (see item 159 below).

The first edition of the collection was published by Heinemann in 1950 with decorative pen drawings by Evadne Rowan. The drawing of 'Little Fan' on p. 8 was the sole representation of E.A.'s work in The New Golden Land Anthology *ed. Judith Elkin (see item A17).*

62. 1958 BRIEF TO COUNSEL by Henry Cecil [Credit] [vig.] with a Foreword by the Hon. Mr. Justice Devlin one of Her Majesty's Judges of the High Court of Justice. London: Michael Joseph, [1958].

Crown 8° in sixteens. 200 × 125 mm. (8 × 5 in.). Pp. [7] 8–190 ([2] *Also by Henry Cecil* [10 titles]; [3] t.p.; [4] imprint: *First published ... 1958. Set and pr. in G.B. by Tonbridge Printers Ltd, Peach Hall Works, Tonbridge, Kent, in Baskerville eleven on thirteen point, on paper made by Henry Bruce At Currie, Midlothian, and bound by Key & Whiting, Canonbury Road, London N.1.*; [5] *Contents*; [6] *List of illustrations*; [7]–9 *Foreword*; 11–182 text; 183–185 *Appendix*; [187]–190 *Index*). § Cream antique wove paper. 28 pen drawings: t.p. vig. and 2 vig. headpieces, 25 full-page drawings in text with letterpress legends. § Black linson boards. D.j. pen drawing with hand-lettering by E.A., part of the latter incorporated in a 2-colour separation on front and spine; letterpress ads. on rear.

REPRINTED: five times before 1972, when a second ed. of the text appeared with an author's preface explaining legal changes. In 1982 a third ed. 'Illus.

by Edward Ardizzone, R.A.' was published 'rev. by His Honour Edgar Dennis Smith ... with a new foreword by The Rt. Hon. the Lord Edmund-Davies ...'. Chichester: Barry Rose.

1958 U.S. EDITION: New York: Harper Brothers (communicated).

At this period E.A. spent much gleeful time sketching at the Law Courts and sketchbook 1 at the Ashmolean Museum contains work related to some of the illustrations noted here.

62.1 1958 THE COMEDIES [by] William Shakespeare [2-colour vig.] with an Introduction by Tyrone Guthrie and Illustrations by E.A. New York: The Heritage Press, [1958].

Medium 8°. 240 × 150 mm. (9½ × 5¾ in.). Pp. [4] v–xlviii [1] 2–1120 ([i] half-title; [iii] t.p.; [iv] colophon: *The text of the Heritage Shakespeare is that of* Collins Tudor Shakespeare, *ed. by Professor Peter Alexander and first published in 1951 ...*; v *Contents*; [vi] *Editor's note*; vii–xxiii *Introduction* and *Acknowledgements* by P. Alexander; xxiv–xxxii *Preliminary matter to the First Folio (1623)*; xxxv–xlvii Intro. by Tyrone Guthrie; xlviii *A Note on the Illustrations* by E.A.; [1]–1100 text of 14 plays, each preceded by an introduction; [1101]–1120 *Glossary*). § Creamy thin laid paper. T.p. vig. and 28 pen drawings (2 per play) each with 2-colour overlays and letterpress legends with quotation and source. § Quarter canvas, decorated paper boards, with dec. titling in maroon and gilt. Maroon slip-case.

1986 'COLLECTORS' EDITION': Norwalk, CT., Easton Press (not seen).In the series described at item 8 above, advertised as in blue leather gilt, a.e.g.

Listed in the 1972 Hand-list at item 31 under a 1951 date, which was, in fact, the original date of Peter Alexander's edited text. The two other volumes in the Heritage Shakespeare were the Histories *illus. by John Farleigh (1958) and the* Tragedies *illus. by Agnes Miller Parker (1959), who also illustrated the* Poems *(1958). E.A.'s 'Note' on p. xlviii outlines his view that 'the illustrator's job is to create a visual background which the reader can people with the author's characters; or, to put it another way, to stimulate the reader's imagination rather than do all his imagining for him'. He goes on to apply this to his pairs of illustrations, one of each being placed vertically on the page, the other horizontally as a quasi stage-set.*

63. 1958 JIM AT THE CORNER [by] Eleanor Farjeon [vig.] [Credit]. London: Oxford University Press, 1958.

Small foolscap 4° in eights. 202 × 148 mm. (8 × 6 in.). Pp. [8] 101 [3] ([i] half-title; [ii] *Books by E. F.*; [iii] t.p.; [iv] imprint: *First published by Basil Blackwell 1934 ... Printed in G.B. by Richard Clay and Company, Ltd., Bungay, Suffolk*; [v] verse dedication to Virginia Bell; [vii] *Contents*; 1–101 text; [102] tailpiece). § Antique wove paper. 30 pen drawings: t.p. vig., contents page headpiece, 10 chapter headpieces incorporating decorated initials, 16 drawings in text, 2 tailpieces. § White linen boards with simplified block of t.p. drawing on front. D.j. in line and watercolour with hand-lettering throughout by E.A. (signed) on front and spine.

1958 U.S. ISSUE: New York: Henry Z. Walck, Inc. English sheets.

1986 'REVISED EDITION': Aylesbury: John Goodchild. A page-for-page resetting of the text, with two illustrations taken back a page to avoid facing a chapter headpiece. The 'revision' (made by the publisher) is of phrasing on pp. 29–30, where references to mariners 'feeling each other' in a thick fog are changed to phrases like 'bumping into each other'.

1986 PAPERBACK EDITION: London: Methuen Children's Books Ltd (a Magnet Book). Crown 8° reprint of the foregoing.

1990 U.S. PAPERBACK EDITION: New York: Alfred A. Knopf (Bullseye Books).

TRANSLATION: 1990 [Japanese] Tokyo: Tuttle Mori Agency. 150 × 105 mm. Wrappers.

First published in 1934 (as noted in the imprint) with three 'other stories' and line illustrations by Irene Mountfort. The jokey dedication was here 'to my Sea-Faring Ancestor for, after all, Miss Dean Fish, how do you know I didn't have one'.[6]

6. Helen Dean Fish was an American children's book editor (she was the first to publish *Dr. Dolittle*) who liked to visit famous English writers. She took tea with E.F. in Hampstead and the tea 'came out of a fascinating double caddy made by a seafaring ancestor'. See her article collected from the *Horn Book* of February 1930 in *A Hornbook Sampler* (Boston, 1959) pp. 255–258.

64. 1958 MIMFF ROBINSON [by] H. J. Kaeser Translated by Ruth Michaelis Jena and Arthur Ratcliff [Credit]. London: Oxford University Press, 1958.

Demy 8°. 213 × 133 mm. (8½ × 5¼ in.). Pp. vii [1] 184 ([i] half-title; [ii] frontis.; [iii] t.p.; [iv] imprint: *Pr. in G.B. by Morrison and Gibb Limited, London and Edinburgh*; v Contents; vii *Illustrations*; 1–184 text). § Antique wove paper. Frontis. and 7 full-page drawings in text, all with letterpress legends and page references. § Dark green cloth boards; sheets later bound in red linson. D.j. a wrap-round colour wash drawing hand-lettered throughout by E.A. Endpapers a scenic watercolour, repeated front and rear.

Fourth and last of the stories about Mimff 'the boy who knew no fear'.

65. 1958 PINKY PIE [by] Eleanor Estes [vig.] [Credit]. New York: Harcourt, Brace and Company, [1958].

Large crown 8° in sixteens. 202 × 130 mm. (8 × 5¼ in.). Pp. [8] 9–192 ([3] t.p.; [4] dedication: *To Helena* and imprint: *Pr. in the U.S.A. 1958*; [5] Contents; [7] fly-title; 9–192 text). § Antique wove paper. T.p. vig. and 20 drawings in text, with a 'follow-the-dots' design hand-lettered by E.A. occupying p. 144. § Pink buckram boards with an enlarged portion of the drawing on p. 41 (cat and typewriter) on front lower right in dark blue. D.j. pale turquoise wash with drawing and hand-lettering by E.A. on front and spine and a colour-separation in peach, letterpress ads. on rear. The rear flap incorporates the dog-and-cat motif from the jacket front.

REPRINTED: at least 6 times in the U.S.A.

1959 ENGLISH EDITION: London: Constable & Co.

66. 1958 THE STORY OF JOSEPH by Walter de la Mare [Credit] [vig.]. London: Faber and Faber, [1958].

Small foolscap 4° in eights. 210 × 153 mm. (8¼ × 6 in.). Pp. [6] 7–83 [1] ([3] half-title; [4] *By the same author*; [5] t.p.; [6] imprint: *First published in this edition 1958 ... Pr. in G.B. by Latimer Trend & Co Ltd Plymouth*; 7–83 text). § Off-white smooth cartridge paper. T.p. vig. and 9 drawings in text. § Paper boards with drawing on front developing that on p. 7, hand-lettered by E.A. and with 3-colour separations; typographic spine; drawing from p. 32 repeated on the grey separation of rear cover. D.j. as binding.

The text is taken from de la Mare's Stories from the Bible *which was first published in 1929 with illustrations by Claudia Guercio. This was followed by editions in 1933, illus. John Farleigh, and 1947, illus. Irene Hawkins. E.A. illustrated three excerpts: the stories of* Joseph, *above, of* Moses *(item 73 below), and of* Samuel and Saul *(item 83 below), and then a complete edition (item 90 below). This last called upon drawings made for the earlier stories and, in the case of* Joseph, *E.A. redrew the illustrations on pp. 49, 61 and 70 in order to change the figure of Benjamin from that of a child to a young man.*

All the drawings reprinted in the complete Stories *are more happily reproduced on its thinner, creamier antique wove paper than on the stock used in the excerpts.*

67. 1959 ELFRIDA AND THE PIG by John Symonds [Credit] [vig.]. London, Toronto, Wellington, Sydney: George G. Harrap & Co. Ltd, [1959].

Crown 4°. 246 × 180 mm. (9¾ × 7¼ in.). Pp. [7] 8–48 ([1] half-title; [4] frontis.: *The clever child was called Elfrida*; [5] t.p.; [6] imprint: *First published in G.B. 1959 … Composed in Bell type and pr. by Western Printing Services Ltd., Bristol*; [7]–48 text). § Off-white cartridge paper. 17 pen drawings: frontis.; t.p. vig., 15 in text, with letterpress legends. § Pea-green linson boards, outline block of Elfrida and the pig from the illus. on p. 28 on front in black, spine lettering black. D.j. central panel on front with drawing and 3-colour overlays, upper and lower panels reversed-out titling on green wash by E.A.; spine lettered in black by E.A.; letterpress ads. on rear.

TRANSLATION: 1960 [Swedish] *Elfrida och Grisen*. Trs. Maj Britt Paul-Pont. London, Stockholm, New York: Sven-Erik Berghs Förlag.

68. 1959 EXPLOITS OF DON QUIXOTE Retold by James Reeves [Credit] [vig. in sanguine]. London and Glasgow: Blackie, [1959].

Demy 8°. 215 × 145 mm. (8½ × 5½ in.). Pp. [16] 17–219 [5] + 12 insets ([1] half-title; [2] publisher's addresses in London, Glasgow and Bombay;

inserted frontis.; [3] t.p.; [4] imprint: *Pr. in G.B. by Blackie & Son. Ltd., Glasgow ... 1959*; [5] *Contents*; [7] *Illustrations in colour*; [9–11] *Introduction* signed *J.R., Chalfont St. Giles, 1959*; [13] dedication: *To Susannah, Quentin and Dominic Clemence and Joanna and Sarah Ardizzone*; [15] fly-title; 17–219 text, with inserted colour plates facing pp. 18, 32, 49, 64, 81, 97, 112, 144, 161, 177 and 192). § Cream offset cartridge paper, the insets on a slightly whiter stock. 12 watercolours with letterpress legends locating the chapter from which the illustration is taken; 60 pen drawings: t.p. vig. (as noted), 21 chapter headpieces, 7 tailpieces, 31 in text. § Red linen boards with block of Don Quixote and Sancho Panza on front in gilt. D.j. a wrap-round watercolour (featuring 3 Quixotes) hand-lettered throughout by E.A. Endpapers a double-spread watercolour repeated front and rear.

Head-piece from *Exploits of Don Quixote* (1959 item 68)

1960 U.S. EDITION: New York: Henry Z. Walck, Inc.

1977 CHEAP REPRINT: London etc.: Blackie. Reprinted by Robert Mac-Lehose and Company Ltd, Glasgow, with the prelims slightly modified and without the colour plates. Simultaneously published as a paperback.

In a by no means uncritical survey of E.A.'s illustrative work, Edward Hodnett (Sources p. 284) singles out the Exploits *and especially its 'superb full-page wa-ter-colours', as 'one of the most satisfying of ... English editions of this classic'.*

69. 1959 FATHER BROWN STORIES [by] G. K. Chesterton. Illustrations by E.A. London: The Folio Society, 1959.

Medium 8°. 227 × 149 mm. (8¾ × 5½ in.). Pp. [9] 2–270 [2] ([i] half-title; [ii] frontis.; [iii] t.p.; [iv] imprint: *Pr. and bound in G.B. by W. & J. Mackay & Co. Ltd. Chatham. Set in 11 point Imprint leaded 1 point*; [v] *Contents* [14 stories]; [vii] *Illustrations*; [1]–270 text). § Off-white cartridge paper. Frontis. and 13 full-page pen drawings. § Grey-brown linen boards, maroon morocco label gilt, dark red endpapers. Mottled rose red slip-case. § *Ref:* Nash 132.

MS. DRAWINGS: the property of the Folio Society.

70. 1959 THE GODSTONE AND THE BLACKYMOR by T. H. White [Credit]. London: Jonathan Cape, 1959 [large vig. scene above title].

Crown 8°. 198 × 130 mm. (7¾ × 5⅛ in.). Pp. [8] 9–224 ([1] half-title; [2] *Other books by T. H. White*; [3] t.p. [4] imprint: *First published 1959 … Pr. in G.B. by Butler & Tanner Ltd. … Bound by A.W. Bain & Co. Ltd., London*; [5] *Contents*; [7] dedication: *Love to Dawn*; 9–224 text). § Antique wove paper. 27 pen drawings: t.p. vig., 12 chapter headpieces incorporating decorated initials, 4 full-page drawings, 10 in text. § 'Horizontally shade-striped vellum' paper boards with a slightly reduced version of the drawing on p. 90 blocked on the front in black, gilt titling in a dark green panel on spine. D.j. a repeat of the drawing on p. 76 on front with hand-lettering by E.A. on front and spine with 2-colour separation; letterpress ads. on rear.

1959 U.S. EDITION: New York: Putnam, not using E.A.'s d.j. and with the illus. slightly reorganised. Later (prudently?) retitled *A Western Wind*.

1960 REPRINT SOCIETY EDITION: London: 'by arrangement with Jonathan Cape'. Pr. at Oxford by the Alden Press; t.p. vig. centred; terracotta cloth.

MS. DRAWINGS: many dispersed. Sketchbook 26 in the Ashmolean Museum is E.A.'s Irish diary, written in 1958 while working on the book (see opposite).

Opposite: Page from E.A.'s Irish diary, written while working on *The Godstone and the Blackymor* (1959 item 70)

Sept: 12 · 1·

Arrive at Ballina about 3.00 —
Accosted by tall Gent. while enquiring about
a bus. Am led by him to a bar &
bought & enormous whiskey. Find to
my surprise that he was plastered (or worse?)
Pompous deportment. reminded me of a
Cross between Micawber & one of ye Americans
in Martin Chuzzlewit.

Kicked violently on ye ankle & informed
in a vast conspiratorial whisper that
ye other occupant in the bar. a dark
young man in a raincoat was a
Nationalist. that he, my companion, was
an ex officer of ye Dublin Constabulary
in ye troubles & we must leave
at once in case ye Nationalist
might insult me. (all tolomey i think)
troth vast. stay in another
bar & to my relief he left me

In 1943–1944, while writing Mistress Masham's Repose *T. H. White determined upon becoming a writer for children and wrote to David Garnett on the subject of getting an illustrator (see* The White/Garnett Letters *1968, pp. 140–142). Bewailing the death of 'Pont' (Graham Laidler) he goes on to mention 'a person called Ardizzone who does quite discerning ink washes' but decides against the idea. Garnett agrees, saying 'Ardizzone only draws drunks leaning against bars – an illustrator of genius but not for your books'. When* Mistress Masham *was first published in New York in 1946 it had line-drawings of vigorous specificity by Frtiz Eichenberg. The English edition of 1947 was unillustrated and (pace Garnett) E.A.'s genius would have been perfectly attuned to it.*

71. 1959 HOLIDAY TRENCH [by] Joan Ballantyne [vig.] Illustrations by E.A. Edinburgh: Thomas Nelson and Sons Ltd., [1959].

Demy 8°. 218 × 137 mm. (8⅝ × 5½ in.). Pp. [8] 120 ([ii] frontis. vig.; [iii] t.p.; [iv] publisher's slug, copyright and imprint: *Pr. in G.B. by Thomas Nelson and Sons Ltd. Edinburgh*; [v] *Contents*; [vii] *List of Illustrations*; 1–120 text*)*. § Antique wove paper. 13 pen drawings: frontis. and one for each chapter. The t.p. vig. is a repeat of the concluding drawing. § Blue cloth boards. D.j. blue wash, titling etc. on three pink panelled overlays on front and spine hand-lettered by E.A.; central plain white panel on front with a reproduction of the drawing on p. 54.

A sequel, Kidnappers at Coombe, *is described at item 79 below. The drawings for the above book were sold (without the artist's knowledge) at Sotheby's on 20 April 1971.*

72. 1959 THE NINE LIVES OF ISLAND MACKENZIE [by] Ursula Moray Williams [vig.] [Credit]. [London]: Chatto and Windus, [1959].

Foolscap 4°. 208 × 165 mm. (8½ × 6½ in.). Pp. [9] 10–128 ([1] half-title; [2] *By the same author*; [3] t.p.; [4] imprint: *Pr. in G.B. by T. & A. Constable Ltd., Edinburgh*. Canadian agent: *Clarke Irwin … Toronto*; [5] dedication: *To Christopher and Charles Bunbury*; [7] *Contents*; [9]–128 text). § Antique wove paper. 25 pen drawings: t.p. vig. as above, 13 chapter headpieces incorporating decorative initials, 7 in text. § Dark green linson boards;

endpapers a double-spread pen drawing with 2-colour separation repeated front and rear. D.j. a pen drawing developing the t.p. vig. with 2-colour separation and hand-lettering on front and spine by E.A.; letterpress blurb within a pink dec. frame on rear.

REPRINTED: in laminated paper boards by Chatto, 1979, and as a crown 8° paperback by Transworld Publishers Ltd., 1980 (Carousel Books).

1960 U.S. EDITION: New York: Wm. Morrow.

TRANSLATION: 1988 [Swedish] *Den Skeppsbrutne Mackenzie.* Trs. Ingegärd Martinell. Stockholm: Sjöstrands Förlag.

The Chatto & Windus archive at Reading University yields a businesslike letter from E.A. to Norah Smallwood setting out his terms for doing the book, which he 'likes very much' (a 'Royalty basis' and an advance of £150). He suggests the present format for the book and sends a copy of Lottie *(item 57 above) saying that it 'has been hideously designed (not by me)' but may show 'how one can get almost an effect of colour using black line only'.*

73. 1959 THE STORY OF MOSES by Walter de la Mare. [Credit] [vig.]. London: Faber and Faber, [1959].

Small foolscap 4° in eights. 210 × 152 mm. (8⅝ × 6 in.). Pp. [6] 7–110 [2] ([3] half-title; [4] imprint: *First published in this edition 1959 … Pr. in G.B. by Latimer Trend & Co Ltd Plymouth*; 7–110 text). § Off-white smooth cartridge paper. T.p. vig., and 9 drawings in text (one per chapter). § Paper boards as item 66, the front cover picture based on the drawing on p. 14, the rear pen drawing an enlargement of the t.p. vig. D.j. as binding.

MS. DRAWINGS: The cover design in pen and ink and watercolour is in the V & A Dept. of Prints and Drawings.

All the drawings were used again in item 90 below, the vignette being somewhat reduced. For companion volumes and other information see items 66 above and 83 below.

74. 1959 TITUS IN TROUBLE [large 2-colour vig.] By James Reeves [Credit]. London: The Bodley Head, [1959].

Demy 4° in eights. 280 × 213 mm. (11½ × 8⅜ in.). Pp. [48] ([1] t.p.; [2] imprint: *First published 1959 … Pr. in G.B. … by A. & M. Weston Ltd., South Wigston, Leicestershire. Set in Monotype Plantin*; [3–48] text). § Off-white cartridge paper. 43 illustrations: 16 pen drawings, including t.p. vig. with single tint in green, 7 ditto, including 1 double-page spread with single tint in pink, 20 line and watercolour drawings, including 3 double-page spreads. § Paper boards, the front in 3 panels with titling etc. by E.A. and a reproduction of the colour illus. on p. 14 in centre, letterpress spine, rear a pale blue wash. D.j. as binding with the colour portrait of Titus from p. 3 on inner front flap.

1960 U.S. EDITION: New York: Henry Z. Walck, Inc.

1969 SECOND EDITION: the format reduced to a large crown 4° but with E.A.'s illus. reproduced the same size as in the 1959 ed.

1972 SECOND U.S. EDITION: New York: Henry Z. Walck, Inc. Follows the 1969 edition.

TRANSLATION: 1962 [Swedish] *Titus på Äventyr*. Trs. Britt G. Hallqvist. Stockholm: Jupiter.

VARIA: drawings from *Titus* were used on a small card bookmark issued by The Bodley Head for publicity. They also produced a single-fold pre-publication order form reproducing the first three pages of the book.

MS. DRAWINGS: Lilly Library, University of Indiana at Bloomington (incomplete); 2 watercolour drawings are in the Kerlan Coll. of the University of Minnesota.

75. 1960 BOYHOODS OF GREAT COMPOSERS Book One by Catherine Gough [Credit] [vig.]. London, Melbourne, Toronto: Oxford University Press, [1960]. (The Young Reader's Guide to Music [I]).

Small foolscap 4° in eights. 209 × 150 mm. (8¼ × 5⅞ in.). Pp. [9] 2–53 [3] ([i] half-title; [ii] *Other books in this series …*; [iii] t.p.; [iv] imprint, dated 1960; [v] *Introduction*; [vii] *List of Contents* (Handel, Mozart, Schubert, Mendelssohn, Grieg, Elgar); [1]–53 text; [55] imprint: *Pr. in G.B. by*

Richard Clay & Co. Ltd., Bungay, Suffolk). § Thickish off–white cartridge paper. 25 pen drawings: t.p. vig. after part of the drawing on p. 9, 6 chapter headpieces, 18 in text (3 per chapter). § Laminated yellow paper boards with an enlarged version of the drawing on p. [1] on front in brown, end-papers a pattern of 12 illus. taken from the book, reduced and printed ultramarine, repeated front and rear; no d.j.

REPRINTED: four times to 1969, later issues bound in dark green linson with d.j. whose centre panel front reproduces the drawing on p. [1] reversed out.

TRANSLATION: 1962 [Afrikaans] *Kinderjare van die Groot Komponiste.* Trs. Arnold van Wyk. Cape Town: Oxford University Press.

See item 101 below for Book Two *and a note on the combined edition.*

76. 1960 ELEANOR FARJEON'S BOOK. Stories • Verses • Plays By Eleanor Farjeon. Chosen by Eleanor Graham and illustrated by E.A. [vig.]. Harmondsworth: Penguin Books, 1960. (Puffin Story Books no. 141).

Small crown 8° mostly in sixteens. 180 × 110 mm. (7⅛ × 4¼ in.). Pp. [6] 7–207 [1] ([1] blurb; [3] t.p.; [4] imprint: *This selection first published 1960 … Made and pr. in G.B. by Western Printing Services Ltd., Bristol;* [5–6] *Contents;* 7–[208] text). § M.f. printing paper (now browning to edges). 34 pen drawings: t.p. vig., 9 chapter headpieces, 22 in text, 2 tailpieces. § Publisher's wrappers with wrap-round pen drawing with additional 4-colour separation hand-lettered by E.A.; series panel with typographic lettering (reversed) and device at foot.

MS. DRAWINGS: 3 were catalogued for sale by Nial and Margaret Devitt in their second Ardizzone cat. (see Sources p. 281).

The selection consists of 30 pieces (prose, verse, a play-text, a masque, a dia-logue) from various books by E.F. Four drawings by E.A. had been previously published in The Little Bookroom *(item 45 above) six would later be used in* Kaleidoscope *(item 102 below), two in* Italian Peepshow *(item 77), while three can be seen as preparatory drawings for work in* The Old Nurse's Stocking Basket *(item 117).*

77. 1960 ITALIAN PEEPSHOW [by] Eleanor Farjeon [vig.] [Credit]. London: Oxford University Press, 1960.

Small foolscap 4° in eights. 203 × 150 mm. (8 × 6 in.). Pp. [8] 96 ([i] half-title; [ii] *Books by E.F.* (12 titles); [iii] t.p.; [iv] imprint: *First published in the United States by Frederick A. Stokes Company, 1926. First published in this ed. 1960. Pr. in G.B. by Western Printing Services Ltd. Bristol*; [v] dedication: *For Bridget and Chloe and Nan for whom this book began*; [vii] *Contents*; 1–96 text). § Creamy cartridge paper. 25 pen drawings: t.p. vig., 11 chapter headpieces, 1 tailpiece, 12 in text. § Red cloth boards. D.j. line and water-colour drawing hand-lettered by E.A. on front and spine, printed 4-colour half-tone, ad. on rear for *Jim at the Corner* with a drawing by E.A. from that book.

1960 U.S. ISSUE: New York: Henry Z. Walck, Inc. English sheets.

Eleven short stories with an Italian setting; two drawings were also published in the preceding item. The book is a revised edition of Italian Peepshow and Other Tales *illus. Rosalind Thornycroft (New York: Frederick A. Stokes Co., 1926).*

78. 1960 JOHNNY THE CLOCKMAKER [large colour drawing] by E.A. London – New York – Toronto: Oxford University Press, [1960] [all hand-lettered by E.A.].

Crown 4°. Pp. [48] ([1] t.p.; [2] dedication and imprint: *For my Grand-daughter Susannah* [in round-hand by E.A.] *Pr. in G.B. by W.S. Cowell Ltd. …*; [3–48] text). § 45 illustrations: t.p. vig. and 20 in watercolour with black line on Kodatrace, 24 pen drawings, two of which are highly technical studies of horological components. § Binding and d.j. conform to those of the 'Tim' books.

REPRINTED: 1971, 1980 (issued as both hardback and paperback).

1960 U.S. EDITION: New York: Henry Z. Walck, Inc.

TRANSLATIONS:
1960 [Swedish] *John Klockmakare*. Trs. Britt G. Hallqvist. Stockholm: Sven-Erik Bergh. Reprinted in 1980.

1961 [German] *Jonny der Uhrmacher*. Trs. Tilde Michels. Munich: Lentz.
1974 [Zulu] *Ujani Umenzi Wekilogo*. Trs. W.S. Naude. Durban: Qualitas.
1998 [Japanese] Trs. Kimiko Abe. Tokyo: Koguma Publishing Co.

MS. DRAWINGS: a dummy version of the book with ms. and pen and pencil sketches is in the Kerlan Collection of the University of Minnesota.

A certain amount of authorial agitation comes to the surface during Johnny's progress towards publication. By 1959 E.A. was regarded as one of the country's most distinguished illustrators; a booming market for children's books was bringing in demands for his services; but the royalty arrangements on the 'Tim' books – the foundation of his success – were still based on the formula produced during the difficult 1949 production of Tim to the Rescue. *The need to re-arrange American terms following O.U.P.'s handing over of their New York operation to H.Z. Walck seems to have brought things to a head and in a long letter to the publisher early in 1959 E.A. makes a strong case for a revision of the royalty payments, 'with* Johnny the Clockmaker *to come and ... plans for another "Tim" ...'. (He was a keen mathematician and his computation that the series had sold 'all in all over 100,000 copies' is probably accurate.)*

No reply to his appeal is on record and, although he protested his loyalty to the Press, the incident was to fuel repercussions later (see note to item 103 below). Unfortunately, as Johnny *was going through the press, there also occurred a bungling of the colour-proofs and the artist launched 'a tirade' against 'all concerned at Cowell's', wondering if he might cut their throats with a cheese cutter as (he believed) the commandos were trained to do.*

Fortunately improvements were made – it was 'worth while making a fuss', he said – and he was pleased with the finished product. This follows the pattern of the 'Tim' series, but with its intrepid youthful hero engaged in less elemental struggles, and, along with items 23.1, 25 and 103, it shows how well the formula could be adapted. Among readers who have taken an especial pleasure in the slight shift of emphasis is Eleanor Farjeon, who wrote to the author on 14 December 1960: 'Dearest of Teds, not being 6½ I had the most wonderful time yesterday reading and seeing your perfect story – one of your masterpieces ...' She rejoices in the recovery of her sight and dwells at some length on elements in the tale and the illustrations that evoked her admiration. Incomprehensibly the book seems to have been reprinted only twice, as noted above. It was, however, selected for the National Book League's exhibition of the 100 Best Books of 1961.

79. 1960 KIDNAPPERS AT COOMBE [by] Joan Ballantyne. Illustrations by E.A. Edinburgh: Thomas Nelson and Sons Ltd., [1960].

Demy 8° in eights, the first and last leaves pastedowns. 218 × 140 mm. (8⅝ × 5½ in.). Pp. [10] 103 [3] ([i] half-title; [iv] frontis.; [v] t.p.; [vi] publisher's slug and copyright notice dated 1960; [vii] *Contents*; [ix] *List of Illustrations*; 1–203 text; [204] imprint: *Pr. in G.B. by Thomas Nelson and Sons Ltd., Edinburgh*). § Antique wove paper. 18 pen drawings: frontis. and one in text of each chapter except chapter 3. § Green glazed cloth boards. D.j. green wash, titling etc. similar to that for *Holiday Trench* (its forerunner, item 71 above) with the central drawing a repeat of that on p. 183.

80. 1960 MERRY ENGLAND by Cyril Ray Illustrations by E.A. [publisher's device]. London: Vista Books, [1960].

Large demy 8°. 226 × 150 mm. (9 × 6 in.). Pp. [8] 9–208 including unnumbered plate pages ([i] half-title; [ii] 2-colour frontis.; [3] t.p.; [4] imprint: *First published in 1960 … Pr. by Mouton & Co. Ltd. The Hague*; [5] *Foreword*; [6] dedication: *To dear Liz, my companion on many of the jaunts and frolics recorded here, which made them twice as much fun*; [7–8] 2-colour headpiece; *Contents*; 9–208 text). § Off-white cartridge paper. 23 pen drawings with single colour overlays: frontis., contents-page headpiece and 12 full-page with peach, 5 with pale yellow, 4 with dark green. § Grey cloth boards. D.j. pen drawing with 3-colour overlays and hand-lettering by E.A. on front and spine, rear with publisher's device only.

MS. DRAWINGS: seven exhibited for sale by Chris Beetles in 1997 (cat. nos. 479–485).

81. 1960 THE PENNY FIDDLE Poems for Children by Robert Graves [Credit]. London: Cassell, [1960] [hand-lettered by E.A. within a 2-colour pictorial design bled to the edge].

Foolscap 4° in eights. 215 × 160 mm. (8½ × 6⅜ in.). Pp. [7] 8–62 [2], variably paginated ([1] half-title; [3] t.p.; [4] imprint: *First published 1960 … Pr. in G.B. by R. & R. Clark Limited, Edinburgh*; [5] dedication: *To Tomás on his eighth birthday*; [7] *Contents*; 8–[63] text; [64] 2-colour tailpiece). § Off-white cartridge paper. 43 pen drawings with a single colour separation, alternating peach and green: t.p. design and tailpiece as noted, with 41 drawings variably placed on pages or spreads throughout the text. § Green linson boards. D.j. pen drawing with 3-colour overlays, hand-lettered by E.A. on front and spine, rear blank. § *Ref:* Higginson A92.

1961 U.S. EDITION: Garden City, New York: Doubleday & Company, Inc., in medium 8° format (230 × 153 mm).

See also item 106 below.

82. 1960 THE RIB OF THE GREEN UMBRELLA [by] Naomi Mitchison. With Drawings by E.A. London: Collins, 1960.

Large crown 8°. 198 × 130 mm. (7⅞ × 5¼ in.). Pp. [4] 5–160 ([1] half-title; [2] *By the same author;* [3] t.p.; [4] imprint: *Pr. in G.B. Collins Clear-Type Press: London and Glasgow;* 5–160 text). § Off-white cartridge paper. 20 pen drawings: 1 chapter headpiece, 19 in text. § Green linson boards, black spine, with block of the drawing on p. 112 in silver on lower right of the front board. D.j. pen drawings based on those on pp. 5 and 67 with 2-colour overlays and hand-lettering by E.A. on front and spine, rear letterpress ads.

83. 1960 THE STORY OF SAMUEL AND SAUL by Walter de la Mare. [Credit] [vig.]. London: Faber and Faber, [1960].

Small foolscap 4° in eights. 210 × 152 mm. (8¼ × 6 in.). Pp. [6] 7–112 ([1] half-title; [2] *By the same Author;* [3] t.p.; [4] imprint: *First published in this edition 1960 … Pr. in G.B. by Latimer Trend & Co Ltd Plymouth …;* [5] section-title: *Samuel;* 7–36 text; [37] section-title: *Saul;* 39–112 text). § Off-white smooth cartridge paper. 9 pen drawings: t.p. vig., 1 in text of *Samuel,* 6 in *Saul,* final tailpiece. § Paper boards as item 66; the illus. on the front a development of that on p. 94, that on the rear a repeat of the one on p. 53. D.j. as binding.

The three chapters of Samuel *are here furnished with only one illustration, for 'The Capture of the Ark'. In item 90 below new drawings are provided of 'The Childhood of Samuel' and 'The Ark is Restored'. The drawings for* Saul *are used unchanged. See also note at item 66 above.*

84. 1960 THE WITCH FAMILY [by] Eleanor Estes [vig.] [Credit]. New York: Harcourt, Brace and Company, [1960].

Large crown 8° in sixteens. 202 × 133 mm. (8 × 5¼ in.). Pp. [12] 13–186 [6] ([3] half-title; [4] *By the same author …*; [5] t.p.; [6] imprint: *Pr. in the U.S.A. 1960*; [7] dedication, set as a vertical column: *For R. and H. and M.S. and W. and M. and P. and YOU*; [9] *Contents*; [11] fly-title; 13–186 text). § Antique wove paper. 19 pen drawings: t.p. vig. and one per chapter, one of which is full-page, 4 partial double-page spreads and 12 in text. § Turquoise linen boards with an additional vig. design by E.A. blocked front centre. D.j. pen drawings on front and spine with blue and pink overlays hand-lettered by E.A. throughout.

[n.d.] PAPERBACK EDITION: New York: Harcourt, Brace & World Inc. (a Voyager Book).

1962 ENGLISH EDITION: London: Constable and Company Limited. Reprinted three times to 1977, the imprint changing to Kestrel Books; also a paperback reprint 1975, London: Universal-Tandem Publishing (Target Books), with wrapper-front by a (justly) unacknowledged draughtsman.

85. 1961 THE ADVENTURES OF HUCKLEBERRY FINN [by] Mark Twain [Credit]. London, Melbourne, Toronto: Heinemann, [1961]. (The New Windmill Series).

Small crown 8° in eights, later in sixteens. 183 × 118 mm. (7¼ × 4¾ in.). Pp. [6] 312 [2] ([i] half-title and blurb; [ii] frontis.; [iii] t.p.; [iv] imprint: *First published 1884. First published in the New Windmill series 1961 … Pr. in G.B. by Morrison & Gibb Ltd. London and Edinburgh*; [v] author's *Notice* and *Explanatory* note; 1–312 text). § Off-white m.f. printing paper. 37 pen drawings: frontis. (a composite of five portraits hand-lettered by E.A.); 4 full-page, 32 in text. § Linson boards, mostly dark green, typographic titling reversed white with white central panel on front blocked in pale brown with an illus. of Huck enlarged from part of the drawing on p. 18.

REPRINTED: many times.

The New Windmill Series was a notable collection of full-text editions published for the educational market and edited by Anne and Ian Serraillier.

86. 1961 THE ADVENTURES OF TOM SAWYER [by] Mark Twain [Credit]. London, Melbourne, Toronto: Heinemann, [1961]. (The New Windmill Series).

Specification as previous item, with pp. [6] 242 [2]. § 30 pen drawings: frontis. designed as above; 5 full-page, 24 in text. § Linson boards as above but mostly pale brown with dark green blocking on front panel and a drawing of Tom enlarged from that on frontis.

REPRINTED: many times.

87. 1961 DOWN IN THE CELLAR [by] Nicholas Stuart Gray [Credit]. London: Dennis Dobson, [1961].

Crown 8°. 191 × 126 mm. (7¾ × 5 in.). Pp. [6] 7–203 [1] ([1] half-title; [3] t.p.; [4] dedication and imprint: *To Maurice and Albourne Farm ... Pr. in G.B. by W. & J. Mackay & Co. Ltd., Chatham*; [5] *Contents*; 7–203 text). § Antique wove paper. 14 pen-drawn chapter headpieces incorporating a drawn initial. § Green/brown mottled linson boards. D.j. white paper with pale peach wash and drawing and hand-lettering in black and red by E.A. on front and spine; ads. on rear.

88. 1961 FOLK SONGS OF ENGLAND, IRELAND, SCOTLAND AND WALES Selected and Edited by William Cole, Arranged for Piano and Guitar by Norman Monath. Drawings by E.A. [2-colour vig.]. Garden City, New York: Doubleday & Company, Inc. 1961 [titling set within a 2-colour canopy by E.A., later used above the title of several songs].

U.S. imperial 8°. 278 × 205 mm. (11 × 8 in.). Pp. [5] vi–xi [1] 243 [1] ([i] dec. half-title; [ii] *Anthologies edited by William Cole*; [iii] t.p.; [iv] *Acknowledgements ... and imprint: Typography by Diana Klemin ... Pr. in the U.S.A. ...*; [v]–viii *Contents* (one decorated page for each country); ix–xi *Introduction* by William Cole and *Note on the Arrangements* by Norman Monath; 1–243 text). § Antique wove paper. 126 pen drawings all with a single colour overlay varying between green in the first and last two gatherings and pink, purple and pale yellow in four each of the successive gatherings between. These drawings consist of 4 full-page fly-titles; 31 canopy headpieces with 12 repeated at least once with that featuring song-birds repeated 32 times; 2 plain headpieces; 57 tailpieces with 3 repeated once and one designed as a double-page spread; 24 drawings in text with one repeated; and 8 small vignettes with 5 repeated several times. § Pale beige linen boards with 9 simple outline images of items appearing among the illustrations on front. D.j. pen decorations with 3-colour overlays and hand-lettering by E.A. on front and spine, with a reduction of the material on p. 16 ('Greensleeves') printed black on rear.

1969 PAPERBACK REPRINTS: without colour and with a typographic cover New York: Cornerstone Library, distributed by Simon & Schuster; subsequently issued with the original design on the front wrapper with 2-colour overlays. Miami, FL.: Warner Bros. Publications Inc.

Not published in England.

89. 1961 HURDY-GURDY. Selected Poems by James Reeves [vig.] [Credit]. London, Melbourne, Toronto: Heinemann, [1961].

Small demy 8° in fours. 215 × 132 mm. (8½ × 5⅜ in.). Pp. [4] 5–48 ([1] half-title; [2] *Some other books by J. R.*; [3] t.p.; [4] notes and imprint: *Pr. in G.B. by The Windmill Press Ltd., Kingswood, Surrey*; [5–6] *Contents*; 7–48 text). § 13 pen drawings all previously published: 6 from item 35 above (with one repeat), 3 from item 61, and 4 from item 58. § White linson over card covers, cut flush, with a specially designed wrap-round pen drawing by E.A. hand-lettered on front and with a separated yellow overlay.

90. 1961 STORIES FROM THE BIBLE by Walter de la Mare [Credit] [vig.]. London: Faber and Faber, [1961].

Royal 8°. 233 × 150 mm. (9½ × 6 in.). Pp. [6] 7–420 ([1] half-title; [2] other books for children by W.D.L.M.; [3] t.p.; [4] imprint: *First published in 1929. Reprinted in this ed. 1961 … Pr. in G.B. by Latimer Trend & Co Ltd Plymouth*; [5] dedication: *To Fridy*; [7–8] *Contents*; 9–15 *Introduction*; [17] section-title: *The Garden of Eden*; 19–420 text, with section-titles at [39] *The Flood*; [59] *Joseph*; [131] *Moses* + vig.; [217] *The Wilderness*; [245]

Samson; [293] *Samuel*; [325] *Saul*; [392] *David*). § Cream offset cartridge paper. 46 pen drawings, of which one is duplicated in reduced size to provide the t.p. vig. In addition to this item there are vigs. on three of the nine section-titles, 2 chapter headpieces, 40 drawings in text, and a tailpiece to 'Saul'. Of this assemblage, seven drawings had already appeared in item 66 above, ten in item 73, and nine in item 83, giving a total of 20 new images in the present book. § Yellow linen boards with eight miniature illustrations set into an architectural design, including *putti,* printed in black line and two colours and hand-lettered by E.A. on front, repeated on rear, with his titling and a further figure-drawing (Moses) on spine. Pale yellow endpapers, top edge stained green. D.j. as binding.

Vignette from *Stories from the Bible* (1961 item 90)

1961 U.S. EDITION: New York: Alfred A. Knopf (A Borzoi Book), manufactured in U.S.A.: white laid paper; red cloth binding with a publisher's design blindstamped on front; d.j. as English ed. but with mauve replacing yellow as base colour and drawn lettering not by E.A.

1963 REPRINT SOCIETY EDITION: in red cloth with gilt spine; red d.j. incorporating the drawing from p. 61. (see Nial & Margaret Devitt's first Ardizzone cat. no. 82).

MS. DRAWINGS: proofs of the binding design have been seen coloured dark green.

For a note on this full text and the related excerpts see item 66 above.

91. 1961 THE ISLAND OF FISH IN THE TREES [dec. rule] by Eva-Lis Wuorio [Credit] [device]. Cleveland and New York: The World Publishing Company, [1962] [title and publishing details in swash lettering; rule and device printed bright blue].

Medium 8°. 227 × 155 mm. (9 × 6 in.). Pp. [6] 7–59 [5] ([1] half-title; [2] colour frontis.; [3] t.p. [4] imprint: *Pr. in the U.S.A. Published simultaneously in Canada by Nelson, Foster & Scott Ltd.*; [5] dedication: *For Toni of Barcelona and Carina of Santa Eulalie because they are children of this same sea*; 7–59 text and plates; [61] *About the author*; [62] edition numbers). § Stiffish cream cartridge paper. Frontis. and 6 double-spreads, all dark-brown line and watercolour, occupying pp. [14–15], [22–23], [30–31], [38–39], [42–43], [54–55]. § Wrap-round line and watercolour drawing, hand-lettered throughout by E.A., on cloth boards (U.S. library binding). D.j. as binding. A publisher's presentation binding in half blue morocco with marbled paper sides has been seen.

1964 ENGLISH EDITION: London: Dennis Dobson. *Pr. and bound in G.B. by Thomas Nelson (Printers) Ltd. London and Edinburgh.* Pp. 56. Similar format and collation, but the first and last leaves of the outer gatherings are paste-downs and the endpapers dec. with 'fishtrees' from illus. on p. [19]. The note on the author, a Finn who had lived in Canada and the U.S.A. and is here writing about Formentera, an island in the Balearics, has been placed on the rear jacket-flap.

The book was selected by the New York Times *and the American Institute of Graphic Arts as one of the Best Illustrated Children's Books of 1962.*

92. 1962 J.M. BARRIE'S PETER PAN [in sanguine] The Story of the Play Presented by Eleanor Graham and E.A. [vig.]. [Leicester]: Brockhampton Press, [1962].

Medium 8°. 227 × 158 mm. (9 × 6¼ in.). Pp. [6] 7–163 [1] ([1] half-title; [3] t.p.; [4] *Do you know that this book is part of the J. M. Barrie 'Peter Pan Bequest'? ... and imprint: First edition 1962. Published by Brockhampton Press Ltd., ... Pr. in G.B. by Richard Clay and Company Ltd., Bungay, Suffolk* + copyrights; [5] *Contents* [vig.]; 7–163 text; [164] vig.). § Thickish off-white cartridge paper. 55 pen drawings: t.p. vig., contents-page vig.,

9 chapter headpieces, 4 tailpieces, 40 in text, several being spot drawings at the edges of the text-block. § Bright blue linen boards, gilt titling on spine. D.j. pen and watercolour design, hand-lettered throughout by E.A. The design depicts an array of characters from the play, repeated front and rear with a portrait of Peter Pan on spine. Pale blue endpapers.

REPRINTED: ten times to 1992; the second impression (labelled 'Gift Edition') and all subsequent incorporate the six plates from the U.S. ed. described below, but not, of course, the t.p.

1963 U.S. EDITION: New York: Charles Scribner's Sons, augmented as follows: Similar format. Pp. [6] 7–175 [1] + 7 insets ([1] half-title with vig.; inset t.p. replicating the watercolour design on the front of the British d.j. with the U.S. publisher lettered-in by E.A. in lower cartouche, bequest, copyright and imprint notes etc. on verso: *Pr. in the U.S.A. A – 7.63 (UJ).* *L.C. no. 63–14737;* [3] *Contents;* [5] *List of Color Illustrations;* 7–163 text with watercolour insets facing pp. 34, 64, 82, 117, 130 and 140; [164] vig.; 165–167 *A Note from Eleanor Graham;* 169–172 biographical note on J.M. Barrie; 173 ditto on Eleanor Graham; 175 ditto on E.A.). Darkish cream cartridge paper, giving a richer finish to the printing of the line blocks. 54 pen drawings, as English ed. but omitting the vig. on the contents page[7]. Pale green linen boards with the final tailpiece blocked on front in darker metallic green. Laminated d.j., a lithographed watercolour design hand-lettered by E.A. on front and spine (not found in the British ed.), repeat of the half-title vig., enlarged, on rear.

TRANSLATION: 1992 [Russian] Tr. Nina Demourova. Moscow: Slovo, 1991. Illus. with 54 pen drawings only, with 2 placed in the final leaves containing statements on contents and publicity matters.

For a general note on the texts and illustrations of Peter Pan *from 1904 onwards see Appendix IV.*

7. Note too that the drawing reproduced on p. 142 of the U.S. edition has been cropped on both sides in its earlier appearance in the English ed.

93. 1962 LONDON SINCE 1912 by John Hayes. London: Her Majesty's Stationery Office, 1962.

Oblong large post 8°. 135 × 210 mm. (5⅜ × 8¼ in.). Pp. [1] 2–32, a single gathering ([1] t.p.; 2 *Illustrations* [sources] … *The illus. on pp. 11, 12, 17 and 21 were especially drawn for this booklet by E.A.* and imprint: *Pr. in England under the authority of H.M.S.O. by The Curwen Press, Plaistow, E.13.* …; 3 *Preface* by D. B. Harden, Director of the London Museum; 4–32 text). § Antique wove paper. 6 pen drawings by E.A. § Thick paper wrappers, the front with monochrome photograph and black letterpress titling on a yellow panel.

The booklet on 'London's changing scene' was written to accompany an exhibition celebrating the 50th anniversary of the London Museum.

94. 1962 MRS. MALONE [by] Eleanor Farjeon [Credit]. London: Oxford University Press, 1962.

Demy 16°, the first and last leaves pastedowns. 140 × 110 mm. (5½ × 4⅜ in.). Pp. [24] ([1] half-title; [2] vig.; [3] t.p.; [4] imprint: *Pr. in G.B. at the Baynard Press, London, S.W.9.*; [5–24] text). § Off-white cartridge paper. 17 pen drawings, as vigs. throughout the text, that on p. [2] is a repeat of the one on p. [12]. § Paper boards with a wrap-round watercolour, printed by 3-colour offset with orange-red spine strip, the same hue used for front and rear free and pastedown endpapers. D.j. as binding with the rear flap and ad. for E.F.'s *The Children's Bells* including a drawing from that book by Peggy Fortnum. What may be a late binding in thin card and a d.j. has also been reported.

Vignette from *Mrs. Malone* (1962 item 94)

1962 U.S. ISSUE: New York: Henry Z. Walck, Inc. English sheets.

TRANSLATIONS:
1996 [Japanese]. Tokyo: Koguma. Trs. Kimiko Abe and Keiko Ibaraki and including an afterword by the former (with a translation of E.F.'s verse tribute to E.A. and a reprint of the English verses).
1999 [Korean]. Eric Yang Agency.

Mrs. Malone *was first published, with decorations by David Knight, by Michael Joseph in 1950. In the course of correspondence over the present edition E.A. remarks that he has 'the germ of a splendid story for "Tim the Wanderer" – my final "Tim" book'.*

Richmal Crompton's 'Outlaws' from *Naughty Children* (1962 item 95).
Here E.A. enters territory sacrosanct to Thomas Henry,
the original illustrator of the 'William' books

95. 1962 NAUGHTY CHILDREN an Anthology Compiled by Christianna Brand [i.e. Mary Christianna Lewis *née* Milne] [vig.] [Credit]. London: Victor Gollancz Ltd. 1962.

Demy 8° in sixteens. 215 × 135 mm. (8½ × 5⅜ in.). Pp. [7] 8–318 [2] ([1] half-title; [3] t.p.; [4] imprint: *Pr. in G.B. by the Camelot Press Ltd., London and Southampton*; [5] dedication: *To my darling daughter Tora* … [and 10 other girls] … *and to all the other nice little girls I know* [2-line quote from Catherine Sinclair's *Holiday House*]; [7]–10 *Contents*; [11]–13 *Foreword*; [15]–314 text; [315] epigraph: 3-line quote from a letter by Mozart; [317]–318 *Acknowledgements*). § Antique wove paper. 43 pen drawings, that of the boy Mozart repeated once and that of 'Pet Marjorie' five times. § Pale blue linson boards. D.j. a pen drawing with 2-colour separation and hand-lettering by E.A. on front and spine; reproduction of the t.p. vig. on rear.

REPRINTED: 1965.

1963 U.S. EDITION: New York: E.P. Dutton & Co. Inc. (printed in the U.S.; leaf [A]14 a cancel) with 39 drawings only by E.A., a result of the replacements of excerpts from *Uncle Tom's Cabin* and *Oliver Twist* by unillustrated pieces (excerpts from P. G. Wodehouse's *Mike,* Charlotte Yonge's *Heartsease,* 'The Plum Cake' (anon) and 'Birth of Tree Toad' by Bob Davis*)*. Substitutions have also been made for 'Harry the Arrogant Boy and Sambo' (Trego Webb's 'Sleepy Maria' and Keats's 'Naughty Boy') and R.H. Barham's 'Legend of Jarvis's Jetty' (Wolcott Gibbs's 'Ring Out Wild Bells'). The red buckram binding has a reduced block of the illus. from p. 243; the d.j. replaces E.A.'s lettering with letterpress titling.

VARIA: the Mozart drawing was used as a heading for a set of sheets of writing paper sold by the Royal Academy of Arts; Pet Marjorie was used on the envelopes, and she also appeared on the lid of a paint-box sold by the Academy.

For the first appearance of Nurse Matilda in this anthology (pp. 29–33) see the note to item 110 below. Christianna Brand's involvement throughout the collection is a joy and particular note should be made of pp. 84–85 where the naughtiness of E.A.'s own children is celebrated.

96. 1962 A RING OF BELLS Poems of John Betjeman. Introduced and Selected by Irene Slade [vig.] Illustrations by E.A. London: John Murray, [1962].

Demy 8°. 216 × 135 mm. (8½ × 5⅜ in.). Pp. [4] v–[vi] 129 [1] ([i] half-title; [ii] *J.B.'s other works* …; [iii] t.p.; [iv] imprint: *Made and pr. in G.B. by William Clowes and Sons, Limited, London and Beccles and published by John*

Murray (Publishers) Ltd … 1962; v *Contents*; 1–5 *Introduction* by Irene Slade; 7 illus. section-title: *Poems of Childhood*; 9–105 text, including 8 further section-titles; 107–129 *Notes*). § Off-white cartridge paper. 13 pen drawings; t.p. vig.; 6 full-page section-titles; paired drawings on 3 section-titles. § Linson boards, a wrap-round scenic design in heavy pen-work with 3-colour overlays hand-lettered in lighter pen by E.A., the sub-title qualified as '… selected for the young'. D.j. as binding.

1963 U.S. EDITION: Boston: Houghton Mifflin.

1964 PAPERBACK ISSUE: John Murray Paperbacks. Apparently the same sheets in glazed paper wrappers with the t.p. vig. on front with green overlay.

1964 SCHOOL EDITION: The Albemarle Library For Schools. Creamy-yellow linson with block from p. 61 on front with a mid-green overlay. No d.j. (communicated).

97. 1962 SAILOR RUMBELOW AND BRITANNIA [by] James Reeves [Credit]. London, Melbourne, Toronto: Heinemann, [1962].

Large crown 8°. 208 × 135 mm. (8¼ × 5⅜ in.). Pp. [10] 115 [3] ([iii] half-title; [iv] *Books by J. R.*; [v] t.p.; [vi] imprint: *Pr. in G.B. by the Windmill Press Ltd., Kingswood, Surrey*; [vii] vig. *Contents*; [ix] fly-title; 1–115 text). § Off-white cartridge paper. 20 pen drawings: 3 chapter headpieces, 17 in text with the vig. at head of contents page being a reduced version of the illus. on p. 26. § Pale blue linen boards. D.j. pen decorations with two-colour overlays incorporating the illus. on p. 1, with hand-lettering by E.A. on front and spine; letterpress ads. at rear incorporating part of a drawing for *Prefabulous Animiles*.

1962 U.S. EDITION: New York: E.P. Dutton & Co. Inc. under the title *Sailor Rumbelow and Other Stories*. The book includes the six stories from the English ed. together with the five published earlier in England as *Pigeons and Princesses* (item 52 above).

The six stories in the book include retellings of the folk tales 'Rapunzel' and 'Simple Jack' furnished with three and two illus. respectively.

98. 1962 THE SINGING CUPBOARD [by] Dana Faralla [Credit]. London and Glasgow: Blackie, [1962].

Small foolscap 4° in eights, the first and last leaves pastedowns. 202 × 145 mm. (8¼ × 5¾ in.). Pp. [12] 13–90 [4] + [2] ([3] vig.; [5] half-title; [7] t.p.; [8] imprint: *This book is set in 12 Monotype Caslon* [sic] *and printed letter-press on Premium Offset at the Villafield Press, Bishopbriggs … 1962*; [9] *Contents*; [10] dedication: *To Ulla and Nils*; [11] fly-title; 13–90 text; [91] vig. tailpiece). § White offset paper (as noted above). 26 pen drawings, including 9 tailpieces. The vig. on p. [3] is a repeat of that on p. 28. § Blue linson boards. D.j. wrap-round watercolour, hand-lettered by E.A.

1963 U.S. EDITION: Philadelphia & New York: J.B. Lippincott Co.

The blurb on the front flap states this to be 'the hundredth book which E.A. has illustrated' a claim which is correct if The Singing Cupboard *be the last of the ten books noted here which E.A. illustrated in 1962.*

99. 1962 THE STORY OF LET'S MAKE AN OPERA! by Eric Crozier [Credit] [vig.]. London, Melbourne, Toronto: Oxford University Press, 1962. (The Young Reader's Guide to Music [V]).

Small foolscap 4° in eights. 208 × 148 mm. (8¼ × 5 ⅝ in.). Pp. [6] 71 [3] ([i] half-title; [ii] *Other books in this series*; [iii] t.p.; [iv] imprint etc.: *The music of the original stage work … is by Benjamin Britten. This adaptation, by the original librettist, is published by arrangement with Boosey & Hawkes Music Publishers Ltd. … Pr. in G.B. 1962*; [v] *Contents*; 1–71 text; [73] *A note on the Original Work … with further imprint: Pr. and bound by Barnicotts Limited at the Wessex Press, Taunton, Somerset*). § Creamy smooth cart-ridge paper. 24 pen drawings, including t.p. vig. § Glazed paper boards, brown and yellow, with an additional drawing by E.A. blocked in dark green on yellow on upper front. No d.j.

'The design for the endpapers [printed on pale green-faced paper] incorporates reproductions of parts of the Audience Songs …' (p. 2), a (faint) reversed out image of E.A.'s illus. on p. 37.

100. 1962 TIM'S FRIEND TOWSER [colour vig.] by E.A. London, New York, Toronto: Oxford University Press, [1962] [all hand-lettered by E.A.].

Crown 4°. Size, make-up and binding follow the design of item 30 above, with t.p. vignette and 18 drawings in watercolour with black line Kodatrace, and 26 pen drawings. The dedication is *For my Grandson Quentin*.

REPRINTED: once before 1989.

1962 U.S. EDITION: New York: Henry Z. Walck, Inc. Pr. in the U.S.A. Here, and in later volumes in the series, the inclusion of New York in the original British t.p. imprint seems to be mistaken.

OTHER REPRINTS: and the year 2000 reoriginations as noted at item 34 above.

TRANSLATIONS:
1962 [Swedish] *Tim och den Hemliga Hunden*. Trs. Britt G. Hallqvist. Stockholm: Bergh.
1969 [Japanese] Tokyo: Kaisei-Sha.
2001 [Japanese] Trs. Chihiro Nakagawa. Tokyo: Fukuinkan Shoten.

VARIA:
1979 *Ceramics:* The watercolours from the front cover and from p. 34 figured on two of the three plates manufactured by Royal Grafton for the International Year of the Child. For the other, see item 34 above.
1987 *Tape cassette:* One of *Six Seaworthy Adventures* as noted at item 4 above (p. 34).

101. 1963 BOYHOODS OF GREAT COMPOSERS Book Two by Catherine Gough [Credit] [vig.]. London, Melbourne, Toronto: Oxford University Press, 1963. (The Young Reader's Guides to Music [IX]).

Uniform with *Book One* (item 75), the pen drawings of the composers (Bach, Beethoven, Chopin, Verdi, Tchaikovsky, Vaughan Williams) similarly organised, with a freshly drawn t.p. vig. Laminated orange paper boards with the drawing from p. 1 in green; peach endpapers with 2 large pen drawings repeated front and rear; no d.j.

The two Books (this and item 75) were issued in a combined edition in 1968. The stories were re-arranged in one chronological sequence and the title-page followed the style of Book One. The binding was turquoise cloth boards and a d.j. in blue and grey with two drawings from the book on the front and two on the back.

102. 1963 KALEIDOSCOPE [by] Eleanor Farjeon [vig.] [Credit]. London: Oxford University Press, 1963.

Demy 8°. 215 × 135 mm. (8½ × 5¼ in.). Pp. [6] vii–x [2] 3–157 [1] ([i] half-title; [iii] t.p. [iv] imprint: *Made and pr. in G.B. by Morrison and Gibb Ltd., London and Edinburgh*; [v] dedication: *To* [drawing of pea-flower and pod, i.e. George E. Earle]; [vi] *Acknowledgement. The drawings on pages 3, 20, 28, 33, 80 and 122 originally appeared in Eleanor Farjeon's Book, published by Puffin Books*; vii–viii *Contents*; ix–x *Foreword*, dated *Hampstead 1963*; [1] section-title: *The Eye of the Earth*; 3–[158] text). § Creamy antique wove paper. 28 pen drawings (of which six have been previously published, as noted above): 21 chapter headpieces, 7 in text. The t.p. vig. is a reduced reproduction of the drawing on p. 45. § Plum-red cloth boards. D.j. a watercolour, hand-lettered by E.A. front and spine; letterpress ad. on rear with E.A. drawing from *The Little Bookroom*.

REPRINTED: Aylesbury: John Goodchild Publishers, 1986.

1963 U.S. EDITION: New York: Henry Z. Walck, Inc. Pr. in the U.S.A. Red linen boards, the headpiece from p. 18 blocked on front, E.A. cartouche and lettering blocked on spine.

First published in extended form, unillustrated, by Collins in 1928. The author's Foreword to the above edition explains that the earlier version was a conflation of stories which stemmed from childhood memories of 'a friend' with 'fantasies which really had nothing to do' with these recollections. These fantasies have now been excised to give unity to the stories about Anthony – who was, in fact, George Earle, the man with whom E.F. lived from 1920 until his death in 1949. As she notes in the Foreword, his nickname was 'Pod'.

103. 1963 PETER THE WANDERER [colour vig.] by E.A. London, New York, Toronto: Oxford University Press, [1963].

Crown 4°. Size, make-up and binding follow the design of item 30 above, with the type set by the Monotyping Services and printed, as usual, by Cowell's. Illustrations are t.p. vig. and 21 drawings in pen and watercolour and 24 pen drawings. The dedication is *To my grandchildren, Joanna, Sarah, Timothy and Rebecca, and also to Kaye Webb with love.*

1964 U.S. EDITION: New York: Henry Z. Walck Inc., with the U.S. printer using a stronger blue which gives the colour-work a darker hue.

MANUSCRIPT: a holograph manuscript with an illus. t.p. reading *Tim the Wanderer. Rough Draft. E.A.* (later addition: *Recast as Peter the Wanderer*) is in the Dept. of Special Collections in the library of the University of California at Los Angeles. It consists of 46 pp. of text and drawings in black ink, bound, with title and ink drawing on the upper board (communicated).

As has been noted at item 94 above, this story was early conceived as another adventure for Tim, and so it remained when the draft was submitted to O.U.P. simultaneously with the illustrated ms. of Diana and her Rhinoceros *(item 107). Both evoked concern in the editorial departments in London and at Walck's in New York, and 'Tim' drew some inexplicit doubts from several independent readers. As a result, E.A. recalled his draft and refashioned the story ('I have sweated blood on it'), sensibly changing the hero's name, if not his personality, in order to redirect readers' expectations into new channels.*

As for Diana, *E.A. rightly judged that his draft needed no such revision. Dismayed by the lack of editorial enthusiasm he wrote firmly, if not brusquely: 'Authors may well be the worst judges of their own work. But alas we are also stubborn in defence of our creatures. I won't alter a word of it'. Having regained it, he offered it to the Bodley Head, whose happy acceptance of it further weakened his sense of loyalty to Oxford.*

104. 1963 STIG OF THE DUMP by Clive King [vig.] [Credit]. Harmondsworth: Penguin Books, [1963]. (Puffin Story Books no. 196).

Small crown 8° in tens. 180 × 110 mm. (7¼ × 4¼ in.). Pp. [6] 7–156 [4] ([i] blurb; [3] t.p.; [4] dedication *For C.J.K.* and imprint: *Made and pr. in G.B. by Hazell Watson & Viney Ltd. Aylesbury and Slough. Set in Linotype*

Baskerville; [5] *Contents*; 7–[157] text; [159] *About the Author*.). § Off-white cheap antique wove paper (now browning to edges). 27 pen drawings: t.p. vig., 9 chapter headpieces, 17 in text. § Publisher's glazed paper wrappers, wrap-round pen and watercolour illus. (combining elements from the t.p. vig. and the drawing on p. 76) hand-lettered by E.A., series panel, letter-press, with Puffin device reversed out, at foot.

REPRINTED: 53 times to 1999, with changes to the wrapper design, that for the 1981 reprint showing two stills from a 10-part serial shown on Thames Television.

1965 NEW EDITION: London: Hamish Hamilton. Demy 8°. Pp. [7] 8–158 [2]. White cartridge paper. Tan linson boards. D.j. orange printed front and spine with 2 ovals printed yellow reproducing the drawings from pp. [54] and 46.

REPRINTED: London: Kestrel Books, 1980. D.j. printed blue, with the t.p. drawing enlarged on front as a watercolour.

VARIA: 1983 *Cassette cover:* an enlargement of the drawing on p. 40 was used on the lid of the cassette box of the 'Cover to Cover' reading of *Stig* by Martin Jarvis.

MS. DRAWINGS: 15 including that for the cover were exhibited for sale by Chris Beetles in 1993 (cat. nos. 462–476).

Soon after her arrival at Penguin as editor of Puffin Books in 1961 Kaye Webb determined upon a limited programme of original publishing alongside the customary reprints. With A Parcel of Trees *by William Mayne,* Stig *was the first of the titles to appear. Its success, leading to constant reprinting, often on inferior paper in the paperback editions, demonstrates how easy it is to produce travesties of the artist's fine-line work.*

105. 1964 THE ALLEY [vig.] [by] Eleanor Estes [Credit]. New York: Harcourt, Brace & World, Inc., [1964].

U.S. demy 8° in sixteens. 204 × 130 mm. (8 × 5¼ in.). Pp. [12] 11–283 [3] ([1] half-title; [2] *By the same author* (10 titles); [3] t.p.; [4] imprint: *Pr. in the*

U.S.A.; [5] dedication: *To the memory of Mama Sadie*; [7] *Contents*; [9] fly-title; 11–283 text). § Antique wove paper. 23 pen drawings: t.p. vig. and one each in text of 20 chapters, two for chapter 3. § Lemon yellow linen boards with block from drawing on p. 34 in dark grey on front. D.j. white paper with pen drawings and hand-lettering by E.A. on front and spine with 2-colour overlays; ads. on rear.

Not published in Great Britain. A sequel appears at item 158 below.

106. 1964 ANN AT HIGHWOOD HALL Poems for Children by Robert Graves [Credit]. London: Cassell, [1964] [hand-lettered by E.A. on panels within a full-page pen drawing with one colour separation, bled to edge].

Foolscap 4° in eights. 215 × 160 mm. (8½ × 6⅜ in.). Pp. [8] 38 [2] ([i] half-title; [iii] t.p.; [iv] imprint: *First published 1964 ... Pr. in G.B. by the Camelot Press Ltd., London and Southampton*; [v] *Contents*; [vii] dedication: *To my grandchildren Georgina and David Graves with love*; 1–[39] text; [40] tail-piece). § Thick white cartridge paper. 35 pen drawings with a single colour separation, alternating peach and green: t.p. design and tailpiece, as noted, with 33 drawings variably placed throughout text (cf. item 81 above). § Pale blue linson boards. D.j. pen drawing, based on the design on pp. 2–3, with architectural pediment for title, with three colour overlays, hand-lettered by E.A. on front and spine, rear blank. § *Ref:* Higginson A110.

1966 U.S. EDITION: New York: Garden City: Doubleday & Company, Inc.

The harsh paper of the London edition is not hospitable to E.A.'s pen draw-ing or to the ink of the separated colours. The U.S. ed. with taller pages (233 × 150 mm) and wove paper, is more satisfactory.

107. 1964 DIANA AND HER RHINOCEROS [by] E.A. [vig.]. London: The Bodley Head, [1964].

Oblong crown 4°. 196 × 254 mm. (7¾ × 10 in.). Pp. [2] 3–32 ([1] t.p.; [2] dedication: *For my Grandchildren Susannah, Quentin and Dominic who live at 43 Queen's Road, Richmond, Surrey, England* and imprint: *Set in Mono-type Plantin ... Pr. and bound in G.B. ... by William Clowes & Sons Ltd.,*

Beccles; 3–32 text). § White cartridge paper. 16 drawings in line and watercolour; 12 pen drawings including t.p. vig. § Paper boards with watercolour drawing and hand-lettering by E.A. on front and spine, large oval watercolour in dotted frame on rear. D.j. as binding.

From *Diana and her Rhinoceros* (1964 item 107, reduced)

REPRINTED: 1968, 1973, 1979.

1964 U.S. ISSUE: New York: Henry Z. Walck, Inc. English sheets.

1983 PAPERBACK EDITION: Methuen Children's Books. (A Magnet Book). 152 × 188 mm.

1993 PAPERBACK EDITION: The Bodley Head. (Red Fox Books). Oblong crown 4°.

TRANSLATIONS:
1979 [Afrikaans] *Dientje en die Renoster*. Trs. Louise Steyn. Cape Town: Human & Rousseau.
2001 [Japanese] Trs. Kimiko Abe. Tokyo: Koguma.

The setting for Diana's story bears a strong resemblance to the house then occupied by its dedicatees. The picture that adorns the sitting-room wall on p. 3 is clearly a version of E.A.'s image of 'The Drinkers' (see item C49 below).

108. 1964 HELLO ELEPHANT by Jan Wahl [Credit]. [large 2-colour drawing]. New York, Chicago, San Francisco: Holt, Rinehart and Winston, [1964].

Small oblong crown 8°. 126 × 167 mm. (6⅝ × 5 in.). Pp. [32] ([1] t.p.; [2] imprint: *Pr. in the U.S.A. ...*; [3] dedication: *For Lisa: this is a long ago story*; [4–31] text; [32] notes on author and illustrator). § Smooth white cartridge paper. T.p. vig. and 14 drawings across the spread with alternate separations in pinkish brown and pale pea-green. § Pale blue antique paper boards with title and line drawing from p. 31 in turquoise on front. D.j. white paper with line drawing, 2-colour overlays, and hand-lettering by E.A. on front, blue overall wash on blank rear and typographic lettering in black and blue on pink spine. Endpapers of heavy mottled blue paper front and rear. A publisher's presentation binding in three-quarters red morocco with red cloth sides has also been seen.

Published simultaneously by the Canadian branch of Holt, but not available in Great Britain.

— **1964** THE JUPITER BOOK OF SONGS & RHYMES FOR THE VERY YOUNG. [Leicester(?): Brockhampton Press, deleted] [manuscript title-page, with a decorative surround of drawings, in ink over pencil].

Crown 4°. Pp. 48, in a publisher's blank dummy which has been used by E.A. to complete the first draft of a work which progressed no farther. The text consists of a letterpress setting of 16 rhymes divided in order to make a sequence through the rectos, with the versos left blank for musical settings. The text is illustrated by E.A. throughout in blue ink over pencil, and the dummy has been given a d.j. in line and watercolour, whose decorative drawings around the titling include a self-portrait (for a reproduction see colour plate I). The book was probably planned as a venture in association with Jupiter Records. The reasons for its abandonment are not known. See overleaf for a reproduction of one of the mocked-up text pages.

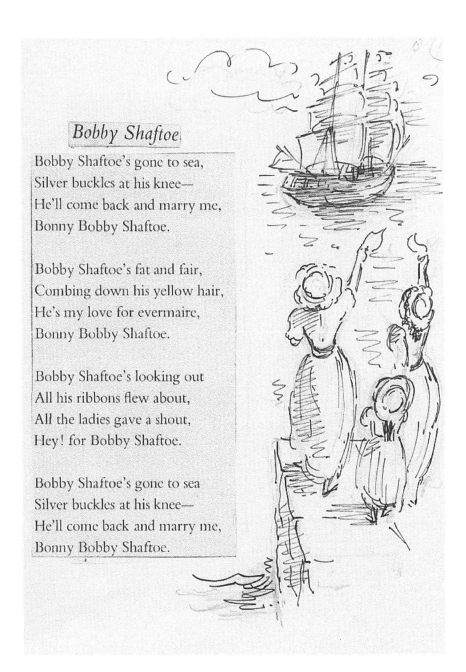

Bobby Shaftoe

Bobby Shaftoe's gone to sea,
Silver buckles at his knee—
He'll come back and marry me,
Bonny Bobby Shaftoe.

Bobby Shaftoe's fat and fair,
Combing down his yellow hair,
He's my love for evermaire,
Bonny Bobby Shaftoe.

Bobby Shaftoe's looking out
All his ribbons flew about,
All the ladies gave a shout,
Hey! for Bobby Shaftoe.

Bobby Shaftoe's gone to sea
Silver buckles at his knee—
He'll come back and marry me,
Bonny Bobby Shaftoe.

Text page from the unpublished
Jupiter Book of Songs and Rhymes (1964, reduced)

109. 1964 THE LAND OF RIGHT UP AND DOWN by Eva-Lis Wuorio [Credit]. Cleveland and New York: The World Publishing Company, [1964].

Royal 8°. 228 × 160 mm. (9 × 6⅜ in.) Pp. [8] 9–60 [4] with three bifolia inset between pp. 10–11, 32–33, 58–59 ([1] half-title; [3] *By the same author and artist* ...; [4] vig. frontis.; [5] t.p.; [6] imprint: *Pr. in the U.S.A. ... Published simultaneously in Canada by Nelson Foster & Scott Ltd.*; [7] dedication: *For my Mother and her little friends Pilar, Meritxell, Maribelle, and Xavier of Arinsal in Andorra*; 9–60 text; [61] tailpiece; [63] *About the author and artist*; [64] edition numbers: *1–5 68–64*). § Cream cartridge paper, plates on the same stock. Three double-page spread watercolours; 20 pen drawings: vig. frontis., 1 chapter headpiece, 16 in text, 2 tailpieces. § Pea-green linen boards blocked in blue on front after the drawing on p. 55. D.j. wrap-round watercolour, an extension of the second colour-spread, hand-lettered throughout by E.A. A publisher's presentation binding in half blue morocco with marbled paper sides has been seen.

1964 ENGLISH EDITION: London: Dennis Dobson. Material re-arranged to give four gatherings of 8 leaves with the colour plates printed as part of the gathering. (The vibrancy of the colour-mix is lessened by an over-emphatic printing of the cyan plate.) The paper-board binding employs the d.j. design.

110. 1964 NURSE MATILDA [by] Christianna Brand [i.e. Mary Christianna Lewis *née* Milne] [Credit]. Leicester: Brockhampton Press, [1964].

Pot 8°. 152 × 97 mm. (6 × 3⅞ in.). Pp. [4] 5–127 [1] ([1] half-title; [2] portrait vig. frontis.; [3] t.p.; [4] dedication: *To Tora – and to our Hilde, with love* and imprint: *First edition 1964 ... Pr. in G.B. by Jarrold & Sons Ltd., Norwich*; 5–[128] text). § Featherweight antique wove paper. 40 pen drawings: vig. frontis., 10 historiated initials, 27 in text, including 1 full-page composite of 3 small scenes, 2 tailpieces. § Green paper boards, pictorial design and lettering by E.A. blocked in gilt on front and spine. D.j. watercolour version of the binding design; the front and rear flaps carry, respectively, photographs of the author and the illustrator as children in best party togs. Red end-papers, all edges stained red, red silk marker.

REPRINTED: eight times to 1979.

1964 U.S. EDITION: New York: E. P. Dutton & Co. Inc. 164 × 110 mm. Pr. in U.S.A. Pale blue linen boards, block from p. 35 in maroon on front. (A later ed. is recorded as Boston: Gregg Press, 1980. Not seen.)

The evolution of Matilda: left, detail from *Naughty Children* (1962 item 95); right, vignette from *Nurse Matilda* (1964 item 110)

1973 PAPERBACK REPRINTS: Leicester: Brockhampton Press. Small crown 8°, reprinted many times, later by Hodder & Stoughton (Knight Books). Early in the 1980s a cover was briefly introduced illus. by Julia Whatley.

1988 'LIBRARY EDITION': Bath: The Chivers Press. (Swift Children's Books). Crown 8°, photographed from the Brockhampton/Hodder text. Laminated paper boards.

TRANSLATIONS:

1966 [German] *Matilda die Seltsame Kinderfrau*. Trs. Jella Lepman. Zürich: Atlantis Verlag.

1966 [Swedish] *Den Fantastika Matilda*. Trs. Stig Kassman. Stockholm: Bonnier.

1979 [French] *Chère Mathilda*. Trs. René Escudié, Paris: Fernand Nathan.

Nurse Matilda first stepped into print in the much-abbreviated version of the present book written for Naughty Children *(item 95, pp. 29–43), although as early as 1939 E.A. had proposed 'a new book' to O.U.P. on 'The Strange Story of Nurse Matilda'. From what Christianna Brand says in* Naughty Children, *however, this 'very old story' came down to her from her great-grandfather – a family story which 'has taken many different forms'. She added that she was 'going to write it into a much longer story which I hope you will one day read.'*

As Christianna Brand's cousin, E.A. was himself part of the family who shared the original tale (and the children's names here, and in the earlier version, echo those of the Ardizzone ménage). The collaboration between the cousins, aided and abetted by the Brockhampton Press production team[8], led to one of the happiest children's books ever produced – and the decline in quality of many of the reprints noted above is painful to behold.

Two sequels written by Christianna Brand were published by Brockhampton in 1967 and 1974. Their design follows the above volume closely; the differences are noted below at nos. 136 and 168.

111. 1964 THE STORY OF JACKIE THIMBLE by James Reeves [vig.] [Credit]. New York: E. P. Dutton & Co., Inc., [1964].

Foolscap 8°, a single gathering of 16 leaves. 163 × 106 mm. (6½ × 4¼ in.). Pp. [4] 5–31 [1] ([1] t.p.; [2] imprint etc.: *Text and illus. copyright 1964. All rights reserved. Pr. in the U.S.A. First edition … published simultaneously in Canada by Clarke, Irwin & Company Ltd. Toronto & Vancouver*; [3]–31 text). § Antique wove paper. 25 pen drawings: t.p. vig., the remainder variably placed on the spreads. § Rose-pink linen boards, t.p. vig. blocked in black on front, drawing at top of p. 6 on rear; bright yellow endpapers. D.j. pen drawings front and rear, based on similar drawings on pp. [4] and 11, with 2-colour separation.

8. Antony Kamm, who edited the book at Brockhampton, reports that a standard octavo volume was intended (perhaps like the U.S. ed?) but that it was E.A. who suggested the quasi-Victorian make-up that was used.

1965 ENGLISH EDITION: London: Chatto & Windus. Imprint: *Pr. in G.B. by Morrison & Gibb Ltd., London and Edinburgh.* As U.S. ed. but with yellow linson boards; no separate endpapers.

From 1973 the text was included in Reeves's Complete Poems for Children *(see item 159 below).*

112. 1964 SWANHILDA-OF-THE-SWANS [by] Dana Faralla [Credit]. London and Glasgow: Blackie, [1964].

Pot 4° in eights, the first and last leaves pastedowns. 202 × 150 mm. (8 × 6 in.). Pp. [14] 15–92 [4] ([5] vig.; [7] half-title; [9] t.p.; [10] imprint: *Pr. in G.B. by Blackie & Son Ltd., Glasgow ... 1964*; 15–92 text; [93] vig.). § Off-white cartridge paper. 25 pen drawings, including one spread across lower portion of pp. 56–57. The vigs. on pp. [5] and [93] are repeats of the drawings on pp. 88 and 29. § Blue linson boards. D.j. wrap-round water-colour., hand-lettered by E.A. throughout.

113. 1964 THE THIRTY-NINE STEPS by John Buchan [vig.] With a Colour Frontispiece and Line Drawings in the Text by E.A. London: J. M. Dent & Sons Ltd. New York: E. P. Dutton & Co. Inc., [1964].

Large post 8°. 210 × 132 mm. (8¼ × 5¼ in.). Pp. [12] 3–145 [9] + inset frontis. ([iii] half-title; frontis.; [v] t.p.; [vi] imprint: *Made in G.B. at the Aldine Press, Letchworth, Herts, 1964* and biographical note on the author by *R.L.G*[reen]; [vii] dedication: *To Thomas Arthur Nelson, Lothian and Border Horse* and ten-line address: '*My dear Tommy ...*'; [ix] *Contents*; [1] fly-title; 3–145 text; [146–150] blank + [4] pp. ads. on a thinner stock). § Creamy cartridge paper. 4-colour half-tone frontis. + 15 pen drawings: 10 chapter head-pieces, 2 tailpieces and 3 in text; the t.p. vig. a reduced repeat of the drawing on p. 59. § Decorated cloth boards in series styling with series dec. endpapers. Series d.j. with a reduced version of the half-tone frontis. on front.

REPRINTED: 1967.

1992 PAPERBACK EDITION: London: J.M. Dent. Crown 8°, the frontis. adapted for the wrapper front.

MS. DRAWINGS: In 1988 J. M. Dent was taken over by Weidenfeld & Nicolson, before which, on 19 June 1987, 'drawings for book illustrations' from the Dent archives were sold by Sotheby's in no fewer than 136 lots. Lot 734 comprised the frontis. watercolour and text drawings for the above title, with some additional proofs etc. See also note at item 138 below.

First published in 1915 and the first of what Buchan described as his 'precipitous yarns' from which his real fame dates (Roger Lancelyn Green in his biographical note).

114. 1964 THREE TALL TALES Chosen from Traditional Sources by James Reeves [Credit]. [London, New York, Toronto]: Abelard-Schuman, [1964] [all hand-lettered by E.A. and placed within a double-page title-spread in line and 3 colours].

Crown 4° in eights, the first and last leaves pastedowns. 252 × 175 mm. (10 × 6⅞ in.). Pp. [48] ([2–3] front endpapers; [4–5] t.p. spread; [6–7] first opening of text, with copyright 1964 on p. [6]; [8–45] text continued, with final imprint: *Lithographed in G.B. by A. & M. Weston, Ltd., South Wigston*; [46–47] rear endpapers). § A stiffish white offset paper. 31 drawings including those on endpapers: t.p. and 14 pen drawings in text with three-colour overlays; 15 pen-drawings in text and endpaper spreads with single colour (peach) overlay. § Pale blue linson boards. D.j. wrap-round pen-drawn design, introducing characters from the tales, with 3-colour overlays, hand-lettered by E.A. Endpapers pen-drawn with a similar purpose, with single, peach overlay. (See also p. 309).

Of the three tales: 'The Cat and the Mouse' is from J. O. Halliwell's Popular Rhymes and Nursery Tales *(London, 1849); 'Sir Gammer Vance' is from Joseph Jacobs's* More English Fairy Tales *(London, 1894); and 'Tuflongbo' is adapted from a chapter in Holme Lee's* Legends from Fairy Land *(1860).*

115. 1965 KNOW ABOUT ENGLISH LAW [by] Henry Cecil [Credit]. London and Glasgow: Blackie, [1965].

Foolscap 4° in eights, the first and last leaves pastedowns. 203 × 142 mm. (8 × 5⅞ in.). Pp. [6] 7–59 [1] ([1] half-title; [2] vig. frontis.; [3] t.p.; [4] imprint: *Pr. in G.B. by Blackie & Son Limited, Glasgow. 1965*; [5] *Contents*; 7–59 text). § Cream cartridge paper. 17 pen drawings: frontis., 8 full-page (two of which face each other as a 'broken spread'), 8 in text. § Orange linson boards; d.j. centre panel front with a line and watercolour drawing by E.A., similar to part of the frontis., reproduced as a half-tone.

1974 REVISED EDITION: as *Learn About English Law*. London: William Luscombe Publisher Ltd. Pp. 56 (not seen).

As with item 62 above, the court scenes have a relationship to the drawings in Sketchbook 1.

Vignette from *The Milldale Riot* (1965 item 116)

116. 1965 THE MILLDALE RIOT by Freda P. Nichols. Illustrated by Diz. London: Ginn and Company Ltd., [1965]. (Active Readers: Second Series).

Small crown 8°. 176 × 120 mm. (7 × 4¾ in.). Pp. vi 154 ([i] t.p.; [ii] imprint: *Pr. in G.B. by R. & R. Clark Ltd., Edinburgh* with lists of *The Active Readers* first and second series in 'interest ages' of 9–13 and 10–15 respectively; iii–iv *About This Book* and *Acknowledgements*; v *Contents*; vi frontis.; 1–154 text). § Off-white cartridge paper. 28 pen drawings: frontispiece, 6 full-page, 21 in text, including 1 chapter headpiece and 1 final tailpiece.

Diagrams etc. in the glossary are by another hand. § Cream linson boards with series pattern and titling in orange and black. Endpapers are maps and an illus. production diagram (designed by Freda Nichols) printed 3-tone black.

REPRINTED: 1969, 1970.

The only book using E.A.'s cartoon signature in the title-page credit. At the time when the 1972 Hand-list *was being compiled E.A. remarked on the particular satisfaction that he enjoyed in making the drawings for this school reader.*

117. 1965 THE OLD NURSE'S STOCKING BASKET [by] Eleanor Farjeon [vig.] [Credit]. London: Oxford University Press, 1965.

Foolscap 4° in eights. 202 × 148 mm. (8 × 5¾ in.). Pp. [7] 2–102 ([i] half-title; [iii] t.p.; [iv] imprint etc.: *First published in 1931. First … in this edition 1965 … Pr. in G.B. by Western Printing Services Ltd., Bristol*; [v] *Contents*; [1]–102 text). § Creamy antique wove paper. 24 pen drawings: t.p. vig.; 3 chapter headpieces; 20 in text, that on p. 94 being a development of the image on p. 106 of item 26 above. § Yellow cloth boards. D.j. in line and watercolour, hand-lettered by E.A. front and spine; ad. for, with block from, item 102 on rear.

1965 U.S. ISSUE: New York: Henry Z. Walck, Inc. English sheets.

1981 PAPERBACK EDITION: Harmondsworth: Puffin Books in assoc. with O.U.P. (A Young Puffin). Crown 8°. Pp. [6] 7–77 [3].

TRANSLATION: [n.d.] [Siamese] Bangkok: Amarin. 185 × 125 mm. Card wrappers.

First published in 1931 by the University of London Press, with illustrations by E. H. Whydale. A second edition appeared from the same publisher in 1949, with illustrations by Philip Gough. The drawings of the Old Nurse on the d.j. and on pp. [1] and 6 here are portrayals of Eleanor Farjeon herself.

118. 1965 OLD PERISHER by Diana Ross [colour vig.] with drawings by E.A. London: Faber and Faber, [1965].

Crown 4° in eights. 245 × 180 mm. (9¾ × 7¼ in.). Pp. [32] ([1] t.p.; [2] imprint: *Pr. in G.B. by Latimer Trend & Co. Ltd., Whitstable. 1965*; [3–32] text). § White cartridge paper. Twelve 4-colour line separations: t.p. vig.; 4 occupying much of double-page spreads; 7 in text, including tailpiece; 15 pen drawings. § Paper boards with line separation in 4 colours and hand-lettering by E.A. on front; letterpress spine; rear blank. D.j. as binding.

119. 1965 SARAH AND SIMON AND NO RED PAINT [2-colour vig.] by E.A. London: Constable Young Books Ltd.; Longmans Canada Ltd, [1965]. ('A Value Book').

Small crown 4° in eights. 230 × 185 mm. (9⅛ × 7¼ in.). Pp. [2] 3–48 ([1] t.p.; [2] dedication and imprint: *To my grandson Timothy. Pr. in G.B. by Hazells Offset Ltd. Slough, Bucks. 1965*; 3–48 text). § Featherweight antique wove paper, browning at edges. 43 pen drawings on Kodatrace, with single-colour washes, sepia and pale green on alternate page-openings: t.p. vig., 5 drawings across the upper two-thirds of double-page spread, 37 in text. § Linson boards with wrap-round illustration in line and watercolour printed down, typographic titling front and rear. No d.j.

1966 U.S. EDITION: New York: Delacorte Press. Pr. in the U.S.A. with the colour overlays alternating green/sepia rather than sepia/green as above.

1974 SECOND PRINTING: London: Kestrel Books. Issued with a d.j. which replicates the design on the binding.

The 'Value Books' were a ploy by Grace Hogarth, children's books editor at Constable's, to bring new picture books, illustrated by leading illustrators, to as large a public as possible by reducing production costs. Sarah and Simon *was published alongside the Grimms'* Snow White and Rose Red, *illus. by Barbara Cooney (both at 7/6 net) at a time when a 48-page picture book such as* Tim and Ginger *(next item) would be twice the price. Although further books in this series appeared in 1966 (see item 129 below) the experiment was discontinued.*

120. 1965 TIM AND GINGER by E.A. [colour vig.]. London, New York, Toronto: Oxford University Press, [1965].

Crown 4°. Size, make-up, binding follow the design of item 30 above, with t.p. vig. and 18 drawings in pen and watercolour and 25 pen drawings. The dedication is *To my grandchildren, Daniel and Hannah*.

REPRINTED: five times to 1989.

1965 U.S. EDITION: New York: Henry Z. Walck, Inc. Pr. in the U.S.A.

OTHER REPRINTS: and the year 2000 reoriginations as noted at item 34 above.

TRANSLATIONS:
1981 [Swedish] *Tim och Ginger*. Trs. Britt G. Hallqvist. Malmö: Bergh.
2001 [Japanese] Trs. Chihiro Nakagawa. Tokyo: Fukuinkan Shoten.
2002 [Norwegian] *Tim og Rødtopp*. Trs. Marianne Danielsen. Stavanger: Sandvik.
2002 [Finnish] *Tim och Tidvattnet*. Trs. Ulf Hyltén-Cavallius. Helsingborg: Go·boken.

MS. DRAWINGS: Toronto Public Library: Osborne and Lillian H. Smith Collections. See J. Shefrin, *Box of Delights; 600 Years of Children's Books* (catalogue). Toronto: Friends of the Collections, 1995 (item 162).

VARIA: 1987 *Tape cassette:* One of *Six Seaworthy Adventures* as noted at item 4 above (p. 34).

121. 1965 TIMOTHY'S SONG [vig.] by William J. Lederer [Credit]. New York: W.W. Norton & Company, Inc., [1965].

Narrow crown 8°. 183 × 120 mm. (7½ × 4¾ in.). Pp. [10] 9–41 [5] ([1] half-title; [3] t.p.; [4] imprint: *First Edition. Pr. in the U.S.A.; published simultaneously in Canada by George J. McLeod Limited, Toronto 1965*; [5] dedication: *For Brian, Jon and Bruce – who were the first to hear this story*; [7] fly-title; 9–41 text; [43] *About the Author*; [44] *About the Artist*). § Off-white cartridge paper. 17 pen drawings: t.p. vig., head- and tailpiece, 9 in text and 5 spread variably across the gutter. § Pale blue coarse linen boards. D.j. line and watercolour drawing hand-lettered by E.A. on front and spine.

1966 ENGLISH EDITION: London: Lutterworth Press. (As the descend-ant of the Religious Tract Society, the Lutterworth Press was a highly appropriate firm to undertake English publication of this latterday religious tract.)

122. 1965 THE TRUANTS AND OTHER POEMS FOR CHILDREN [by] John Walsh [Credit]. London: Heinemann, [1965].

Crown 8°, the first and last leaves pastedowns. 198 × 127 mm. (7¾ × 5 in.). Pp. [8] 79 [1] ([i] half-title and vig.; [iii] t.p.; [iv] imprint: *Pr. in G.B. by Bookprint Limited, Kingswood, Surrey 1965*; [v] dedication: *To Moira Doolan*; [vii] *Contents*; 1–[80] text). § Off-white cartridge paper. 40 pen drawings: half-title vig. and 39 in text. § Green glazed cloth boards. D.j. green-printed, lettering by E.A. in white panels on front and spine, enlarged reproduc-tion of the drawing on p. 43 in central oval panel on front.

REPRINTED: 1967, 1971.

1968 U.S. ISSUE: Chicago: Rand McNally. English sheets

123. 1965 THE YEAR ROUND [by] Leonard Clark [large 2-colour drawing] [Credit]. [London]: Rupert Hart-Davis Educational Pub-lications, 1965.

Small crown 8°, a single gathering of 16 leaves. 183 × 122 mm. (7¼ × 4¾ in.). Pp. [32] ([1] t.p.; [2] *Contents*; [3] contents continued and imprint: *Pr. in G.B. by Bristol Typesetting Co. Ltd.*; [4] dedication: *For Michael and Betty*; [5–36] text). § Stiffish white cartridge paper. 27 illustrations/dec-orations: t.p. drawing, the rest variously disposed with pale peach or pale green overlays for each opening. § The leaves stapled into glazed paper boards with a repeat of the drawing by E.A. on p. [6] on front. (N.B. it appears that some copies may have been made up for the author with an extra bifolium round the gathering and the whole sewn into the boards. E.A.'s copy has been signed by L.C. on the first blank of these extra leaves.)

VARIA: 1978 *Four Songs*. A South Leigh Press poster card. Broadside 415 × 295 mm folded twice laterally and once vertically to give six panels 140 × 295 mm on which are reproduced, within a dec. border, E.A.'s four 'season titles' for the book (two with 4-line stanzas) and two other illus., also with 4-line stanzas all hand-lettered by the publishers. One fold on the reverse forms the title, as above, with another pen drawing from the book, faced by the imprint: *The year round poster and greeting card. Illus. by E.A. © 1978 The South Leigh Press ... London SW6 5SP.*

124. 1966 DADDY-LONG-LEGS [by] Jean Webster [vig.] with New Illustrations by E.A. [Leicester]: Brockhampton Press, [1966].

Large crown 8°, the first and last leaves pastedowns. 202 × 135 mm. (8 × 5¼ in.). Pp. [6] 7–183 [1] + 8 insets ([1] half-title; [3] t.p.; [4] imprint: *First published 1912 ... Pr. in G.B. by C. Tinling & Co. Ltd, Leicester;* [5] dedication: *To You;* 7–[184] text). § Antique wove paper, with the insets on a smoother grey stock. 9 pen drawings: t.p. vig. and 8 full-page drawings, sometimes anticipating events in the text, on grey paper placed as conjugates around sigs. B, E, H and L. 34 further drawings in text by the author. § Pale blue imitation pebble-grain cloth, purple panel gilt on spine. D.j. a gallery of pictures in line and watercolour, hand-lettered, by E.A. on front and spine, plain blue wash on rear. The blurb numbers the book among seven 'Brockhampton 20th Century Classics'. Also issued in a binding of white 'Ivorex' boards with maroon leather label in a matching slip-case designed for presentation to authors, illustrators and other worthies.

REPRINTED: 1969.

1967 U.S. EDITION: New York: Meredith.

First published in 1912 with the text illustrations by Jean Webster retained here.

125. 1966 THE DRAGON by Archibald Marshall [large vig.] [Credit]. [London]: Hamish Hamilton, [1966].

Oblong small crown 4° in eights. 185 × 235 mm. (7¼ × 9¼ in.). Pp. [32] ([1] t.p.; [2] imprint: *First published in G.B. 1930. Pr. by A. & M. Weston Ltd, Wigston, Leicestershire, 1966;* [3–32] text). § Dead white cartridge

paper. 27 illustrations: 10 line and watercolour drawings, 5 covering portions of a double-page spread; 17 pen drawings: t.p. vig., tailpiece and 15 in
text. § Linson boards with line and watercolour design, hand-lettered by
E.A. printed down on front and spine, rear cover blank. D.j. as binding
with letterpress ad. for *The Eleanor Farjeon Book* (next item) on rear with
the drawing from p. [159] of that book.

1967 U.S. EDITION: New York: Dutton.

MS. DRAWINGS: Sketchbook 35 contains several preparatory drafts, especially of the dragon.

'The Dragon' was first published in Punch *and appeared in Marshall's* Simple
Stories from Punch *in 1930, illus. by George Morrow. Publication of the U.S.
edition occasioned a review in* Book Week *(Spring Children's Books, 2 May
1967 p. 24), by E.A.'s great contemporary, Maurice Sendak, who felt that his
work was too often taken for granted:* The Dragon *'is a charming example of
the various and unique abilities of this artist who is possibly the supreme contemporary example of the genuine illustrator. He works easy magic in* The Dragon
*and these whirlwind-rendered watercolours – that look careless to the dull-minded
– are some of his finest'. The review in which this occurs is reprinted in Sendak's*
Caldecott & Co.; Notes on Books and Pictures *(New York: Michael di
Capua Books; London: The Bodley Head, 1988, pp. 133–137).*

126. 1966 THE ELEANOR FARJEON BOOK: a Tribute to her
Life and Work 1881–1965. Introduction by Naomi Lewis [Credit]. London:
Hamish Hamilton, [1966].

Demy 8° in sixteens. 215 × 132 mm. (8¾ × 5¼ in.). Pp. [7] 2–184 [2] ([i]
half-title; [iii] t.p.; [iv] imprint: *Pr. in G.B. by Western Printing Services Ltd,
Bristol, 1966*; [v] *Contents*; [1]–10 *Introduction*; [11]–184 text). § White
cartridge paper. 13 pen drawings: headpiece vigs. to *Introduction* and 12
contributions. § Plum linson boards. D.j. line and watercolour drawings,
hand-lettered by E.A. (with typographic additions) on front and spine, letterpress ads. on rear.

1966 U.S. ISSUE: New York: Henry Z. Walck. English sheets. Salmon
pink linen boards, blue-lettered spine.

Opposite: Page from *The Eleanor Farjeon Book* (1966 item 126)

TEA WITH ELEANOR FARJEON

Rumer Godden

SHE CAME to meet you at her blue front door that let you in beside the bow window that stretched across the sturdy little house front. She would be wearing a comfortable flowered dress, in china blue and white perhaps—"I don't buy clothes. I wear my old ones"—her feet in equally comfortable strap buttoned shoes, her hair gathered up out of the way, her cheeks rosy, though she was so often ill, and her eyes clear behind her spectacles as she beamed at you; "beaming" was the right word for Eleanor Farjeon, a beam that shone and lit you. Unlike most of us, she was not ashamed of showing her feelings and, if the sight of you made her happy, happiness enfolded you. There was never

The text is by Mary Norton, Gillian Avery, Eilís Dillon, James Reeves, Rosemary Sutcliff, Ruth Ainsworth, Patricia Lynch, Ian Serraillier, William Mayne, Barbara Willard and Dorothy Clewes, with a valedictory portrait, 'Tea with Eleanor Farjeon', by Rumer Godden. In 1980, Avery's contribution, 'The Italian Boy', with E.A.'s illus. from p. 79, was published in All Made of Fantasy, *ed. Marjorie and Jeremy Rowe. This ring-bound collection of stories for children was from the theatre in Chipping Norton 'to help raise funds to keep theatre alive in North Oxfordshire.'*

127. 1966 THE GROWING SUMMER [by] Noel Streatfeild [Credit]. St. James's Place, London: Collins, 1966.

Large crown 8°. 198 × 130 mm. (7¾ × 5⅛ in.). Pp. [8] 9–223 [1] ([1] half-title; [2] *by the same author ...*; [3] t.p.; [4] acknowledgement and imprint: *Pr. in G.B. Collins Clear-Type Press London and Glasgow*; [5–6] *Contents*; [7] dedication: *For Elizabeth Enright because I so greatly admire her books*; 9–[224] text). § Antique wove paper. 21 pen drawings in text. § Dark blue linson boards. D.j. line and watercolour drawing front and spine, typographic titling, ads. at rear.

1967 U.S. EDITION: as *The Magic Summer*. New York: Random House, Inc. Pr. in U.S.A., with the drawing on p. 10 of the English ed. repeated on the t.p.

1968 PAPERBACK EDITION: Harmondsworth: Penguin Books. (Puffin Story Book no. 293). Small crown 8°. Pp. [10] 11–216.

2000 PAPERBACK EDITION: London: Collins Children's Books. Pp. [6] 7–236 [4]. Photo on front wrapper.

128. 1966 THE LAND OF GREEN GINGER by Noel Langley [vig.] [Credit]. [Third edition]. Harmondsworth: Penguin Books, [1966]. (Puffin Story Books no. 256).

Small crown 8°. 180 × 110 mm. (7¼ × 4¼ in.). 'Perfect' binding, no quires. Pp. [6] 7–189 [3] ([1] blurb; [3] t.p.; [4] imprint etc.: *First published as* The Tale of the Land of Green Ginger *by Arthur Barker 1937. This re-written version published in Puffin Books 1966. Made and pr. in G.B. by Richard Clay (The Chaucer Press) Ltd, Bungay, Suffolk. Set in Monotype Baskerville*;

[5–6] *Contents*; 7–189 text; [191–192] ads.). § Mechanical m.f. printing paper, browning to edges. 43 pen drawings in text, that on p. 166 repeated as t.p. vig. § Publisher's wrappers with wrap-round pen drawing with 4-colour separation hand-lettered by E.A.; series panel with typographic lettering and device at foot.

REPRINTED: 1970, 1972.

1975 NEW EDITION: Harmondsworth: Penguin books. Small crown 8° Pp. 157. Revised throughout, with the excision of chapter 8 and of seven illustrations (leaving a total of 36, one repeated). The removal thus of the character Nosi Parka has required E.A. to substitute Silver Bud and Abu Ali for his portrait on the rear wrapper.

1977 HARDBACK EDITION: of 1966 text: London: Kestrel Books. Crown 8°. Pp. 197 [3]; illus. as above with a different t.p. vig. D.j. hand-lettered by E.A. with 3 vigs. from the book front and rear printed 4-colour half tone.

2001 NEW EDITION: of 1975 text and illustrations: London: Faber & Faber (Faber Children's Classics series). 197 × 122 mm. Pp. [6] 115 [7].

This spoof sequel to the tale of Aladdin has appeared in various guises. The first edition published, as noted above, by Arthur Barker in 1937 was a luxurious production, a royal quarto (287 × 200 mm) of 144 pp. with 19 coloured illustrations by the author in the text and with the dedication For John and Tim Allison. *In 1947 Barker published a second edition (so designated) brought into conformity with the economic stringencies of the period. The format was reduced to that of a foolscap quarto (210 × 155 mm) with 123 pages of inferior antique wove paper, but there were now 33 pen drawings by the author in the text (several based on the earlier designs), together with one full-page drawing and a hand-lettered and decorated title-page. There were slight modifications to the story and the dedication disappeared. As described on its imprint page, the first Puffin edition is indeed 're-written' throughout and is given an additional adventure to end with ('Chapter the Twelve and a Halfth, which Brings the Story to its Close') and rejoices in a welter of capitalization. Much of that disappears in the 1975 revision, where the removal of 'Chapter the Eighth' brings the number back to twelve. For a comparison of E.A.'s drawings with Langley's own see overleaf*

Above and left:
the Genie of the Lamp,
a comparison of the styles
of E.A. and Noel Langley
when illustrating
The Land of Green Ginger
(1966 and 1947 respectively,
see item 128)

129. 1966 THE LITTLE GIRL AND THE TINY DOLL [large 2-colour vig.] by Edward & Aingelda Ardizzone. London: Constable Young Books Ltd. Toronto: Longmans Canada Ltd., [1966]. ('A Value Book').

Specification as for item 119 above, the dedication now *To Miss Irene Theobald*. § Featherweight antique wove paper, browning to edges. 43 pen drawings as item 119, the overlays in lilac and pale yellow: t.p. vig., 7 drawings across spread, 35 in text. § Binding as item 119.

1967 U.S. EDITION: New York: Delacorte.

1973 SECOND AND THIRD PRINTINGS: Harmondsworth: Longman Young Books. D.j. repeats the binding design.

1978 FOURTH PRINTING: Harmondsworth: Kestrel Books. D.j. repeats the binding design.

1979 SECOND EDITION: Harmondsworth: Penguin Books. (A Young Puffin). Crown 8°. Pp. [8] 9–53 [11, including 8 pp. editorial matter and ads.]. Slightly revised (and improved) text, the illus. photographically reduced reproductions of the original pen drawings, without overlays. Blue series wrapper with a new line and watercolour drawing on front.

TRANSLATION: 1983 [Afrikaans] *Die Dogtertjie end die Duimpiepop*. Trs. Louise Steyn. Cape Town: Human & Rousseau.

Aingelda Ardizzone is the artist's daughter-in-law, widow of his son Philip. The story has also been published with illustrations by Emma Chichester Clark in the anthology compiled by Laura Cecil, The Kingfisher Book of Toy Stories *(London: Kingfisher, 2000).*

130. 1966 LONG AGO WHEN I WAS YOUNG [by] E. Nesbit [Credit] [vig.]. London: Ronald Whiting & Wheaton, [1966].

Foolscap 4° in eights. 203 × 162 mm. (8 × 6⅜ in.). Pp. [10] 11–127 [1] ([1] half-title; [3] t.p.; [4] imprint: *Pr. in G.B. by A. Wheaton & Co. Ltd, Exeter. 1966 … Published simultaneously in Canada by the Ryerson Press*; [5] *Acknowledgement*; [7] *Contents*; [9] *List of Illustrations*; 11–25 *About this Book* by Noel Streatfeild; [27]–127 text). § White laid paper watermarked

'Abbey Mills Greenfield'. 26 pen drawings: t.p. vig., headpiece to introduction, 12 chapter heads incorporating dec. initials; 12 in text (one to each
chapter), with letterpress legends. § Dark brown linen boards. D.j. printed
brown with 3 panels pale blue on white on front, the central one with an
enlarged version of the drawing on the t.p., 2 panels on spine with letterpress titling, and 1 on rear with a reduction of the drawing on p. 11.

REPRINT: London: Macdonald & Jane's, 1974. White cartridge paper;
maroon linson boards, also the basic colour for d.j.

1966 U.S. EDITION: New York: Franklin Watts.

1987 ENLARGED REPRINT: London: Beehive Books, an imprint of Macdonald & Co. (Publishers) Ltd. Small crown 4°. Text and illus. reproduced
photographically (but slightly enlarged) from the original ed., the t.p. vig.
omitted and replaced by a repeat of drawing on p. 105. Six inset watercolour illus. by George Buchanan have been added on conjugate leaves to
face pp. 32, 49, 64, 81, 96 and 113, with letterpress legends referring to
the page to which the illustration relates. Prelims reorganised to allow a
list of these plates, below which is a repeat of E.A.'s drawing on p. 89. Tan
linson boards with gilt lettering on front and spine. D.j. cream art paper
with typographic lettering and two additional watercolours by Buchanan
on front and rear. Creamy yellow endpapers.

MS. DRAWINGS: Toronto Public Library: Osborne & Lillian H. Smith
Collections.

*The text was published as 'My School-Days' in twelve of the weekly numbers
of the* Girl's Own Paper *from 10 October 1896 to 11 September 1897, the
episodes so spread that they would also occur in the monthly bind-ups of the
weekly parts. In her life of E. Nesbit,* A Woman of Passion *(London: Hutchinson, 1987), Julia Briggs suggests that the process of writing the episodes played
an important part in the fashioning of the work that would prove 'the great trans-
formation' in Nesbit's writing. This was of course* The Story of the Treasure
Seekers, *the 'ur-version' of which appeared in the magazine* Father Christmas *(as by 'Ethel Mortimer') in December 1897.*

Chapter Two

LONG DIVISION

I SPENT a year in the select boarding establishment for young ladies and gentlemen at Stamford, and I venture to think that I should have preferred a penal settlement. Miss Fairfield, whose school it was, was tall and pale and dark, and I thought her as good and beautiful as an angel. I don't know now whether she was really beautiful, but I know she was good. And her mother – dear soul – had a sympathy with small folk

36

Page with head-piece and initial from
Long Ago when I was Young (1966 item 130, margins not indicated)

131. 1966 THE MUFFLETUMPS [in pale yellow] The Story of Four Dolls by Jan Wahl [Credit] [all framed at sides and bottom by a pen drawing with pale yellow overlay]. New York., Chicago, San Francisco: Holt, Rinehart & Winston, [1966].

Oblong 8°. 150 × 202 mm. (8 × 6 in.). Pp. [48] ([1] half-title; [3] t.p.; [4] imprint: *Pr. in the U.S.A. ...*; [5] dedication: *Shirley Kervish, they are for you*; [6–47] text; [48] *Notes* on author and illustrator). § White cartridge paper. 33 pen drawings: t.p., 10 double-page spreads, 22 on single pages with one colour-separation alternating between yellow and blue-grey for each opening. § Bright yellow paper boards impressed front bottom left in blue with part of the drawing from p. [33] (dancing dolls), blue letterpress spine. D.j. a version of the whole drawing on p. [33], mostly hand-lettered by E.A., with 3 colour separations on front, letterpress titling on spine, rear blank. Endpapers printed with yellow vertical lines approx. 7 mm apart, front and rear.

Published simultaneously by the Canadian Branch of Holt, but not available in Great Britain (more's the pity).

132. 1966 THE SECRET SHOEMAKERS AND OTHER STORIES Freely Adapted by James Reeves [Credit] from *Kinder-un* [sic] *Hausmärchen* by the Brothers Grimm. London, New York, Toronto: Abelard-Schuman, [1966].

Small foolscap 4° in eights. 203 × 157 mm. (8¼ × 6¼ in.). Pp. [6] 7–96 ([1] half-title; [3] t.p.; [4] *By the same author* and publisher's addresses; [5] *Contents* (12 stories); 7–96 text, with imprint on p. 96: *Pr. in G.B. by C. Tinling and Co. Ltd. Liverpool, London and Prescot*). § Thick white offset cartridge paper. 29 pen drawings: 2 chapter headpieces, 3 tailpieces, 24 in text (some inspired by Cruikshank; see opposite). § Yellow linson boards. D.j. yellow wash with an enlarged version of the drawing on p. 12 on front with red overlay and an additional drawing of a goose on rear, letterpress titling throughout.

1967 U.S. ISSUE: New York: Abelard-Schumann Ltd. English sheets with corrected t.p.

1969 PAPERBACK EDITION: Harmondsworth: Penguin Books. (A Young Puffin). Small crown 8°. With redrawn cover illus. front and rear by E.A.

In *The Secret Shoemakers* (1966 item 132) we find E.A. (top right and
bottom) cunningly dividing into two a borrowing from one of
George Cruikshank's etchings for Edgar Taylor's translation of
the Grimms' *German Popular Stories* (1823, top left)

133. 1967 KALI AND THE GOLDEN MIRROR [by] Eva-Lis Wuorio [Credit]. Cleveland and New York: The World Publishing Company, [1967].

U.S. royal 8°. 227 × 163 mm. (9 × 6⅜ in.). Pp. [8] 9–64 + inset bifolia between pp. 24–25, 48–49 and 56–57 ([1] half-title; [3] *By E.-L.W.* (4 titles); [4] frontis.; [5] t.p.; [6] imprint: *Published simultaneously in Canada by Nelson, Foster & Scott Ltd … Pr. in the U.S.A.*; [7] dedication: *For my friend Katie Harris with love*; 9–64 text). § Smooth creamy cartridge paper. 21 illustrations: 3 inset double-spread drawings in pen and watercolour; 18 pen drawings: frontis., 3 tailpieces, 14 in text. § Bright yellow linen boards blocked with an enlarged version of the frontis. in red. D.j. wrap-round scenic picture in pen and watercolour hand-lettered throughout by E.A.

Not published in Great Britain.

134. 1967 A LIKELY PLACE by Paula Fox [vig.] [Credit]. New York: The Macmillan Company, [1967].

Large crown 8°. 207 × 135 mm. (8¼ × 5⅜ in.). Pp. [6] 57 [1] ([i] half-title; [iii] t.p.; [iv] imprint: *Pr. in the U.S.A. …*; [v] dedication: *For Adam*; 1–[58] text). § Off-white cartridge paper. 21 line drawings: t.p. vig.; 4 chapter headpieces; 1 tailpiece; 14 in text; vig. on final blank. § Lemon yellow linen boards, blocked in black on front with a simplified version of the drawing on p. 43. Yellow d.j., typographic lettering with a different version of the drawing on p. [4] on front with a green overlay; repeat of the drawing on p. 120 on rear.

1967 ENGLISH IMPRESSION: London: Macmillan, reprinted photographically from the U.S. ed. with consequent loss of definition in the line blocks.

1989 SCHOOL EDITION: Boston: Houghton Mifflin. 215 × 134 mm. Pp. 69 [3], including intro. for pupils, 'roundtable' discussions ('Compare Mr. Madruga's situation with Lewis'), notes, glossary, etc. Glazed card wrappers.

MS. DRAWINGS: The de Grummond Coll. of the University of Southern Mississippi.

In 1977 Piccolo Pan Books published a paperback ed. of the text with 25 line illus. by Trevor Stubley which do not measure up to their predecessors in either consistency or organisation.

135. 1967 MIRANDA THE GREAT [by] Eleanor Estes [vig.] [Credit]. New York: Harcourt, Brace & World, Inc., [1967].

Foolscap 4° in eights. 205 × 163 mm. (8⅛ × 6½ in.). Pp. [10] 11–79 [1] ([1] half-title; [2] *By the same author*; [3] t.p.; [4] imprint: *Pr. in the U.S.A. 1967*; [5] dedication: *To Ruth*; [7] *Contents*; [9] fly-title; 11–[80] text). § White cartridge paper. 29 pen drawings: t.p. vig., 10 chapter headpieces, 3 drawings occupying much of a double-page spread; 9 in text; 6 tailpieces. § Yellow ochre linen with enlarged portion of the headpiece to chapter 5 (Miranda with kittens) impressed front lower right in black. D.j. enlarged and redrawn version of the t.p. vig. hand-lettered by E.A. on front and spine with 2 colour separations, rear letterpress ads.

Not published in Great Britain.

136. 1967 NURSE MATILDA GOES TO TOWN [by] Christianna Brand [Credit]. Leicester: Brockhampton Press, [1967].

Specification closely matching that of *Nurse Matilda* (item 110 above) with the following differences: p. [4] imprint *Cox & Wyman Ltd, London, Fakenham and Reading*; [6] dedication: *to Simon Taylor my godson*. § 46 pen drawings (including a repeat of the frontis. vig. from item 110): 1 chapterhead with dec. initial, 7 historiated initials, 1 drawing across the spread, 29 in text, 2 paired drawings on 2 pages, 1 headpiece to the music for the song *Mama Must Go Now* (see overleaf), 2 tailpieces. § Binding as for item 110 but with shades of blue replacing red throughout. D.j. ditto but the 2 photographs replaced by one on rear flap of young Christianna Brand with *her* Nurse Matilda. Some copies, as item 124 above, were issued in a presentation binding of white 'Ivorex' boards with maroon leather label in a matching slip-case.

1968 U.S. EDITION: New York: Dutton.

1975 PAPERBACK EDITION: London: Hodder & Stoughton. (Knight Books). Reprinted an unspecified no. of times, with a Julia Whately wrapper used briefly during the early 1980s (see item 110 above).

1989 'LIBRARY EDITION': as for item 110 above.

Ma - ma must go now, time for your bed now;

On your white pil-low lay your lit-tle head now.

The dark is a friend, so we'll turn out the light,

To-day's at an end, so dar - lings, good night!

Page from *Nurse Matilda goes to Town* (1967 item 136)

137. 1967 RHYMING WILL by James Reeves [Credit] [all hand-lettered by E.A. and framed by a pen drawing with Will and street-audience in lower half. Publisher given on verso of title-leaf].

Oblong crown 4° in eights. 182 × 242 mm. (7⅜ × 9½ in.). Pp. [32] ([1] t.p.; [2] imprint: *First published in G.B. 1967 by Hamish Hamilton Ltd. … London W.C.1. … Printed by A. & M. Weston Ltd, Wigston, Leicester-shire* and dedication: *To Daniel Ardizzone and Cristina Capparucci*; [3–32] text). § White cartridge paper. 22 illustrations: 11 in line and water-colour, four covering double-page spreads; 11 pen drawings: t.p. drawing and 6 on single pages, four covering double-page spreads. § Linson boards with watercolour design hand-lettered by E.A. on front and spine, rear blank. D.j. as binding with ad. for and drawing from *The Dragon* (item 125 above) on rear.

1968 U.S. EDITION: New York: McGraw-Hill.

TRANSLATION: 1971 [Afrikaans] *Willie Rympies*. Trs. E. P. du Plessis. Pretoria: Human & Rousseau. Pr. in England.

In his Preface to The James Reeves Story Book *(item 175 below) the author gives the following account of the inception of* Rhyming Will: *'This was the result of an inspiration on Ted's part when he suggested that I write a tale in which the hero is unable to speak except in verse. I treasured the idea and let it ripen in the back of my mind until it could be harvested. The resulting col-laboration was one of our happiest and has given much pleasure both to Ted's and my family and friends.'*

138. 1967 THE STUFFED DOG [by] John Symonds [Credit]. London: J. M. Dent & Sons Ltd., [1967].

Large crown 8°, the final leaf a pastedown. 210 × 135 mm. (8⅜ × 5¼ in.). Pp. [6] 7–60 [2] ([1] half-title; [2] *Other Books by John Symonds* …; [3] t.p.; [4] imprint: *Made in G.B. at the Aldine Press, Letchworth, Herts … 1967*; [5] dedication: *To Carole Hanania*; 7–60 text). § White cartridge paper. 13 pen drawings in text, with letterpress legends, except for the final tail-piece. § Blue linson boards with formal dec. front and spine in gilt and dark blue. Unlike the rear pastedown, the front endpapers are the genuine thing on a different paper stock. D.j. front a watercolour partially hand-lettered by E.A., letterpress spine, ads. at rear.

MS. DRAWINGS: As noted at item 113 above, Sotheby's auctioned some of the J. M. Dent archive on 19 June 1987, including the 13 drawings and the d.j. design for the above title.

139. 1967 TRAVELS WITH A DONKEY IN THE CEVENNES [by] Robert Louis Stevenson. Drawings by E.A. London: The Folio Society, 1967 [printed in black and olive green, the title interlined with author, illustrator and publisher entries].

Narrow crown 8°. 213 × 128 mm. (8⅜ × 5 in.). Pp. [10] 11–135 [1] ([2] frontis.; [3] t.p.; [4] imprint: *First published in 1879. Set in Monotype Bell 11 on 13 point. Pr. and bound by W. & J. Mackay & Co. Ltd, Chatham*; [5] introductory letter from R.L.S. to Sidney Colvin; [7] *Contents*; [9] section-title: *Velay*; 11–[136] text). § White cartridge paper. 31 pen drawings: frontis., 5 on section-titles, 18 chapter headpieces, 5 in text, 2 tailpieces. § Green cloth boards, the front and rear printed with a line drawing across the spine by E.A., tan endpapers and top edge. Green paper-board slip-case. § *Ref*: Nash 242.

MS. DRAWINGS: Sketchbook 10, pp. 34–55, has drafts made by the artist on a visit to the Cevennes.

Nash records 11 reprints to 1993, with an enlarged leaf size in 1981. He also notes that the chapter headpieces originally 'incorporated capital letters felt by the designer (Peter Guy) to be unusable; the artist was amused at his request to remove them, and conceded [over-modestly] "I always was a ham-fisted letterer"'.

140. 1968 ROBINSON CRUSOE his Life and Strange Surprising Adventures by Daniel Defoe. Edited with a Foreword by Kathleen Lines [Credit]. London: The Nonesuch Press, [1968]. (A Nonesuch Cygnet) [Printed as a double-page title with (i) the subtitle and publisher, and (ii) the editorial and series details printed in facing boxes framed with fleurons, each also featuring the Nonesuch Cygnet device wood-engraved by Joan Hassall].

Royal 8°. 235 × 150 mm. (9½ × 5¾ in.). Pp. [10] 11–281 [7] ([8–9] title-spread; [10] imprint: Robinson Crusoe *was first published in 1719. This edition first published 1968 … Designed by Sir Francis Meynell. Set in 11 point Ehrhardt leaded 2 points. Pr. and made in G.B. by William Clowes and*

Sons, Limited, London and Beccles ...; 11–14 *Foreword* by Kathleen Lines; [15] frontis.; 17–272 text; 275–276 *Epilogue. Robinson Crusoe's Return to his Island* ...; 279–281 *Glossary*). § Cream imitation vellum paper, very responsive to the detail of the line blocks. 68 pen drawings: full-page frontis., 25 headpieces placed below the synopsis at the head of each chapter; 38 in text; final tailpiece; additional drawing on rear endpaper. § Greeny blue linen boards, titling and device on upper and titling on spine all gilt; matching endpapers, the front free one with the drawing on p. 139 reversed white, the rear free one with an otherwise unused drawing reversed white. D.j. blue, series design. § *Ref:* Dreyfus 140.

See Dreyfus 140 and pp. 127–130, detailing the editing of the Cygnets and quoting E.A.'s letter in which he expressed his pleasure at seeing his drawings 'embedded in a book of this quality'.

141. 1968 TIM TO THE LIGHTHOUSE by E.A. [colour vig.]. London, New York, Toronto: Oxford University Press, [1968] [all hand-lettered by E.A.].

Crown 4°. Size, make-up and binding follow the design of item 30 above, with t.p. vig. and 19 drawings in pen and watercolour, and 22 pen drawings including a labelled cut-through section-drawing of a lighthouse. The dedication is *To my cousin Christianna Brand and to my tenth grandchild Jessica.*

REPRINTED: twice to 1989

1968 U.S. EDITION: New York: Henry Z. Walck, Inc. Pr. in the U.S.A.

OTHER REPRINTS: and the 2000 reoriginations noted at item 34 above.

TRANSLATIONS:
1979 [French] *Le Phare: une Aventure de Tim* Trs. Catherine Chaîne. Paris: L'Ecole des Loisirs, 1979. Pr. in Italy.
1984 [German] *Tim und der Leuchtturm.* Trs. Michaela Bach. Munich: Lentz; paperback 1984 Ravensburg: Maier.
2001 [Japanese] Trs. Chihiro Nakagawa. Tokyo: Fukuinkan Shoten.

VARIA: 1987 *Tape cassette:* One of *Six Seaworthy Adventures* as noted at item 4 above (p. 34).

142. 1968 UPSIDE DOWN WILLIE [by] Dorothy Clewes [Credit] [2-colour vig.]. London: Hamish Hamilton, [1968]. (Gazelle Books).

Small crown 8°. 183 × 122 mm. (7¼ × 4¾ in.). Pp. [4] 5–48 ([1] half-title; [2] list of 10 Gazelle Books; [3] t.p. [4] imprint: *Reproduced by photo-lithography and made at the Pitman Press, Bath ... 1968* and dedication: *For Robert Gregory Jr.*; 5–48 text). § Bulky cream antique wove paper. 23 pen drawings with a single overlay, including t.p. vig. and 2 drawings across the spread. § White linson boards overprinted with Gazelle series design in 3 colours incorporating a front panel by E.A., ads. at rear. D.j. as binding.

The first of three books by Dorothy Clewes about Willie (see item 147 and 149 below). In 1991 they were published together by Julia MacRae Books as The Adventures of Willie *with E.A.'s illustrations replaced by monochrome half-tones by Caroline Crossland.*

143. 1969 THE ANGEL AND THE DONKEY by James Reeves [large vig.] [Credit]. London: Hamish Hamilton, [1969].

Oblong crown 4° in eights. 184 × 243 mm. (7¼ × 9 ⅝ in.). Pp. [32] ([1] t.p.; [2] imprint: *Printed by offset in G.B. by William Clowes and Sons Ltd. London and Beccles 1969. Author's Note – The Story of Balaam, as related in the* Book of Numbers, *has complexities and even inconsistencies which make it necessary, if it is to be adapted for young readers, to simplify it ... readers curious to know what happened to the Moabites will find the sequel to the story in ...* Numbers *Chapters XXII and XXIII*; [3–32] text). § White offset cartridge paper. 24 illustrations: 10 drawings in red line and water-colour, with 5 being double-page spreads; 14 pen drawings including t.p. vig. and 2 drawings across the spread. § Paper boards, an additional line and watercolour drawing, hand-lettered by E.A., on front, plain rear printed orange, yellow spine with black letterpress titling. D.j. as binding.

1970 U.S. EDITION: New York: McGraw-Hill.

TRANSLATION: 1974 [Afrikaans] *Die Koning en die Waarsêer*. Trs. Hester Heese. Durban: Qualitas.

MS. DRAWINGS: Sketchbook 35 contains some drafts related to this book.

The story of Balaam's Ass does not appear in the brief account of the Wilderness Years in The Story of Moses *(item 73 above) where the Moabites are mentioned as a friendly tribe.*

144. 1969 DO YOU REMEMBER WHAT HAPPENED by Jean Chapman [Credit] [2-colour vig.]. [London, Sydney, Melbourne, Singapore]: Angus and Robertson, [1969].

Demy 8°. 215 × 138 mm. (8½ × 5½ in.). Pp. [40] ([1] half-title; [2] imprint: *First published 1969. Made and pr. photolitho in G.B. by Ebenezer Baylis and Son, Ltd, The Trinity Press, Worcester, and London* …; [5–39] text; [40] *And, so happenings come every day. Some to remember for ever*). § Thickish smooth white cartridge paper. 37 pen drawings with a single colour overlay, alternating peach and apple-green through the page-openings: t.p. vig., the remaining illustrations positioned to accompany 32 poetically observed 'moments' in child-life. § Plum linson boards. D.j. a pen drawing with 2-colour overlays, hand-lettered by E.A., repeated front and rear, hand-lettering and letterpress on spine. § *Ref:* Marcie Muir, *Australian Children's Books: a Bibliography* (Melbourne Univ. Press, 1992) vol. I., 1384; vol. II., 1577.

1973 ABRIDGED EDITION: London: Transworld Publishers Ltd. (Storychair Books). Oblong foolscap 8°. 24 pp., the observed 'moments' abridged to 19, with 22 of E.A.'s drawings, printed either monochrome or with a varied sequence of pink or blue-green overlays. Laminated paper wrappers with series design incorporating the t.p. vig. from the hardback ed. on front and the drawing from p. [15] on rear. See Muir, *op. cit. infra* vol. II., 1577.

The question mark required by the title is never used.

145. 1969 JOHNNY'S BAD DAY transferred to 150.1 under the title *The Wrong Side of the Bed.*

146. 1969 A RIOT OF QUIET [2-colour vig.] by Virginia Sicotte [Credit]. New York, Chicago, San Francisco: Holt, Rinehart and Winston, [1969].

Small crown 8°. 177 × 135 mm. (7 × 5⅜ in.). Pp. [32] ([1] half-title; [2] blank, with overall peach wash; [3] t.p.; [4] imprint: *Pr. in the U.S.A. ... Published simultaneously in Canada by Holt, Rinehart and Winston of Canada Ltd.*; [5] dedication: *To the Little People*; [4–31] text; [32] notes on author, illustrator and book: ... *The text is set in Monotype Perpetua and the title ... in Optima Semi-Bold; the book is printed by offset* ...). § Thick, creamy offset cartridge paper. 21 pen drawings with grey wash and a single colour overlay alternating between openings of pale peach and pale apple-green: t.p. vig. with six of the illustrations as spreads. § Pale buff ribbed paper boards with an adaptation of the t.p. vig. stamped in dark green lower right of front, letterpress spine, rear blank, olive green endpapers. D.j. adaptations of the pen and wash drawings on pp. [30–31] and on t.p. on front and rear with two additional colours, hand-lettered by E.A. on front; typographic spine. A publisher's presentation binding in three-quarters red morocco with red cloth sides has also been seen.

A 'mood book' typical of its time. E.A. contributes atmospheric illustrations to versified phrases signifying quietness: '... A bean, sprouting / An oyster, pouting ...'. The book is here placed under the copyright date given for author and artist. The Library of Congress no. is L.C. 70-80314. No edition was published in Great Britain.

147. 1969 SPECIAL BRANCH WILLIE [by] Dorothy Clewes [Credit] [2-colour vig.]. London: Hamish Hamilton, [1969]. (Gazelle Books).

Specification as for item 142 above, the dedication *For Michael Gregory*. With 24 2-colour illustrations, including t.p. vig. and 3 across the spread.

1971 PAPERBACK EDITION: London: Armada Books. Pp. 32. The colour separation on the line illus. is a lurid blue.

The second of three stories 'for the very young' about Willie. See also items 142 and 149.

148. 1970 DICK WHITTINGTON Retold by Kathleen Lines [large vig.] [Credit]. London, Sydney, Toronto: The Bodley Head, [1970]. (Fairy Tale Picture Books).

Small royal 8°. 228 × 164 mm. (9 × 6½ in.). Pp. [4] 5–42 [6] ([1] half-title; [3] t.p.; [4] *Uniform with this book* (one title), publisher's device and imprint: *Pr. and bound in G.B. by William Clowes & Sons Ltd, Beccles 1970*; 5–44 text; [45] concluding watercolour; [46–48] *About Richard Whittington* signed *K. L. November 1969*). § White cartridge paper. 34 illustrations variously disposed: 16 watercolours with sepia line, 18 pen drawings in sepia, including t.p. vig. § Linen-textured paper boards lithographed with an additional watercolour by E.A. on front; letterpress titling etc.; ads. on rear. D.j. as binding, with a photograph of E.A. and a biographical note on rear flap.

1970 U.S. EDITION: New York: Henry Z. Walck, Inc.

MS. DRAWINGS: An alternative design for the d.j., rejected by the publisher, is in the Free Library of Philadelphia.

'The text of this present edition follows what I believe to be the generally accepted version, with emendations and additions … from historical fact …' (K. Lines p. [48]). For another volume in this series illus. by E.A. see item 154 below.

149. 1970 FIRE-BRIGADE WILLIE [by] Dorothy Clewes [Credit] [2-colour vig.]. London: Hamish Hamilton, [1970]. (Gazelle Books).

Specification as for item 142 above, the dedication *For Nicholas Rathbone who has ideas of his own.* With 25 2-colour illustrations, including t.p. vig. and 3 across the spread.

The third of three stories 'for the very young' about Willie. See also items 142 and 147.

150. 1970 HOME FROM SEA [by] Robert Louis Stevenson: Poems for Young Readers Chosen and Introduced by Ivor Brown [vig.] [Credit]. London, Sydney, Toronto: The Bodley Head, [1970]. (Poetry Selections for Young Readers).

Demy 8°. 215 × 140 mm. (8½ × 5⅜ in.). Pp. [4] 5–80 ([1] half-title; [3] t.p.; [4] imprint: *Pr. and bound in G.B. … by William Clowes & Sons Ltd,*

Beccles. Set in Monotype Baskerville … 1970 and a list of nine other poetry selections in the same format; 5–6 *About Robert Louis Stevenson*; 7–14 *Introduction*; 15–16 *Contents*; [17]–77 text; 79–80 *Index of First Lines*). § Creamy white cartridge paper. 24 pen drawings: 4 section-titles, 20 in text. The t.p. vig. is a reduction of the illustration on p. 41 (for a reproduction see the title-page). § Blue-green linson boards, turquoise endpapers. Typographic d.j. with the section-title illus. for part II on front and portrait of R. L. S. on rear.

The 'Poetry Selections' series started publication in 1964 with a group of Robert Frost's poems You Come Too, *illus. by Cécile Curtis. It ran to a dozen or so volumes over nine years (with Naomi Lewis's selections from Emily Brontë and Christina Rossetti being especially notable) and it has been called 'one of the noblest publishing ventures for children since the War'.*

150.1 1970 THE WRONG SIDE OF THE BED [large 2-colour vig.] by Edward Ardizzone. Garden City, New York: Doubleday & Company, Inc., [1970].

Square crown 8°, a single gathering of 16 leaves. 187 × 144 mm. (7⅜ × 5¾ in.). Pp. [32] ([1] t.p.; [2] imprint: *Pr. in the U.S.A.*; [3–32] 'text'). § Thick, smooth off-white cartridge paper. 31 pen drawings with overlay of a single colour alternating apple-green and peach through the openings: t.p. vig., 2 double-page spreads, 24 full-page, and one spread of 4 half-page vigs. § Seen only in a side-stabbed heavy cloth board binding with a pen drawing based on that on p. 3 blocked on front with 3-colour overlays, hand-lettered by E.A. on front and spine; rear board bright apple-green. D.j. as binding. Peach endpapers.

1970 ENGLISH EDITION: as *Johnny's Bad Day*. London, Sydney, Toronto: The Bodley Head. Same format, but in eights with pastedown first and last leaves. The overlays are muted to alternating pale green and pale peach. Paper boards designed as above, but with overlays and endpapers muted.

'TRANSLATION': 1992 [French] *Triste Journée Pour Johnny*. Paris: Circonflexe. (Aux Couleurs du Temps series). With a 2-page preface by the illustrator Philippe Dumas.

A story told in pictures with no text other than the title. Apparently commissioned by Doubleday, with English rights going to the Bodley Head.

151. 1970 THE YOUNG ARDIZZONE an Autobiographical Fragment [by] E.A. [vig.]. London: Studio Vista, [1970].

Narrow royal 8°. 245 × 135 mm. (9⅞ × 5⅜ in.). Pp. [4] 5–144 ([1] t.p.; [2] imprint: *Set in Ehrhardt. Pr. and bound in G.B. by W.S. Cowell Ltd, at the Butter Market, Ipswich* 1970; [3] *Contents*; 5–144 text). § Thickish dead white cartridge paper. 117 pen drawings, 55 of which have a single colour overlay (16 pale yellow, 10 pale green, 14 pink, 15 mauve). The illustrations are variously disposed to mesh in with the incidents of the autobiography and consist of 11 chapter headpieces, 87 smaller drawings in text (3 pages being assigned respectively to three, two and two drawings free of text), 14 drawings across the spreads, and 5 acting as tailpieces. The monochrome t.p. vig. is a repeat, without overlay, of the drawing at the foot of p. 37. § Green linson boards. Typographic d.j. with an enlarged version of the drawing on p. 15 tinted pale green and pink on front and an enlarged monochrome version of the tinted drawing on p. 31 on rear.

1970 U.S. EDITION: New York: Macmillan.

In 1978 a passage from pp. 55–57 was reprinted with two drawings (reduced and without the colour overlay) in a group of 'Term Time Tales' in Puffin Post *(vol. 12, no. 2, pp. 4–5). For two of the drawings, one an 'adoption', see pp. 40 and 257.*

152. 1971 HOW THE MOON BEGAN a Folktale from Grimm Adapted by James Reeves [Credit]. [London]: Abelard-Schuman, [1971] [all hand-lettered by E.A. on the recto of a double-page pictorial title-spread].

Small crown 4° in eights, the first and last leaves pastedowns. 242 × 170 mm. (9½ × 6⅝ in.). Pp. [48] ([2–3] front endpapers; [4–5] title-spread; [6–45] text, with copyright and publishing dates, but no imprint, at upper outer corner of p. [6]). § Dead white offset cartridge paper. 32 illustrations, plus one solid black oblong representing 'the old state of darkness', variably placed on single or across double pages: 15 pen drawings with a 3-colour wash, 17 pen drawings on a blue-grey ground, including repeat endpaper spreads which are an alternative version of the colour illustration on pp. [28–29]. § Paper boards with a wrap-round colour-wash drawing and spine panel hand-lettered throughout by E.A. D.j. as binding, but the rear flap includes an imprint: *Pr. in G.B.*

1972 U.S. ISSUE: New York: Abelard-Schuman. English sheets but with a label on recto of rear free endpaper: *Pr. in G.B. by Butler & Tanner …* Dark green cloth, three-quarter moon in silver on front.

1973 PAPERBACK EDITION: Abelard-Schuman. (Picture Grasshopper series). *Pr. in G.B. by C. Tinling & Co. Ltd, London and Prescot.* Format as above but [40] pp. and hence lacking the endpaper designs, the left-hand portion of the title spread and the final drawing on p. [45]. Laminated card wrappers.

TRANSLATION: [n.d.] [Japanese] Via Tuttle-Mori.

The story is based on 'Der Mond', no. 175 in the Grimms' Kinder-und-Hausmärchen.

153. 1971 THE SHORT STORIES OF CHARLES DICKENS [vig.] Selected and Introduced by Walter Allen [Credit]. New York: Printed for the Members of the Limited Editions Club, 1971.

Royal 8°. 245 × 165 mm. (9¾ × 6½ in.). Pp. [8] ix–xx [2] 3–423 [5] + 16 insets ([i] half-title; [iii] t.p.; [iv] *The special contents of this edition are copyright ©1971 by The George Macy Companies, Inc.*; [v] *The Contents*; [vii] *The Color Plates*; ix–xx *Introduction* signed *Walter Allen. Coleraine, Northern Ireland, July 1970*; [1] Story-title *The Boarding House*; 3–423 text, including unnumbered title-leaves for the succeeding 15 stories; [425] colophon: *E.A. drew the illustrations which appear in this book … for the fifteen hundred members of The Limited Editions Club for whom this special collection … was made. The edition was designed and printed by Joseph Blumenthal at The Spiral Press in New York. This is copy number … and is signed by the artist … and the designer-printer …*). § White antique laid paper, most leaves watermarked with the roundel of the Limited Editions Club. The plates are on a slightly thicker, unwatermarked stock of a similar laid paper. 35 illustrations: title-page vig. in sepia; 16 full-page inset line-drawings with overlays in pink and grey-green with letterpress legends to face pp. 12, 49, 68, 104, 132, 148, 180, 212, 236, 257, 280, 293, 308, 345, 389, 412; and17 vig. chapter headpieces and final roundel at head of colophon. § Half black canvas boards gilt with marbled paper sides, slip-case to match with letterpress label on spine.

Opposite: From 'The Lamplighter' in *The Short Stories of Charles Dickens* (1971 item 153, margins not indicated)

SECOND IMPRESSION: Norwalk CT.: The Heritage Press, [1971]. Photographic reprint in the series format of the Heritage Press Dickens, conforming to the specifications noted at item 8 above. The gatherings are mostly in sixteens, leading to slight adjustments in the placing of the insets which are printed on the same stock as the text, described as 'vellum-finish cream-white paper'. The colophon roundel is omitted.

— **1972** DAILY TELEGRAPH GUIDE TO THE PLEASURES OF WINE [by] Denis Morris. London & Glasgow: Collins, [1972].

See item C36 below.

154. 1972 THE OLD BALLAD OF THE BABES IN THE WOOD [Credit] [vig.]. London, Sydney, Toronto: The Bodley Head, [1972]. (Fairy Tale Picture Books).

Small royal 8°. 230 × 162 mm. (9⅛ × 6½ in.). Pp. [4] 5–28 [4] ([1] half-title including series title: *A Bodley Head Fairy Tale Picture Book. General Editor: Kathleen Lines* ...; [2] *Uniform with this book* ... (7 titles); [3] t.p.; [4] publisher's device and imprint: *Pr. and bound in G.B. by William Clowes and Sons Ltd, Beccles* ... *1972*; 5–28 text; [29] vig. and note: *About this story*; [30–31] commentary by Kathleen Lines). § White cartridge paper. 19 illustrations variously disposed: 8 watercolours with sepia line; 11 pen-drawings, including t.p. vig., with that on p. [18] reduced to form the vig. on p. [29]. § Linen textured paper boards lithographed with an additional watercolour by E.A. on front; letterpress titling etc.; ads. on rear. D.j. as binding with a reduced copy of the colour pic. on p. 25 on front flap and a photograph of E.A. with a biographical note on rear flap.

1972 U.S. EDITION: New York: Henry Z. Walck, Inc. Yellow linen boards with enlarged block from the drawing on p. [7] on front.

'The ballad used as the text for this picture storybook dates from 1640 (considered to be the standard text and recorded as in the possession of the British Museum)' (K. Lines p. [31]). For another volume in this series illus. by E.A. see item 148 above.

Page from *The Old Ballad of the Babes in the Wood*
(1972 item 154, margins not indicated)

155. 1972 RAIN, RAIN DON'T GO AWAY by Shirley Morgan [2-colour drawing] [Credit]. New York: E.P. Dutton & Co. Inc., [1972].

Small demy 8°. 215 × 145 mm. (8½ × 5⅝ in.). Pp. [16] ([1] t.p.; [2] copyright and imprint: *Pr. in the U.S.A. Published simultaneously in Canada by Clarke, Irwin & Company Ltd., Toronto and Vancouver*; [3] dedication: *To Stephanie and Christopher, who watched the spring rains with such delight*; [4–31] text; [32] notes on author and illustrator and: *The drawings are in black wash combined with an alternating* [separated] *color. The display type is set in Optima and the text type in Janson. The book is printed by offset*). § Thickish off-white cartridge paper. 22 monochrome wash drawings, with alternate overlays in pink and grey: t.p. drawing, 8 across the opening, 13 within single pages. § Side-sewn into bright blue linen boards with part of the drawing on p. [28] blocked in black on lower right corner of front. D.j. with additional wash drawings front and rear. Pale orange endpapers.

1973 ENGLISH EDITION: London: Hutchinson Junior Books. 207 × 143 mm. D.j. with a more colourful version of the drawing on front, that on rear replaced by ads. Plain endpapers.

156. 1972 THE SECOND-BEST CHILDREN IN THE WORLD [by] Mary Lavin [large coloured vig.] [Credit]. [London]: Longman Young Books, [1972].

Crown 4° in eights. 244 × 185 mm. (9⅝ × 7⅜ in.). Pp. [48] ([1] 'frontispiece'; [3] half-title; [5] t.p.; [6] imprint: *Pr. in G.B. by W.S. Cowell Ltd, Ipswich … 1972*; [7] dedication: *To Kathleen MacMahon and Daniel and Hannah Ardizzone*; [9–48] text). § White cartridge paper. 34 colour wash drawings with sepia line, including 'frontispiece' and t.p. vig., variously disposed on single pages and across spreads. § White paper boards with reproductions of the illus. on pp. 18 and 27 on front and rear; letterpress titling. D.j. as binding.

1972 U.S. EDITION: Boston: Houghton Mifflin.

157. 1972 TIM'S LAST VOYAGE [vig.] by E.A. London, Sydney, Toronto: The Bodley Head, [1972].

Crown 4°. Size, make-up, binding follow the design of item 30 above, but with 17 drawings in pen and watercolour and the t.p. vig. and 22 drawings

Opposite: Title-page of *Tim's Last Voyage* (1972
item 157, reduced, margins not indicated)

TIM'S LAST VOYAGE

by
EDWARD ARDIZZONE

The Bodley Head
London — Sydney — Toronto

in line, plus one page with 5 spot drawings showing 'hard days' for the Captain and his crew, printed by William Clowes, Beccles, separations by Colourcraftsmen, Chelmsford. The paper is a white cartridge with a harder surface than that formerly used in the series, and the dedication is: *To all my Grandchildren*.

1972 U.S. EDITION: New York: Henry Z. Walck, Inc.

1984 PAPERBACK EDITION: London: Macmillan Children's Books. (Picturemacs).

1993 PAPERBACK EDITION: London: Random House Children's Books. (Red Fox Paperbacks; bound with *Ship's Cook Ginger*, item 172 below).

2000 NEW EDITION: London: Scholastic Press, as above, but reoriginated from original artwork (see item 34 above).

TRANSLATIONS:
1981 [Japanese] Tokyo: Mizuki Shobo Inc.
2001 [Japanese] Trs. Chihiro Nakagawa. Tokyo: Fukuinkan Shoton

158. 1972 THE TUNNEL OF HUGSY GOODE By Eleanor Estes [Credit]. New York: Harcourt Brace Jovanovich, Inc. [vig.] [1972].

Demy 8° in sixteens. 220 × 132 mm. (8 × 5½ in.). Pp. [8] ix–[x] [2] 3–244 [2] ([i] half-title; [iii] *By the same author* (13 titles); [v] t.p.; [vi] imprint: *Pr. in the U.S.A. First edition 1972*; [vii] dedication: *To C. and T.*; ix–[x] *Contents*; [1] fly-title; [2] map of the Alley and locality; 3–244 text). § Antique wove paper. 27 line drawings in text. § Pale green linen boards. D.j. 2 pen drawings on front, 1 on spine with 2-colour overlays handlettered by E.A.; publisher's name and device on spine, ads. on rear all letterpress.

Not published in Great Britain. The book is a sequel to The Alley *(item 105 above). The original pen drawing for the illus. on p. 40 carries a note to Estes from her editor, Margaret McElderry: 'This doesn't jibe very well with the text. Should we ask E.A. to do over, as it would mean almost an entire new picture? Or could we change that a bit?' To which Estes replies: 'I'll change text'.*

159. 1973 COMPLETE POEMS FOR CHILDREN [by] James Reeves [Credit]. London: Heinemann, [1973].

Large demy 8° in sixteens. 232 × 150 mm. (9¼ × 5¾ in.). Pp. [13] 2–193 [3] ([i] half-title; [ii] *Books by J.R.*; [iii] t.p.; [iv] imprint: *Filmset and printed Offset Litho in G.B. by Cox and Wyman Ltd. London, Fakenham and Reading ... 1973*; [v] dedication: *To Daniel James Irwin*; [vii–xi] Contents; [xii] *Acknowledgements*; [1] section-title: *The Wandering Moon*; 2–[186] text; 188–192 *Index of First Lines*; 193–[195] *Index of Titles*). § Creamy cartridge paper. 4 pen drawings previously unpublished + 40 repeated from previous volumes (see note below). § Grey linson boards. D.j. a wrap-round drawing in line and watercolour hand-lettered throughout by E.A.

A reprint of five books of poems by James Reeves with E.A.'s illus. arranged as follows: pp. [1]–54 The Wandering Moon (item 61 above): all drawings used, but the frontis. transferred to p. [148]; pp. [55]–116 The Blackbird in the Lilac (item 35 above): section-titles only retained, t.p. vig. and all text drawings omitted; pp. [117]–142 Prefabulous Animiles (item 58 above) 11 drawings retained, 29 and portions of three others omitted; pp. [143]–173 Ragged Robin first published as a folio volume illus. in colour by Jane Paton, here reprinted and illus. with four new line drawings by E.A. plus the frontis. from The Wandering Moon; pp. [175–185] The Story of Jackie Thimble (item 111 above) nine drawings retained, t.p. vig. and 14 others omitted.

1986 'REISSUE': the d.j. now laminated. Reprinted by the St Edmundsbury Press, Bury St Edmunds.

1987 PAPERBACK EDITION: as *The Wandering Moon and Other Poems*. Harmondsworth: Puffin Books. Crown 8°.

1994 AUGMENTED REPRINT: pp. [13] 14–267 [5], the contents as above with the addition on pp. [199]–256 of *More Prefabulous Animiles* (item 169 below) with all drawings retained; and on pp. [257]–267 of eight *Additional Poems* from various sources. Of these, 'Gabble-Gabble' is taken from item 126 above with E.A.'s accompanying drawings. Bound in maroon linson boards.

1998 PAPERBACK EDITION: London: Mammoth. Crown 8°. Wrapper a (not inspiring) design by Elisa Trimby. Reprinted 2001 as a 'Classic Mammoth'.

160. 1973 THE LITTLE FIRE ENGINE by Graham Greene [large colour vig.] [Credit] [Second edition]. London, Sydney, Toronto: The Bodley Head, [1973].

Oblong small crown 4° in eights. 177 × 240 mm. (7 × 9½ in.). Pp. [4] 5–48 ([3] t.p.; [4] imprint: *Pr. in G.B. … by William Clowes & Sons Ltd, Beccles. Colour separations by Colourcraftsmen Ltd, Chelmsford. This edition first published 1973*; 5–48 text). § White cartridge paper. 51 illustrations in line and watercolour: t.p. vig.; a central double-spread without text, the remainder varying from spot drawings to drawings across two text pages. § Paper boards with pen and watercolour drawing and hand-lettering by E.A. on front, repeat of drawing on p. 12 on rear; letterpress titling on spine. D.j. as binding.

1973 U.S. ISSUE: Garden City, New York: Doubleday & Co. English sheets.

1977 PAPERBACK EDITION: Harmondsworth: Puffin Books, in association with The Bodley Head. (Picture Puffins). Oblong large crown 8°, a single gathering. Glazed paper wrappers, the illus. on the front reduced and turned through 90° to make a central panel on rear.

TRANSLATIONS:
1974	[Swedish] *Den Lilla Brandsputan*. Trs. Lisa-Christina Persson. Malmö: Bergh.
[c. 1975]	[Afrikaans] *Die Klein Brandweerwaentjie*. Trs. Louise Steyn. Cape Town: Human & Rousseau.
[n.d.]	[Spanish] *El Cochecito de Bomberos*. Trs. Francisco Pabòn Torres. Madrid: Debate
[n.d.]	[Japanese] Tokyo: Bunka Publishing Bureau.

First published in similar format with illustrations by Dorothy Craigie (London: Max Parrish, 1950). For a note on this and its three companion volumes see next item.

161. 1973 THE LITTLE TRAIN by Graham Greene [large colour vig.] [Credit] [Third edition]. London, Sydney, Toronto: The Bodley Head, [1973].

Format and specifications as for previous item, with 35 watercolour drawings, including a double-spread pictorial map (of dubious accuracy) on pp.

20–21, plus a page of exclamatory lettering (*Stop-Boomp-Woosh* ...) reversed white on a grey ground on p. [35], not by E.A. § Binding and d.j. with an additional watercolour drawing on front and a repeat of that on p. [39] on rear.

U.S. ISSUE AND BRITISH PAPERBACK EDITION: following the style and dating for the previous item.

TRANSLATIONS:

1974 [Norwegian] *Det Lille Toget.* Trs. Lotte Holmboe. [Oslo]: J. W. Cappelen. Pr. in England. Also published in the anthology *Barnas Beste.* Oslo: Cappelen, 1985.

1974 [Swedish] *Det Lille Tåget.* Trs. Lisa-Christina Persson. Malmö: Bergh. Pr. in England.

1975 [German] *Die Kleine Lok.* Trs. Alexander Auer and Ilse Walter. Munich: Wilhelm Heyne. (Das Besondere Bilderbuch series). 180 × 130 mm. The illus. reduced and re-arranged to fit the smaller format. Card wrappers redesigned by Christian Diener .

1979 [Spanish] *El Pequeño Tren.* Trs. Francisco Pabòn Torres. Madrid: Debate.

[n.d.] [Japanese] Tokyo: Bunka Publishing Bureau.

The Little Train was first published in 1946 in similar format to the above by Eyre & Spottiswoode, where Greene was a director. Authorship was attributed to its illustrator, Dorothy Craigie, who was at that time Greene's mistress.

In 1957 a second edition was published, re-illustrated by Craigie as a square octavo, to join the three companion volumes noted here (items 160, 166 and 167) which she and Greene had produced for the firm of Max Parrish. The four books varied in format and were issued bound in either pictorial paper boards or plain cloth, both issues with d.j.s.

162. 1973 THE NIGHT RIDE by Aingelda Ardizzone [large colour vig.] Credit]. [London]: Longman Young Books, [1973].

Oblong crown 4° in eights. 180 × 240 mm. (7 × 9½ in.). Pp. [32] ([1] t.p.; [2] dedication: *To my five children*; imprint: *Pr. in G.B. by W.S. Cowell Ltd, 8 Butter Market, Ipswich*; [3–32] text). § Thickish, smooth, dead white cartridge paper. T.p. vig. and 25 watercolours with sepia line, occupying

From *The Night Ride* (1973 item 162, margins not indicated)

much of the page area of both single pages and spreads (see the reproduction opposite). § Paper boards with a predominantly yellow wash, a wide oval additional watercolour on front and a repeat of the final illus. on rear; typographic lettering. D.j. as binding.

1975 U.S. EDITION: New York: Windmill Books.

163. 1974 DIARY OF A WAR ARTIST [large vig.] [by] E.A. London, Sydney, Toronto: The Bodley Head, [1974].

Royal 8°. 247 × 150 mm. (9¾ × 6 in.). Pp. [12] 3–213 [1] (p. [i] half-title; [ii] frontis.; [iii] t.p. , but with author above and title below the vig.; [iv] dedication: *To Catherine*, publisher's device and imprint: *Pr. and bound in G.B. ... by William Clowes & Sons Ltd, Beccles. Set in Monotype Scotch Roman ... 1974*; [v] Contents; vii–[ix] *Introduction*; [1] section-title: *Book I. Sicily – Italy. July 1943 to January 1944*; 3–[214] text, with further section-titles on pp. [97], [123] and [157]). § Thick dead-white cartridge paper. 130 illustrations: frontis. and 35 full-page reproductions from the diary on a half-tone ground, 3 double-page spreads and 22 partial pages thus; t.p vig. and 60 drawings and sketches reproduced as line-blocks in text, with 6 of the same full-page. § Dark blue cloth boards, gilt titling on spine. D.j. a wrap-round picture: *The painting on the jacket is 'Naval Control Post on the Beaches of Normandy, 1944' by E.A. and is reproduced by courtesy of the Trustees of the Imperial War Museum* (rear flap).

164. 1974 THE LAND OF BEULAH. Being an Extract from *The Pilgrim's Progress* by John Bunyan. Newly illustrated by E.A. London: The Bodley Head, [1974].

Royal 12°, a single gathering. 190 × 110 mm. (7½ × 4⅜ in.). Pp. [4] 5–22 [2] ([1] half-title; [3] t.p.; 5–19 text, printed on rectos only; 21–[23] *A Note on the Illustrations* by E.A.; [24] copyright and colophon: *Privately printed in an edition of 350 copies at The Stellar Press Ltd, Hatfield for distribution by the artist and the publisher December 1974*). § Smooth white cartridge paper. 6 pen drawings in text. § White card wrappers. D.j. white paper with parchment finish with a wrap-round drawing by E.A. in ink and grey wash. No lettering.

In his note the artist recounts details of the edition of Pilgrim's Progress *that was given to him as a schoolboy (see item 19 above) and adds 'Looking back I realise now that this book, unwittingly at the time, confirmed me in my desire to be, not only a painter, but an illustrator too'. The passage from Bunyan which he has chosen to illustrate tells of Christian and Hopeful approaching the City and is taken from the Nonesuch Press edition, ed. G.B. Harrison and illus. Karl Michel (London, 1928, pp. 191–194).*

The booklet is from a series issued privately by the publisher at Christmastime. For two other examples in which E.A. was involved see items 179 and A23 below.

165. 1974 THE LION THAT FLEW by James Reeves [large vig.] [Credit]. London: Chatto & Windus, [1974].

Oblong crown 4° in eights. 186 × 245 mm. (7⅜ × 9¾ in.). Pp. [32] ([1] t.p.; [2] imprint: *Pr. in England by Colour Reproductions Ltd., Billericay, Essex*; [4–32] text). § Smooth white cartridge paper. 26 illustrations: 13 in red line and watercolour; 12 pen drawings + t.p. vig. § Laminated paper boards with an additional watercolour drawing and hand lettering by E.A. on front; repeat of t.p. vig. on rear with typographic blurb. No d.j.

166. 1974 THE LITTLE HORSE BUS by Graham Greene [large colour vig.] [Credit] [Second edition]. London, Sydney, Toronto: The Bodley Head, [1974].

Format and specifications as for item 160, with 41 watercolour drawings, including one illus. in black and grey only and one page occupied mostly by an oblong of pale green wash. Binding and d.j. with additional illus. front and rear.

REPRINTED: London: Viking, 1994. 'Published simultaneously in Puffin.' Reprints of all four of the titles were proposed at this time, but only this and the following item were eventualy published.

U.S. AND BRITISH PAPERBACK EDITIONS: as for item 160 above.

TRANSLATIONS:
1974 [Swedish] *Den Lilla Häst Bussen*. Trs. Gunvor Lubbock and Lisa-Christina Persson. Malmö: Bergh. Pr. in G.B.

1975 [German] *Der Kleine Pferdebus*. Trs. Ilse Walter. Vienna/Hamburg: Paul Zsolnay.

1995 [French] *La Petite Voiture à Cheval*. Trs. Catherine Bonhomme, préface de Brian Alderson. Paris: Circonflexe.

[n.d.] [Japanese] Tokyo: Bunka Publishing Bureau.

First published as a square octavo with illustrations by Dorothy Craigie (London: Max Parrish, 1952).

167. 1974 THE LITTLE STEAMROLLER by Graham Greene [large colour vig.] [Credit] [Second edition]. London, Sydney, Toronto: The Bodley Head, [1974].

Format and specifications as for item 160, with 33 watercolour drawings, including a symbolic 'black hand' and a rebus-coded letter. Binding and d.j. with additional illus. front and rear.

REPRINTED: London, 1994, with foregoing item.

U.S. AND BRITISH PAPERBACK EDITIONS: as for item 160 above.

TRANSLATIONS:

1974 [Swedish] *Den Lilla Ångvälten*. Trs. Gunvor Lubbock andLisa-Christina Persson. Malmö: Bergh. Pr. in G.B.

1975 [German] *Die Kleine Dampfwalze*. Trs. Ilse Walter. Vienna/Hamburg: Paul Zsolnay.

[n.d.] [Japanese] Tokyo: Bunka Publishing Bureau.

First published as a square octavo with illustrations by Dorothy Craigie (London: Max Parrish, 1953).

168. 1974 NURSE MATILDA GOES TO HOSPITAL [by] Christianna Brand [Credit]. Leicester: Brockhampton Press, [1974].

Specification closely matching that of *Nurse Matilda* (item 110 above), with imprint as for item 136 and dedication (p. [5]): *To darling Lucy and to Danny and Joel and to all the other children who know that I am a whych.* § 32 pen drawings (including a repeat of the frontis. vig. from item 110): 8 historiated initials, 23 in text. § Binding as for item 110 but boards, edges and endpapers in shades of olive green, the silk marker emerald green. D.j. as item 110 but with a new photograph of the young Christianna and a repeat of that of the young E.A.

SECOND IMPRESSION: London: Hodder & Stoughton, 1985.

1975 LARGE PRINT EDITION: Bath: Chivers (not seen).

The third book about Nurse Matilda: '... But when they had come to the end of the letter, and had dutifully sent love to Avangeleen and Pug and Fiddle and Miss Prom, and had time to look up – the Baby was sitting in its high chair beating cheerfully on a plate with its silver spoon – but Nurse Matilda was gone.'

169. 1975 MORE PREFABULOUS ANIMILES by James Reeves and E.A. [London]: Heinemann, [1975] [all hand-lettered by E.A. in similar fashion to item 58 above].

Small demy 8°. 215 × 135 mm. (8½ × 5⅜ in.). Pp. [8] 1–51 [5] ([i] half-title; [ii] *Other books by J.R.* [20 titles]; [iii] t.p.; [iv] imprint: *Pr. and bound in G.B. by Cox & Wyman Ltd, London, Fakenham and Reading ... 1975*; [v] dedication: *To Philip and Gelda Ardizzone*; [vii] *Contents*; 1–[56] text). § Smooth white cartridge paper. 40 pen drawings illustrating 11 sets of verses: t.p. and 39 illus. varying widely in size and placement on single pages and spreads. § Apple-green linson boards, dec. gilt spine. D.j. in line and watercolour with hand-lettering by E.A. on front, letterpress titling and ads. on rear and spine.

In 1994 the text and drawings were incorporated into the augmented reprint of Reeves's Complete Poems for Children *(item 159).*

170. 1976 ARDIZZONE'S KILVERT. Selections from the Diary of the Rev. Francis Kilvert 1870–79. Edited by William Plomer and abridged for children by Elizabeth Divine [Credit] [publisher's device]. London: Jonathan Cape, [1976].

Small demy 8°. 215 × 133 mm. (8½ × 5¼ in.). Pp. [6] 7–174 [2] ([1] half-title; [3] t.p. [4] dedication: *This abridgment has been a labour of love by*

Elizabeth Divine and is dedicated to her grandchildren, Linden, Caroline and Ewen and imprint: *Selections from the Diary … were first published in three volumes between 1938 and 1940 edited by William Plomer. This abridged edition … Pr. by Butler & Tanner Ltd. Frome and London 1976*; [5] *Note*; 7–174 text; [175] map of Clyro and District; [176] map of Chippenham and District). § Antique wove paper. 32 line drawings in text. § Orange linson boards. Typographic d.j. with E.A.'s drawings on pp. 94 and 30 reproduced front and rear.

MS. DRAWINGS: Sketchbook 64 contains some preparatory drafts for this book.

171. 1977 ARCADIAN BALLADS [printed purple] by James Reeves with illustrations by E.A. [Andoversford]: The Whittington Press, [1977].

Imperial 8°. 280 × 185 mm. (11 × 7½ in.). Pp. [10] ix–[x] [2] 48 [2] ([i] half-title; [iv] frontis.; [v] t.p.; [vi] imprint: *Pr. and published by The Whittington Press, Manor Farm, Andoversford, Gloucestershire … 1977*; [vii] *These poems are based on Ovid's* Metamorphoses, *from which they have been very freely adapted. Only the first* [Pyramus and Thisbe] *is not strictly Arcadian, the legend being Babylonian, not Greek. J.R.*; ix Contents; [x] ballad title: *Pyramus and Thisbe*; 1–48 text, with 4 further ballad title-pages; [49] colophon (see below); [50] device: wood engraving of a cat by Helmuth Weissenborn. § Roughish white wove mould-made paper, with deckle-edges. 18 pen drawings: frontis. and 2 full-page, 3 headpieces, 1 tailpiece, 12 variously disposed on text pages. All printed in purplish sepia. The other specifications are given in the colophon: *200 copies hand-set in 14-point Caslon and printed at Whittington Court by John and Rosalind Randle, Tim Jollands and Miriam Macgregor, on Arches paper* [watermarked 'ARCHES FRANCE']. *The illustrations were printed by lithography at the Senecio Press. 200 cloth copies* [bound in mauve printed floral linen with an oval title label on front], *and 50 leather copies* [in royal blue morocco, single gilt rule front and rear, gilt titling on spine] *with endpapers marbled by Solveig Stone, were bound by Weatherby Woolnough. Printing completed November 1977.* The leather copies were housed in a black board slip-case, the cloth in a rose pink one. Gilt tops to both bindings. § *Ref:* David Butcher, *The Whittington Press: a Bibliography* (Andoversford: Whittington, 1982) 27.

1978 TRADE IMPRESSION: Published by Heinemann Educational Books Ltd. … Pr. in G.B. by Cox & Wyman Ltd., London, Fakenham and Reading. 277 × 188 mm. Pp. [10] 48 [2], collating [1–2]⁸ [3]⁶ [4]⁸. Reprinted offset from the Whittington edition. Heavy white cartridge paper, the 18 illustrations printed black. Dark brown linen boards; d.j. orange-brown laminated paper, E.A.'s drawing on pp. 24–25 blown up to make a wrap-round decoration printed black, titling reversed out white on front and spine. Orange-brown endpapers. Top edge stained brown.

172. 1977 SHIP'S COOK GINGER Another Tim Story [vig.] by E.A. London, Sydney, Toronto: Bodley Head, [1977].

Crown 4°. Size and make-up follow the design of item 30 above, but with 23 drawings in pen and watercolour, and the t.p. vig. and 21 drawings in line. Printer and paper as for item 157, the binding laminated paper boards without d.j. There is no dedication.

REPRINT: London etc.: Random Century Ltd, 1991. (Little Greats). 240 × 183 mm.

1978 U.S. EDITION: New York: Macmillan Publishing Co., Inc.; issued with a d.j.

1985 PAPERBACK EDITION: London: Macmillan Children's Books. (Picturemacs).

1993 PAPERBACK EDITION: London: Random House Children's Books (Red Fox Paperbacks; bound with *Tim's Last Voyage,* item 157 above).

2000 SECOND EDITION: London: Scholastic Press, as above, but reoriginated from original artwork (see item 34 above).

TRANSLATIONS:
1978 [Swedish] *Skeppskocken Ginger.* Trs. Edward Brehmer. Stockholm etc.: Bergh.
1982 [Japanese] Tokyo: Mizuki Shobo Inc.
2001 [Japanese] Trs. Chihiro Nakagawa. Tokyo: Fukuinkan Shoten.

173. 1978 ARDIZZONE'S HANS ANDERSEN [vig. above]
Fourteen Classic Tales. Selected and Illustrated by E.A. Translated by
Stephen Corrin. [Publisher's device] [London]: Andre Deutsch, [1978].

Small royal 8°. 237 × 160 mm. (9⅜ × 6½ in.). Pp. [8] 9–191 [1] ([1] dec.
half-title; [3] t.p.; [4] imprint: *Filmset by Keyspools Limited, Golborne,
Lancs. Pr. in G.B. by Sackville Press, Billericay, Ltd*; [5] *Contents* (14 tales);
[6] *Colour Illustrations*; [7] *Translator's Note* (acknowledging help from
Birgitte Ege and Inger Sørensen and noting some cuts made and 'liberties
taken'); 9–191 text). § White cartridge paper. 47 illustrations: 16 full-page
in line and watercolour with letterpress legends; 31 pen drawings: 20 head-
ings to stories and story-sections, 4 tailpieces, 7 in text. Half-title dec. from
the drawing on p. 152, t.p. vig. a repeat of drawing on p. 21. § Maroon
linson boards, gilt titling front and spine with the drawing on p. 21 repeated
on front. D.j. letterpress titling with repeats from the watercolours on pp.
[158] and [2] front and rear. Front and rear endpapers a double-spread
blow-up of the vig. on p. 110 in rose ink on pink-washed paper. Top edge
stained pink.

Head-piece from 'The Snow Queen' in
Ardizzone's Hans Andersen (1978 item 173)

191

1979 U.S. EDITION: New York: Atheneum.

1989 REVISED EDITION: issued in laminated paper, hardback and paper-back, the colour plates now converted to muddy monochrome half-tones.

TRANSLATION: 1994 [Japanese] Tokyo: Aoitori Bunko. 2 vols. 172 × 112 mm; the colour illus. as in the above 1989 revised ed. Thin card wrappers with laminated d.j.s displaying E.A.'s watercolours for (1) The Little Mermaid and (2) The Snow Queen.

MS. DRAWINGS: Sketchbook 49 contains several pages of draft drawings for the stories. A selling exhibition of the original drawings and water-colours was held at the Mayor Gallery, 15 November–21 December 1978.

174. 1978 A CHILD'S CHRISTMAS IN WALES [by] Dylan Thomas [vig.] [Credit]. London, Toronto, Melbourne: Dent, [1978].

Small crown 4° in twelves, the first and last leaves pastedowns. 240 × 180 mm. (9¾ × 7⅛ in.). Pp. [5] 6–45 [3] ([1–2] pastedown endpaper, the exposed verso washed pale green; [3] free endpaper, washed pale pink [4] imprint etc.: *Text, copyright the Trustees for the copyrights of the late Dylan Thomas … Pr. in G.B. by William Clowes and Sons Ltd, London, Beccles and Colchester … 1978*; [5] t.p.; 6–45 text; [46–48] endpapers as for pp. [1–3]). § Thick smooth white cartridge paper. 31 illustrations, varying between single and double pages: 15 watercolours with black line; 16 line drawings, the t.p. vig. being a repeat of the tailpiece on p. 45. § Paper boards with a wrap-round watercolour hand-lettered in yellow panels on front and spine by E.A. D.j. as binding. Endpapers described above.

REPRINTED: 1979, 1983.

1980 U.S. EDITION: Boston: David R. Godine, Publisher, Inc. Two gatherings of 12 ff. with additional brown-paper endpapers. Rust-red linson boards.

1983 ANNOTATED WORK BOOK EDITION: [Tokyo]: Yamaguchi Shoten, annotated by Atsuko Furomoto. 210 × 140 mm. Pp. [6] iii–iv [1] 2–59 [3]; [1] 2–16 [2] ([i] t.p.; iii–iv introduction in Japanese; [1] fly-title; 2–14 text;

43–59 English/Japanese vocabulary and notes; [60] Japanese imprint; the remaining pages a 'report' for the child-reader to fill in). The illus. are in monochrome line and half-tone throughout. Laminated wrappers as on the English ed.

1986 PAPERBACK EDITION: London: Dent. Format as above.

1993 MINIATURE EDITION: London: Orion. 120 × 93 mm. Laminated paper boards.

1996 PAPERBACK EDITION: Harmondsworth: Puffin Books. Crown 8°, the colour converted to a blotchy monochrome.

TRANSLATIONS:
1978 [Welsh] *Nadolig Plentyn yng Nghymru.* Trs. Bryan Martin Davies. Llandysul, Wales: Gwasg Gomer.
1997 [Japanese]. Tokyo: Zuiun-sya Ltd.

MS. DRAWINGS: Welsh National Centre for Children's Literature, Aberystwyth. At the time of purchase, in 1982, the Centre exhibited the drawings and published an accompanying booklet of 24 pp. with articles by Marcus Crouch, Walford Davis and Paul Ferris, the text in English and Welsh. Along with the Andersen sketches noted in the previous item, sketchbook 49 contains several pages of drafts for this book too.

The story was first published in New York in Harper's Bazaar *in December 1950; it was cobbled together from a BBC radio broadcast made in 1945 and an article published in* Picture Post *27 Dec. 1947. A text of the BBC script is given in* Dylan Thomas: the Broadcasts *ed. Ralph Maud (London: J. M. Dent, 1991). The complete piece was recorded by Caedmon in 1952. A blow-up of the drawing on p. 33 was used in a poster to advertise a show at the Chepstow Museum, 1997–1998.*

175. 1978 THE JAMES REEVES STORY BOOK [Credit] [vig.]. London: Heinemann, [1978].

Large demy 8°. 233 × 150 mm. (9¼ × 6 in.). Pp. [6] 7–207 [1] ([1] half-title; [2] *Other books by J.R.* (12 titles); [3] t.p.; [4] imprint etc.: *Pr. and bound by Cox & Wyman, London, Fakenham and Reading;* [5] *Contents;*

[6] dedication: *For Harriet Fitch and Lucy Ardizzone*; 7–[8] *Preface*; 9–[208] text). § White cartridge paper. T.p. vig. and 46 line drawings, all repeated from previous publications (see below). § Blue linson boards. D.j. line and watercolour drawing, hand-lettered by E.A. on front and spine (the drawing depicts children swarming round a huge book opened to display five miniaturized illustrations to stories in the present selection); ads. on rear.

1986 PAPERBACK REPRINT: as *The Gnome Factory and Other Stories*. Harmondsworth: Puffin Books. Crown 8°. Pp. 200, the cover now (badly) drawn by Elisa Trimby, with E.A.'s design of the open book featuring as a frontispiece.

The contents consist of 19 stories intermingled: from Pigeons and Princesses *(item 52 above) all five stories, with eight out of a possible 19 illus.;* Sailor Rumbelow *(item 97 above) five out of six stories, with 13 out of a possible 17 illus.;* Three Tall Tales *(item 114 above) all stories, with line only versions of eight illus. originally with colour separations;* The Secret Shoemakers *(item 132 above) five out of 12 stories with 11 out of a possible 13 illus.; and* Rhyming Will *(item 137 above) complete text with six line drawings from the picture sequence. Most drawings are enlarged from their earlier printings except for those from* Three Tall Tales *which are reduced. The t.p. vig. is taken from 'The Woodcutter's Third Son' (*Secret Shoemakers*) although that story is not included here. The only new material provided by E.A. for the book is the d.j.*

James Reeves's Preface to the selection is largely devoted to explaining his pleasure at working with E.A. for thirty years or so: '… my favourite illustrator … nor can I call him an illustrator without qualifying the word. He is an artist in his own right, and any author ought to be proud, as I am, to have his genius at my service'. Reeves's account of the collaboration on Rhyming Will *is given in the note to that book above.*

176. 1978 LETTERS FROM MY WINDMILL [by] Alphonse Daudet; Translated with an Introduction by Frederick Davies [vig.] [Credit]. Harmondsworth: Penguin Books, [1978]. (Penguin Classics).

Small crown 8° in sixteens. 180 × 110 mm. (7⅛ × 4¼ in.). Pp. [8] 9–219 [5] ([1] blurb; [3] t.p.; [4] imprint: *Made and pr. in G.B. by Richard Clay (The Chaucer Press) Ltd, Bungay, Suffolk. Set in Monotype Ehrhardt*; [5] translator's dedication: *To George Steiner. Eloquent and wise interpreter of man to man*; [7–8] *Contents*; 9–[23] *Introduction*; 29–30 *Translator's Note and Acknowledgements ... And to Edward Ardizzone (C.B.E.) I owe an immeasurable debt for illustrations which not only capture the spirit of Daudet's elusive charm but which are works of art in their own right;* 31–[41] *Daudet's Preface from the Collected Edition of his Works ...;* 42–[43] *Foreword;* 44–[220] text; [221–224] *More about Penguins and Pelicans).* § Mechanical m.f. paper. 16 line drawings: t.p. vig., 3 full-page, 4 chapter headpieces, 1 tailpiece, and 7 in text. § Laminated paper wrappers with *a detail from 'Harvest ...' by Vincent Van Gogh* on front.

From *Letters from my Windmill* (1978 item 176)

The translator's introduction includes details of the authorship and first publication of the Lettres de mon Moulin, *12 letters serialised in* L'Evénement *in 1866 and 12 in* Le Figaro *in 1868.*

Head-piece from 'The Old Woman and her Pig' in
Ardizzone's English Fairy Tales (1980 item 177)

177. 1980 ARDIZZONE'S ENGLISH FAIRY TALES [dec.
rule] Twelve Classic Tales. Selected and Illustrated by E.A. from the Collection of Joseph Jacobs [publisher's device]. Andre Deutsch, [1980].

Small royal 8°. 234 × 150 mm. (9¼ × 6 in.). Pp. [8] 9–78 [2] ([1] half-
title; [3] t.p.; [4] imprint: *Pr. in G.B. by Ebenezer Baylis and Son Ltd. The
Trinity Press, Worcester, and London*; [5] publisher's note (see below); [7]
Contents; 9–78 text). § A wood-free printing paper, browning to edges.
20 line drawings: 8 chapter headpieces, 3 tailpieces, 2 full-page and 4 in
text of which 2 were formerly published in *The Old Ballad of the Babes in
the Wood* (item 154 above). Fourteen of the new drawings are – unusually – signed with the artist's initials 'E.A.' § Bright blue linson boards,
silver lettering on spine; bright blue matching endpapers. D.j. with typographic lettering and a framed watercolour (here signed) taken from p. 5
of *The Babes in the Wood*.

1987 SECOND IMPRESSION: issued as laminated paper hard- and paperback.

The publisher's note reads: 'When E.A. died in November 1979 he was at work on the illustrations for a selection of twenty-five of the English Folk Tales *collected and edited by the folklorist, Joseph Jacobs. He had illustrated eleven of the stories, which are presented in this book.*

'The illustration for the twelfth story, The Children in the Wood, *first appeared in an edition of this poem published by The Bodley Head in 1972. So did the watercolour reproduced on the jacket. We wish to thank The Bodley Head for generously allowing us to use this work. The original artwork of the watercolour is in the possession of Dr. J. A. Child, who kindly gave us permission to photograph it.'*

Eleven of the stories come from Joseph Jacobs' English Fairy Tales *first published in 1890 with illustrations by John D. Batten. 'The Children in the Wood' comes from the successor volume* More English Fairy Tales *of 1894. One story, 'Tom Tit Tot', with E.A.'s illustration, appeared more or less simultaneously with its first publication in* Vogue *(137, 15, no. 2202, Nov. 1980, pp. 151–152). The book was published on 17 November.*

E.A.'s genius as an illustrator is nowhere better shown than in these drawings made during his final illness. At first sight they seem shadows of what they might have been – sketches awaiting full articulation – but this bareness accentuates the artist's gift for finding the moment for his illustration and enriching it with a rightness of expression, gesture, movement and wit.

— **1981** VISITING DIEPPE by E.A. introduced by Lynton Lamb. London: Warren Editions, 1981.

See item A11 below.

178. 1983 FROM EDWARD ARDIZZONE'S INDIAN DIARY [vig. printed claret]. London: The Bodley Head, [1983].

Small crown 8°, a single gathering. 183 × 112 mm. (7½ × 4⅜ in.). Pp. [2] 3–12 [4] ([1] t.p.; 3–[13] text; [14] copyright and colophon: *These edited extracts and pictures are from* Edward Ardizzone's Indian Diary *to be published ... in 1984. The present booklet is issued in an edition of 225 copes for private distribution by the publisher in December 1983. Pr. in G.B. by The Stellar Press Ltd. Hatfield*; [15] tailpiece vig. printed claret and note on the text).

§ Cream laid paper with Stellar Press watermark. 9 pen sketches reproduced from the diary printed claret: t.p. vig., tailpiece, 7 in text. § Cream laid card wrapper, titled on front *Some Words & Drawings From Edward Ardizzone's Indian Diary 1952–53*, set between thick rules printed claret, with 2 additional sketches (black) above and below; rear cover a further sketch printed claret.

The note on the text records that the extracts are given 'in date sequence but without marks of ellipses' and relate mostly to E.A.'s 'UNESCO involvement with the teaching of printing by silk screen' – which is more fully documented in the following item, where six of the twelve sketches used here may be found, printed black.

179. 1984 INDIAN DIARY 1952–53 [by] E.A. Introduction by Malcolm Muggeridge [drawing]. London, Sydney, Toronto: The Bodley Head, [1984].

Small royal 8°. 247 × 150 mm. (9¾ × 6 in.). Pp. [6] 7–159 [1] ([1] half-title; [3] t.p.; [4] sketch and imprint: *Pr. in G.B. … by Grosvenor Press. Set in Linotron Bembo Special 1984*; [5] *Contents* with sketch; [6] sketch; 7–[9] *Publisher's note*; [10] frontis.; 11–14 *Introduction* by M.M.; [15] fly-title; [16] sketch; 17–[155] text; [156] sketch; [157]–159 *Notes*). § White cartridge paper. 76 illustrations. The publisher has compiled a variegated anthology of E.A.'s Indian drawings which may be summarised as follows: 8 sketches used in prelims and on final pages; 7 double-spread reproductions of diary pages, 47 single-page ditto, 11 pages which include monochrome half-tones of watercolours, 2 half-tone reproductions of privately-owned watercolours based on the diary, and one 3-panel line-drawing first published in *Punch* on 1 July 1953 (there it figured, with a hand-lettered title-drawing, for an article by P.M. Hubbard, 'Don't Turn Round', and the whole was reprinted in *The Pick of Punch* (1954, pp. 24–25). § Blue-grey linson boards, gilt lettered spine. D.j. with typographic titling, a pen and watercolour drawing by E.A. on front and a photographic portrait on rear. Top edge stained dark grey.

The sketches on the t.p. and on pp. 69, 131 and 143 (three sketches) were used in the previous item.

180. 1985 THE ADVENTURES OF TIM. [colour vig.] Six Delight-ful Stories by the Award-Winning Author and Illustrator E.A. [London]: Chancellor Press, [1985].

Crown 4° in eights, the first and last leaves pastedowns. Pp. [15] 16–300 [4] ([5] half-title; [7] t.p.; [8] title copyrights and imprint: *Pr. in Hungary*; [9] *Contents*; [11] *An Introduction to Tim* with colour vig.; [13] fly-title: *Tim and Ginger* with pen drawing repeated from p. 48; [15]–300 texts). § Off-white featherweight antique wove paper. Includes all the illustra-tions from the Tim books (see below). § Laminated paper boards with oval illus. in colour, like d.j.

The following six stories are included in apparently random sequence, each preceded by a title-page with a pen-drawing taken from the text: pp. [13]–60 Tim and Ginger; [61]–108 Tim and Charlotte; [109]–156 Tim's Friend Towser; [157]–204 Tim to the Lighthouse; [205]–252 Tim in Danger; and [253]–300 Tim All Alone.

In bumper-book fashion this compendium is printed on an off-white feather-weight paper, with the watercolours probably reproduced from the O.U.P. film. The result tends to the over-emphatic, especially with the cyan plates, and, while this does not affect the simpler compositions too severely, the line and colour in the more detailed illus. are muddy or gaudy by turns.

— THE GOLDEN AGE by Kenneth Grahame.

In Ardizzone's sketchbook 49 there is tantalizing evidence that, towards the end of his career, he was negotiating over illustrating Kenneth Grah-ame's *The Golden Age* and *Dream Days*. He lists the child characters (e.g. 'Charlotte – not more than 8 – the I of the story') and a specification 'Large Crown. 222 down × 136 mm across. 10 full-page per volume – broken up spots and halves ...'. No more is known of this project, for which his genius was entirely suited, and if he had carried it through with his accus-tomed sensitivity nothing could have been labelled more appropriately '*Finis coronat opus*'.

A: CONTRIBUTIONS TO BOOKS ETC.

A chronological list of works in which the artist participated in some way, but to a lesser extent than in the commissioned or contracted works listed in the previous section. Included are books with single illustrations, usually frontispieces, books with only endpaper designs, and books and one or two periodicals in which E.A. appears as only one among a number of illustrators. Commissions for the design or illustration of dust-jackets and some card-covered publications are separately listed in the next section, but designs for bindings are included here.

A1. 1929 THE 1929 CHRISTMAS TREE ANNUAL [vig., unattributed]. [London]: Published in aid of the Children's Country Holidays Fund by Ernest Benn Limited.

Vignette from *The 1929 Christmas Tree Annual* (item A1)

Crown 4°. 247 × 180 mm. Pp. [4] 5–192 + frontis. by Mabel Lucie Attwell and 3 plates. Illus. by some 20 artists, including Cecil Aldin, L.R. Brightwell and Hilda Cowham. E.A. provides 4 pen drawings signed 'Ardizzone', printed red-brown, in the text of a short extravaganza 'Some Modern Magic' by Stephen King-Hall, pp. 36–64 (E.A.'s brother-in-law and future biographer, Gabriel White, has 4 drawings, printed blue, in a play-text 'Pandora's Box' by Gertrude Jennings immediately following). § Quarter dark blue cloth, glazed paper boards with a design by Alan Rogers on front, ads. on rear. No d.j. seen (called-for?).

E.A.'s earliest-known published illustrations 'contributed', according to the publisher's note, 'free of any charge'. The commission presumably arrived through E.A.'s sister Betty (married to Gabriel White), who was then working for the Children's Country Holiday Fund.

A2. 1941 A HANDY DICKENS Selections ... Made and Introduced by Arthur Machen. With a Frontis. by E.A. London: Constable & Co. Ltd., [1941] [all within a simple fleuron frame].

Small crown 8°. 184 × 110 mm. Pp. [4] v–xviii [1] 2–258 [2]. The inset frontis. by E.A. is a pen and watercolour drawing printed half-tone on coated stock: rustic titling within a lancet window surrounded by 7 small Dickensian scenes redrawn from the images of Phiz (H.K. Browne). Signed 'Ardizzone'. § Dark blue cloth boards, silver lettering on spine. D.j. white paper with a slightly reduced version of the frontis. on front.

A3. 1947 OVER THE HILLS AND FAR AWAY Three Centuries of Holidays by Hartley Kemball Cook. London: George Allen & Unwin Ltd, [1947].

Large crown 8°. 196 × 127 mm. Pp. [6] 7–263 [1] + frontis. and 8 double-sided half-tone plates. § Mushroom grey linen boards, endpapers with 3 parallel horizontal designs showing seaside, coaching and early railway scenes in pen and wash, printed mauve with yellow interlining, signed 'Edward Ardizzone'. D.j. a replication (tracing?) of the endpaper design printed in sepia line and full colour.

A4. 1947 THE STRAND Vol. 114, Issue 684 [London: George Newnes Ltd.] December, 1947.

On pp. 52–66, as a special Christmas feature 'Mr. Ardizzone Presents His Christmas Pantomime Cinderella'. The text consists of an introductory letter to the (adult) reader, surrounded by a baroque design featuring the play's characters, all by E.A., followed by a synopsis of a pantomime version of the story and instructions on making the theatre (anonymous, but known to be by Macdonald Hastings). Interspersed are E.A.'s designs for the proscenium arch, the sets and characters etc., hand-lettered by him and printed in 2, 3 and 4 colours. E.A. also designed the cover for this issue of the magazine, and this image was used by the Trustees of Pollock's Toy Museum on the front of a letter-card sold in aid of the Museum's redevelopment plan, 2001.

An editorial note on p. 66 offers a limited number of the stage sets available separately (none seen – however the Ardizzoddities *display at Harrogate in 2000 included an, albeit rather flimsy, construction of the theatre made by Valerie Alderson from mounted colour-photocopies of the* Strand *materials). For E.A.'s involvement with the* Strand *see item D2 below.*

A5. 1947 TOLLER REPORTS [by] Jeremy Taylor. With Illustrations by War Artists. Bristol: The White Swan Press Ltd., 1947.

Small crown 4°. 246 × 180 mm. Pp. [4] 5–95 [1], including a total of 18 illus. on 16 full-page plates of which 5 are by E.A. § Quarter orange linen, yellow paper boards, red titling on front.

The introduction says of the text that 'these sketches were written between February 1943 and the end of the war … a sort of souvenir book, to recall the humour and even absurdity that went along with [its] stern tasks'. The 'sketches', about an inefficient subaltern, were mostly published in Punch *and the illus. are taken from war artists' work 'by courtesy of the Imperial War Museum'. Four of E.A.'s paintings are reproduced in monochrome from his 'West Country Manoeuvres' sequence, the fifth is 'Soldiers Buying Silks in the Bazaar, Cairo'. Other artists who feature are Thomas Freath, Thomas Hennell, Sam Black, Anthony Gross and Carel Weight.*

A6. 1948 THE ROSE AND THE RING … a Fireside Pantomime … by Mr. M. A. Titmarsh [i.e. W. M. Thackeray]. London: Guilford Press Limited & Wilfrid David Ltd., [1948] [all within illus. frame (see below)].

Crown 8°. 202 × 127 mm. Pp. [6] 128 [2], with Thackeray's illus. and rhymed running-heads. The letterpress t.p. within a rule frame is surrounded by 6 pen drawings by E.A. with pale pink and grey overlays based on Thackeray's own illustrations for the book, first published for Christmas 1854; signed 'E. Ardizzone'. § Pale turquoise cloth boards with E.A.'s sketch of Angelica from p. 28 blocked in silver on a dark brown panel on front. D.j. a pen drawing hand-lettered by E.A. with overlays in yellow, grey and pink, showing Thackeray's characters within the flames of a fireplace, repeated front and rear and signed 'E. Ardizzone', with the artist's hand-lettering on the yellow spine.

The Guilford Press was a subsidiary of Lindsay Drummond formed in 1946 (see item 21 above). When Drummond failed, the stock of this book was acquired by Sidgwick & Jackson who placed their sticker on the verso of the title-leaf. Sheets were later bound in plain blue linson, with the d.j. in pink, with letterpress titling and Thackeray's drawing from p. 22 on the front in blue.

A7. 1949 THE SATURDAY BOOK Being the Ninth Annual Issue of this Celebrated Repository of Curiosities and Looking-Glass of Past and Present. Ed. by Leonard Russell … Designed by Laurence Scarfe. [London]: Hutchinson, October 1949.

Large demy 8°. 230 × 145 mm. Pp. [16] 17–288. E.A.'s only contribution is on p. 35, the title drawing in line with a mauve overlay to a story by Desmond MacCarthy 'The Most Miserable of Men'. § Plain red buckram, d.j. designed by Philip Gough.

A8. 1950 HARVEST Volume Two. The Household [device] Ed. by Vincent Stuart. London: Castle Press, 1950.

Crown 4°. 242 × 185 mm. Pp. [8] 9–82. E.A. provides 2 pen drawings for an article by Nancy Spain on 'The Butler and the Housekeeper', pp. 28–37. § Cloth boards. D.j. by Leslie Hurry.

Harvest was a short-lived miscellany. The initial volume, Travel, *was published in 1948 and was here advertised as available bound together with volume 2 'for subscription only' (a sure sign of a failing enterprise).*

A9. 1951 BRITANNIA, February 1951.

Pages 84–85 are part of a feature on 'The London Scene', with E.A. supplying a short text and 4 pen drawings on the subject of 'My Street'. This follows a similar piece by Anthony Gross on dress showrooms.

A10. 1951 THE ENGLISH INN by John Pudney. Illustrated by Diz.

Demy 4°. 280 × 215 mm. A 4-page central inset, perhaps also separately issued, on antique wove paper within the art-paper gathering of *Vickers Overseas News* (Summer 1951). The outer pages of the bifolium have a title drawing by E.A. with his script-lettering and two others with a purple overlay; the inner pages have two drawings with a yellow overlay. Imprint for the suggested separate issue: *This supplement ... was printed by Fosh & Cross Ltd. by the litho-offset process on a George Mann machine.*

MS. DRAWINGS: Sketchbook 1 has preliminary drafts on pp. 18–19.

A11. 1951 THE GOOD TIME GUIDE TO LONDON [by] Francis Aldor. Art Editor I. Hofbauer. London, Sydney, Toronto, Bombay: George G. Harrap & Co. Ltd., [1951].

Small crown 8°. 183 × 115 mm. Pp. [6] 7–319 [1]. Illus. by 13 named artists, including Fougasse, Francis Marshall, and Feliks Topolski. E.A. provides 8 spot drawings: 7 in 3 or 4 colours, 1 in sepia. § Rose-red cloth boards. D.j. white with border sketches in colour by E.A. on front.

A12. 1951 THE SATURDAY BOOK Being the Eleventh Appearance of this Renowned Repository ... Ed. by Leonard Russell ... Designed by Laurence Scarfe. [London]: Hutchinson, [October, 1951].

Large demy 8°. 228 × 146 mm. Pp. [6] 7–279 [1]. Page 128 announces: *E.A. drew the pictures and wrote the text (including a slight misspelling or two) for the next contribution.* Pages [129–140] bear: *A Diary of a Holiday Afloat,* a facsimile of E.A.'s ms. record of seven days rowing down the Thames in a Jerome K. Jerome-ish boat from Lechlade to Oxford. 20 interspersed pen drawings depict the *splendeurs et misères* encountered by E.A. and his crew, Catherine and Nicholas. See also the following item. This number also has a pen-drawn headpiece and a full-page drawing with one overlay by E.A.

for the story of 'Cupid and the Duchess' by Josephine Blumenfeld (pp. 252–260). § Bright red buckram boards, gilt. Decorative d.j. by Joan Hassall.

REPRINTED: in Judy Taylor's *Sketches for Friends* (see Sources p. 286).

For a facsimile of one of the drawings see p. [10].

A13. 1951 SIGNATURE: a Quadrimestrial of Typography and Graphic Arts. Ed. by Oliver Simon. New Series 13. Plaistow, London, 1951.

Crown 4°. 247 × 185 mm. Pp. [5] 4–62 [4]. Pages 30–35 are an introductory account of 'Visiting Dieppe' by Lynton Lamb, which precedes a facsimile printing of E.A.'s brief diary of a trip taken from Friday 25–Monday 28 May 1951 by E.A., his brother David, and Barnett Freedman (pp. 36–46). The text is much preoccupied with the good things of life (*Gevrey Chambertin 39 – Pommard 45 – and a very old Calvados*) and is illustrated with 19 suitably reverent pen drawings. The work is similar in style to the boating adventure recorded in the preceding item. § Standard card wrappers.

1981 NEW EDITION: as *Visiting Dieppe*. London: Warren Editions. An independently published edition with an introduction by Lynton Lamb, 'from the press of Jonathan and Phillida Gili'. Large crown 8°. 262 × 195 mm. Pp. [28]. Printed at the Curwen Press on St Cuthbert's Fourdrinier mould-made paper; binding by Weatherby Woolnough in quarter red cloth with patterned paper boards by Glyn Boyd Harte. 100 numbered copies were published, together with a further 50 (numbered in roman from I–L) issued in a slip-case with a matching copy of *A Weekend in Dieppe* by Glyn Boyd Harte. The latter was a 'mirror account' describing another visit made thirty years later by Harte, accompanied by Jonathan Gili and Ian Beck. Harte's lithographs were made available separately in various states. See Jonathan Gili, 'Warren Editions' in *Matrix 19* (Winter 1999, pp. 44–57, items 25a and 25b).

1985 REPRINTED: in reduced format in *Private View*, a journal of the Cambridge School of Art (no. 4, Spring 1985, pp.13–17) with Lynton Lamb's essay.

ABRIDGED REPRINT: in Judy Taylor's *Sketches for Friends* (see Sources p. 286).

A14. 1952 THE HUMOUR OF DICKENS Chosen by R. J. Cruik-shank [vig.] with Illustrations by Modern Artists. London: 'News Chronicle' Publications Dept. ..., [1952].

Large crown 8°. 205 × 143 mm. Pp. xiv 145 [1]. Published in aid of the Dickens House Endowment Fund (Walter Dexter memorial) with ten artists, including Giles, Illingworth, Low and Searle, contributing two pen drawings each. E.A. supplies the frontis., 'Dinner at the Veneerings', and the illus. on p. 77, 'Wemmick's Castle', both signed 'Diz'. § Plain grey linen-surface card wrappers cut flush. D.j. printed orange with rustic titling surrounded by character portraits signed 'M.W. 52' (by Mervyn Wilson?). There was also a superior issue bound in red linen boards with gilt-lettered spine, at 5s. net, with a transparent wrapper printed with the cover-design in black. A presentation copy (specially bound?) in full limp red morocco is described in Devitt, *Ardizzone 1* (item 71).

A15. 1952 THE SATURDAY BOOK. Twelfth Issue. Founded by Leonard Russell, ed. by John Hadfield. [London]: Published by Hutchinson, [1952].

Large demy 8°. 228 × 146 mm. Pp. [6] 7–296. The anonymous 'Memoirs of a Batman' (pp. 157–168) are illus. with five spot drawings by E.A. § Rose-red buckram boards. D.j. with shell roundel on a copy of a Georgian wall-paper design in red.

A16. 1953 VOGUE Vol. 109, No. 1791, June 1953.

Pages 120–121 bear a single line and wash drawing over a spread, titled: *E.A. animates a Coronation street scene.*

In his Indian Diary *(item 179 above), on 8 February 1953 in Delhi E.A. records 'Day in my room making a drawing for* Vogue'. *The finished work was despatched on 25 February before he left for Mysore.*

— 1955 THE ILLUSTRATED ILLUSTRATOR [Facsimile excerpts of letters]. See *The Newcomes* (item 42 above).

A17. 1958 A GOLDEN LAND Stories, Poems, Songs New and Old [vig. by Peggy Fortnum] Ed. by James Reeves; Illus. by Gillian Conway and others. London: Constable and Company Ltd., [1958].

Large demy 8°. 236 × 154 mm. Pp. xvi 496. Two previously published complete stories by E.A. are included, illus. with a total of 10 newly-prepared pen drawings: pp. 24–35 *Paul the Hero of the Fire* (item 25 above) and pp. 312–322 *Nicholas and the Fast Moving Diesel* (item 23.1 above).

1973 PAPERBACK EDITION: Harmondsworth: Puffin Books. (A Young Puffin). Crown 8°.

In 1983 'a new edition', The New Golden Land Anthology, was published, edited by Judith Elkin (Kestrel Books), thereby providing socio-literary critics with a comparative exercise. Somewhat disingenuously the editor claims to have retained much of James Reeves's original choice for his anthology, whose 'first place on the nursery bookshelf' had justly been seen as unchallengeable by The Guardian *– but 'much' turns out to be only 33 items out of 116. Both of E.A.'s stories have been deleted and his sole appearance is alongside Reeves's 'Little Fan', newly imported from item 61 above. A paperback edition appeared in 1984 (Puffin Books).*

A18. 1961 GLYNDEBOURNE FESTIVAL OPERA 24 May–20 August 1961. (Festival Programme Book. Tenth edition).

Royal 4°. 305 × 240 mm. Pp. [1] 2–103 [1], including many full-page ads. Pages 69–72 are 'Supplementary Wine Notes No. 23A. June 1960', an account by E.A., reproduced from his handwriting, of a visit to the previous year's performance of *I Puritani* by the Wine Committee of the Royal College of Art. Six pen drawings record stages in the trip and five photographs portray the author and his colleagues at work. § Paper wrappers with yapp edges, with a *trompe l'oeil* wrap-round illus. by Carl Toms.

REPRINTED: in Judy Taylor's *Sketches for Friends* (see Sources p. 286)

A19. 1961 NOT SUCH AN ASS by Henry Cecil. With a Foreword by the Rt. Hon. Lord Justice Devlin … Hutchinson of London, [1961].

Crown 8°. 196 × 125 mm. Pp. [6] 7–208. § Black linson boards, endpapers a pen-drawn court scene by E.A., printed red; repeated front and rear. D.j.

with pen drawings by E.A. on front and spine with two-colour overlay. Typographic titling.

A20. 1960 LAND 10. Ed. D. Wolfers [Farm Journal of the Shell Chemical Co.] Winter 1960/61.

Oblong imperial 8°. 220 × 272 mm. Pp. [2] 3–48, printed on 3 different paper stocks by W.S. Cowell Ltd., Ipswich. Pages 34–40 contain 'The Country Pub' by R. C. Robertson-Glasgow, illus. with photographs and with three pen drawings and a full-page watercolour, bled to edges, by E.A. The watercolour is of a corner of Rodmersham Green, where the artist had his country cottage, and probably still exists somewhere as an independent painting. § Card covers, the front after a painting by Elinor Bellingham-Smith.

A21. 1962 THE LITTLE GREY MEN a Story for the Young in Heart by 'BB'. Illus. by Denys Watkins-Pitchford. Harmondsworth: Penguin Books, [1962]. (Puffin Books no. 160).

Small crown 8°. 180 × 108 mm. Pp. [6] 7–255 [1]. § Series wrappers with a wrap-round pen drawing with 2-colour separations, hand-lettered by E.A.

First published by Eyre & Spottiswoode in 1942, winning the Library Association's Carnegie Medal for that year. The book's author and illustrator are one and the same person.

A22. 1962 THE ORANGE CAROL BOOK Arranged by Mervyn Horder [fleurons]. London: Constable and Co. Ltd., [1962].

Royal 8°. 247 × 157 mm. Pp. vi [2] 88. 53 carols with piano accompaniments: translated texts are given with their originals; with brief notes. § Linson boards printed with an outdoor scene of carollers in line and watercolour, running from front to rear, by E.A., with his hand-lettering on front and spine. Orange typographic d.j. with a panel (72 × 54 mm) cut from front revealing the faces of two of the earnest singers on the binding.

An impression in crown 8° (205 × 140 mm) was published simultaneously, jointly with Stainer & Bell, with the binding design on linson card. The title derives from the publisher's address: 'Constables live in Orange Street' as their slogan had it.

A23. 1965 OPEN THE DOOR [by] Margery Fisher [vig. by Leslie Marshall]. [Leicester]: Brockhampton Press, [1965].

Demy 8°. 220 × 146 mm. Pp. [12] 13–384. A collection of 39 stories and excerpts, grouped so that the young reader is ushered into different kinds of place ('The Garden Gate', 'The Kitchen Door' etc.) and encouraged to reach out to new reading experiences. There are notes and suggestions for further reading and the illus. are mostly from the source of first publication. E.A.'s pen drawing on p. 369 is from Eleanor Farjeon's 'Little Boy Pie' in *Jim at the Corner* (item 63 above), that on p. 87 for Ursula Hourihane's 'Mrs. Cumfitt's Sugar Mice' may be original. § Bright red cloth boards, gilt dec. on front and spine. D.j. a line and watercolour design on front and spine, showing children opening various doors, drawn and hand-lettered throughout by E.A. Top edge stained red. Yellow silk marker.

A24. 1967 IN SEARCH OF ELSIE PIDDOCK; an Echo of Eleanor Farjeon by Denys Blakelock with a Drawing by E.A. [London: The Favil Press, 1967].

Small foolscap 8°. 153 × 112 mm. Pp. [8] on smooth white cartridge paper, 9–24 on laid paper. Pen-drawn frontis. by E.A. on p. [4]. § Blue glazed paper boards, yellow printed label.

A25. 1968 THE OXFORD ILLUSTRATED OLD TESTAMENT with Drawings by Contemporary Artists. London, New York, Toronto: Oxford University Press, 1968–1969.

Royal 8°. 235 × 145 mm. Five volumes. Pagination, including full-page plates, varies through the set. § Each volume is in a different coloured cloth, matched by the d.j.

An ambitious (but surely misguided) project to 'show-case', as the Americans have it, illustrations by 22 artists each of whom appears irregularly throughout the work and provides a comment (repeated from volume to volume) on his/her approach to the commission. E.A.'s contributions are to vol. 2 (Samuel), 13 pen drawings; vol. 4 (Jonah), one pen drawing; and vol. 5 (Ecclesiasticus), 13 pen drawings. His comment reiterates his liking for drawing figures 'in their settings rather as if they were actors on a stage'. He worked in line with watered ink and added a grey wash 'to knit the scene together and heighten the effect'. An exhibition of the drawings prepared for this work was held in the Diploma Gallery of the Royal Academy in 1968 with an 80-page illustrated catalogue.

A26. 1969 MR. VISCONTI [by] Graham Greene. An Extract from 'Travels with my Aunt'. Drawing by E.A. London: The Bodley Head, [1969].

Royal 12°. 190 × 107 mm. Pp. [8] 10 [6]. Frontis. in pen and grey wash by E.A. § Yellow wrappers folded on to card covers, with the frontis. repeated on the front.

'This extract ... is published in an edition of 300 copies for private distribution by the author and publisher for Christmas 1969.' In series with items 164 and 178 above.

A27. 1971 CUT-STEEL AND BERLIN IRON JEWELLERY by Anne Clifford. [London]: Adams & Dart, [1971].

Small foolscap 4°. 210 × 162 mm. Pp. [8] 9–95 [1] + 4 plates. The t.p. spread (pp. [2–3]) is a grey pen and wash drawing bled to edge, signed 'Diz'. § Cream linson boards. D.j. decorated grey laminated paper.

The drawing of an eighteenth-century street scene bears little relation to the subject of the book, which was written by a friend who lived near to the Ardizzones in Kent.

A28. 1972 THE MYSTERIES OF BIRMINGHAM by Brian Gould with an Envoi by William Horner and a Drawing by E.A., R.A. Bedford Park: Naples Press, 1972.

Typescript duplicated on 41 ff. of quarto paper 'for poets' conference held this year in Birmingham'. § Side-stapled into thicker paper covers with E.A.'s drawing on the front 'from a notebook and used by courtesy of the artist, who writes that it may be of a young soldier he met during the war.

A29. 1974 ERIC AND US a Remembrance of George Orwell [by] Jacintha Buddicom [6-line quotation]. Leslie Frewin of London, [1974].

Large crown 8°. 213 × 130 mm. Pp. [10] xi–xxi 165 [5]. Pen-drawn frontis. by E.A. above two lines from a sonnet written by Eric Blair in 1919, first published in this book (p. 87). § Brown linson boards, gilt lettering front and spine. D.j. with photograph on front.

A30. 1974 DOUBLE CROWN CLUB ROLL OF MEMBERS Together with a List of Dinners Since 1924 & the Club Rules [vig.]. Privately Printed, 1974.

Long crown 12°. 203 × 112 mm. Pp. [4] 5–35 [1]. The t.p. vig. is a pen drawing by E.A. The colophon on the final page records 'of this nineteenth edition … 130 copies have been printed by W. &. J. Mackay Ltd, Lordswood, Chatham, Kent. June 1974.' § Brown linen boards with dec. D.C.C. emblem in gilt on front.

For a note on the Club and its menus see item C10 below.

A31. 1974 PUFFIN ANNUAL Number 1 [set above a page of variegated pen drawings by Fritz Wegner indicating some of the contents and faced by the imprint etc.] Edited by Treld Bicknell, Frank Waters, Kaye Webb … Harmondsworth: Puffin Books …, 1974.

Folio. 293 × 210 mm. Pp. [5] 6–125 [3] including pastedowns. § Laminated paper boards.

Amid the mèlange of articles etc. traditional to annuals, E.A. contributes 'Ten Characters in Search of a Story' (pp. [18]–19), an account of some of his favourite characters in the 'Tim' books who can be identified, along with the artist himself, in the facing (muddily printed) illustration which is an enlarged version of a drawing first published on the cover of Young Elizabethan, *noted on page 247 below. The subject, an audience watching a Punch and Judy show, occurs on a grand scale as part of E.A.'s murals designed for the nursery of the P. & O. ship* Canberra.

Opposite: Title-page of the Double Crown
Club *Roll of Members* (1974 item A30)

DOUBLE CROWN CLUB

ROLL OF
MEMBERS

together with the
LIST OF DINNERS since 1924
& the CLUB RULES

PRIVATELY PRINTED

1974

B: BOOK JACKETS

For many illustrators seeking to make their way in the world, commissions to design dust-jackets and wrappers for books can be an important opportunity to gain experience in fashioning a narrative illustration and also to forge a link with publishers' editors. For this reason it seems well to give the following chronological list of the books for which E.A. drew the jackets or wrappers and nothing else. It should be borne in mind that such work is not formally recorded in catalogues and bibliographies and that there may therefore be a number of omissions. The publication-place is London unless otherwise stated.

B1. 1934 Frank Pollard. *All in the Downs*. Constable. *A decorative maritime scene swirling round front and spine in full colour; lettering probably by E.A.; signed 'Ardizzone'.*

B2. 1935 Frank Pollard. *East Indiaman*. Constable. *Quayside scene in full colour, front and spine matching the foregoing design.*

B3. 1938 Len Ortzen. *Down Donkey Row*. Cresset Press. *Two-colour street scene; front and spine hand-lettered.*

B4. 1942 Cyril Hare. *Tragedy at Law*. Faber. *Pen drawing with overlays in 2 colours, hand-lettered by E.A. on front and spine; signed 'DIZ'.*

B5. 1946 Noel Langley. *Music of the Heart*. Arthur Barker. *Full-colour titling on a fairground stage with characters; signed 'DIZ'.*

B6. 1947 Bruce Marshall. *The Red Danube*. Constable. *Pen drawing, an officer with nuns, printed on a pink wash.*

B7. 1948 Ben Lucien Burman. *Blow for a Landing*. Lutterworth Press. *Full-colour 'Mississippi Steamboat at Quayside'. Unsigned and unconfirmed as by E.A.*

B8. 1948 Noel Langley. *There's a Porpoise Close Behind Me*. Arthur Barker. *Not seen.*

B9. 1948 L. A. G. Strong. *Trevannion*. Methuen & Co. Ltd. *Pen portrait of Trevannion in the street of a sea-side town on front only, overlays in three colours with hand-lettering front and spine; signed 'E. Ardizzone'. The original water-colour (around 268 × 173 mm) is in a private coll. in the U.S.A.*

B10. 1951 [Helmut Gernsheim]. *Masterpieces of Victorian Photography 1840– 1900 from the Gernsheim Collection* [a catalogue]. London: The Arts Council … on the occasion of the Festival of Britain. *Card covers. Quasi-Victorian decorative lettering within a pen-drawn frame of active and/or eminent Victorian personages (cf. Dicky Doyle) on front only. Overlays in three colours. Signed 'DIZ'. For a reproduction see overleaf.*

B11. 1951 Cyril Hare. *An English Murder*. Faber. *Butler and corpse, hand-lettered by E.A. on front, horizontal pen scribbles on spine, in two colours.*

B12. 1951 V. S. Pritchett. *Mr. Beluncle*. Chatto and Windus. *Pen-portrait of Mr Beluncle with posters on front in line and two colours, hand-lettered by E.A. front and spine; signed 'DIZ'. The original watercolour (270 × 217 mm), with paste-ons revising Mr Beluncle's portrait and the title-lettering, is in the Chatto and Windus Archive at Reading University Library.*

B13. 1951 Emile Zola. *The Dram-Shop (L'Assomoir)*. Trs. Gerard Hopkins. Hamish Hamilton. *Forceful pen drawing with overlays in two colours on front and spine, panels above and below in a third colour hand-lettered by E.A.; signed 'DIZ'.*

B14. 1953 Julian Franklyn. *The Cockney: a Survey of London Life and Language*. Andre Deutsch. *Pen-drawn street-scene with two-colour overlays on front and spine. Hand-lettered on front by E.A. Signed 'DIZ'. Featured, show-ing the line original, on p. [47] of Peter Curl's* Designing a Book Jacket *(London: Studio Publications, 1956).*

B15. 1954 Cyril Hare. *That Yew Tree's Shade*. Faber. *Atmospheric hill scene; forceful pen drawing with overlays in two colours, hand-lettered by E.A. on front and spine. Signed 'DIZ'.*

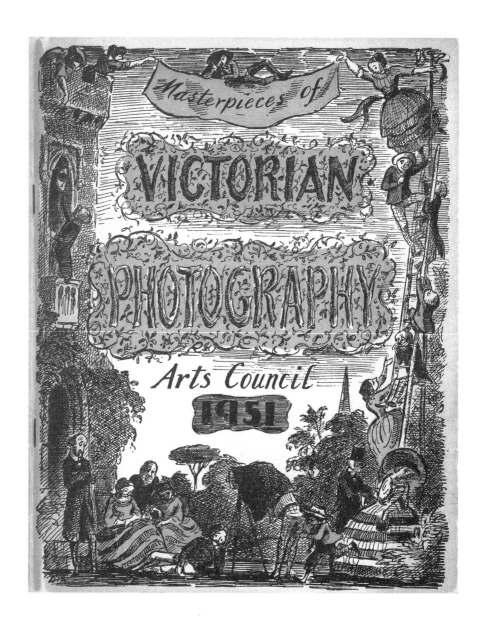

Front cover of *Masterpieces of Victorian Photography* (1951 item B10, reduced)

B16. 1957 Leslie Paul. *The Boy Down Kitchener Street*. Faber. *Pen-drawn suburban street scene (c. 1900) with children at their games on the front and spine; with overlays in three colours, hand-lettered throughout by E.A. and signed 'DIZ'.*

B17. 1957 Adolf Bolm and Ralph Vaughan Williams. *On Christmas Night: a Masque*. Oxford University Press. *Front cover mauve wash with pen drawing of Scrooge and the Ghost of Christmas Present with white highlights. Signed 'DIZ'.*

B18. 1958 Peter Fletcher. *The Long Sunday*. Faber. *'Protestant piety' going to chapel: pen drawing with three-colour overlays hand-lettered by E.A. on front and spine.*

B19. 1958 John Foley. *Bull and Brass*. Cassell. *A cleverly-designed wrap-round jacket in line and three colours for a collection of stories about the 'inmates' of the War Office. The front shows an officer entering the portal, the rear shows him leaving in civilian clothes, and the spine, the officer in the office.*

B20. 1958 Mary F. Thwaite (ed.). *Children's Books of this Century: a First List of Books Covering the Years 1899 to 1956, Chosen for the Library of Children's Literature now Being Formed at Chaucer House*. The Library Association Youth Libraries Section. *Very pale green card wrappers with a drawing of children reading beside bookshelves, hand-lettered cartouche by E.A. 'The illustration on the cover is from a design specially drawn for the Youth Libraries Section by Edward Ardizzone' (p. 3). Signed 'DIZ'. (See section E for an alternative use.)*

B21. 1959 Chris Massie. *When My Ship Comes Home: a Novel*. Faber. *Pen drawing of a boy running along a Norfolk sea-dyke on front and spine, overlays in two colours, hand-lettered throughout by E.A. Signed 'DIZ'.*

B22–29. World's Classics Series. London: Oxford University Press. *Round about 1959 the Press commissioned Lynton Lamb to redesign the jackets for this often rather dowdy-looking series of classics. George Mackie in his monograph on Lamb (London: Scolar Press, 1978) notes the technique that he adopted, which was to draw in black ink on grey paper, using Chinese white for highlights etc. This meant that the grey ground could be inked to any colour in the printing – a more satisfactory means of gaining two colours than using what would have been a substantial over-lay. Lamb asked E.A. to undertake work on some of the titles using this method* *and these follow here in alphabetical order by author with the series number and the date of its first appearance as a World's Classic. The actual dates of the commissions are not available.*

B22. Jane Austen. *Persuasion*. WC 356. 1930. *Peach ground: Anne Elliot at a window.*

B23. Charles Dickens. *The Adventures of Oliver Twist*. WC 8. 1901. *Grey ground: Oliver apprehended.*

B24. Charles Dickens. *Great Expectations*. With six illus. by Warwick Goble. WC 128. 1907. *Lavender ground: Pip and Miss Havisham. Signed 'DIZ'.*

B25. Oliver Goldsmith. *The Vicar of Wakefield*. WC 4. 1901. *Rose-pink ground: the Vicar and his family.*

B26. Tobias Smollett. *Humphry Clinker*. WC 290. 1925. *Khaki ground: signing the document.*

B27. Tobias Smollett. *Roderick Random*. WC 353. 1930. *Blue ground: Roderick on the quayside.*

B28. Laurence Sterne. *Tristram Shandy*. WC 40. 1903. *Pale blue ground. Uncle Toby and Corporal Trim at their fortifications.*

B29. Leo Tolstoy. *Childhood, Boyhood and Youth*. WC 352. 1930. *Pale olive ground: domestic scene.*

B30. 1961 Margery Fisher. *Intent Upon Reading: a Critical Appraisal of Modern Fiction for Children*. Leicester: Brockhampton Press. *Vignette (35 × 45 mm) of a girl sitting reading, set in lower panel of a two-colour typographic jacket and repeated (23 × 30 mm) on spine. Signed 'DIZ'. A slightly enlarged printing was used on the cover of Elizabeth N. Bewick's* Reader's Guide to Children's Books *(Book-list 81 in the New Series published by the Library Association County Libraries Group, 1964).*

B31. 1962 Alex Hamilton. *As If She Were Mine*. New Authors Ltd. *Squaring up in the public bar: pen drawing with overlays in two colours.*

B32. 1964 P. L. Travers. *I Go by Sea, I Go by Land*. New York: a Dell Yearling Book. *Front wrapper 192 × 130 mm (image 157 × 117 mm), black line with blue wash foregrounding two children on a ship, typographic lettering in red. Travers's story of two children evacuated to the U.S. was first published in 1941 with drawings by Gertrude Hermes (London: Peter Davies; New York: Harper). This U.S. paperback edition can only be explained as having been prompted by the film of Travers's* Mary Poppins.

B33. 1970 Kenneth Lindley. *Coastline*. Hutchinson. *Design in four colours, front and spine, based on a watercolour of Southend.*

B34. 1970 *A Piano Recital by Moura Lympany* [charity concert programme]. *Watercolour (198 × 146 mm) of children in a garden; no titling. Signed 'E.A.' on card wrapper.*

B35. 1970 William Woodruff. *Vessel of Sadness*. Chatto and Windus. *Monochrome version of a painting by E.A. reproduced by permission of the Imperial War Museum, running from inner front flap to a portion of the rear cover.*

B36. 1975 Cyril Ray (editor). *The Compleat Imbiber 9*. Collins. *The wrap-round design in line, with a single colour, is repeated on the boards of the binding (see also item C36 below).*

B37. 1978 *Britische Bücher*. The British Council. *A catalogue produced for the Frankfurt Book Fair in card covers with a wrap-round d.j. in line and water-colour by E.A. (featuring, incongruously, two boys fighting on a sea-front). The design was taken from a painting and was not prepared by the artist as a catalogue-cover.*

B38. 1978 Olivia Manning. *The Battle Lost and Won*. Weidenfeld and Nicolson. *Full-colour jacket using on the front the painting 'Wounded Man being Lifted into a Jeep' from the Imperial War Museum.*

Monotype

Hand Composition

From the *Curwen Press Newsletter* (1938 item C1, reduced)

C: COMMERCIAL BROCHURES AND EPHEMERA

While designing book jackets served the double function of doing work for a (fairly) quick return and developing contacts with publishers' editors, more run-of-the-mill commercial work was also of value to those set upon the uncertainties of a career in book-illustration. Payment, of course, usually carried no royalty, but at least it would be more or less on the nail for work which did not require sustained attention.

In the early periods of his career E.A. readily turned his hand to whatever jobs came along and the following selective list of work thus undertaken has been organised according to a chronological sequence rather than a 'classified' one. Access to the categories, which are given at the start of each entry, can be gained through the index.

The miscellaneous character of this section should carry the message that the tally of items has been gathered in a fairly serendipitous way and that no claims are made for its completeness. I should also point out first that the inclusion of greeting cards does not include family Christmas cards (which are discussed in the note to item C8 below) and second that the work done for periodicals which is included in this section consists mainly of 'one-off' commissions. Regular work for periodicals is briefly listed in section D below.

Ephemera such as exhibition catalogues which re-use previously published artwork are (almost entirely) omitted, but may receive mention in the relevant note to the earlier publication.

C1. 1938 *Periodical illus./Postcards*: CURWEN PRESS NEWS-LETTER 15. [Plaistow: Curwen Press, 1938].

Crown 4°. 258 × 185 mm. The initial *Notes & News* announces a 'sidelight' in which E.A. *gives an imaginary and witty interpretation of the printing scene at Plaistow*. 10 pen drawings (around 90 × 136 mm), each showing various departments of the press at work (including a van on the streets and a salesman in a restaurant).

A description of this item is given against the first inset following p. 30 in Matrix *5 (Winter 1985), where eight of the hand-coloured drawings are also illustrated. In an accompanying article John Dreyfus records payment to E.A. for the ten drawings on 30 May 1938 of £31.0.0. An unspecified number of the drawings were also sold in the form of tinted postcards.*

C2. 1939 *Invitation card:* DRAWINGS BY E.A. THE NICHOLSON GALLERY The pleasure of your company is requested at the Private View … 15 March 1939.

Pale salmon-pink card, 168 × 127 mm. Pen drawing above letterpress invitation, all printed blue.

A picture from this exhibition, 'The Office Club', was reproduced in line and wash in the London Mercury *(no. 234, April 1939).*

C3. 1939 *Periodical frontispiece:* SIGNATURE: a Quadrimestrial of Typography and Graphic Arts. Ed. Oliver Simon. No. 11, March 1939. Plaistow: Curwen Press. Lithographed pen drawing, 250 × 185 mm, with E.A.'s script title 'Evening in Maida Vale'. Below is a typographic editorial legend, 'Above: Drawing by E.A. illustrator … [5 titles]'

A very similar image (reversed, and rendered as a chalk lithograph) appears at NAP 12, tentatively dated 1948 and noting E.A.'s pencilled title 'Lovers and a New Moon'.

C4. 1942 *Periodical cover:* PARADE Ed. Major H. L. Ruston … Published for the Three Services in the Middle East and Persia-Iraq Commands. Pr. in Egypt by Al Hidal, Cairo, for the Publishers P. R. (Publications) G.H.Q., M.E.F. No. 123, vol. 10, 19 December 1942.

Cover design (283 × 202 mm) for a Christmas number in two colours entitled 'The Soldiers Dream' or 'Christmas Eve at the Local'. Hand-lettered throughout (including ten speech-bubbles) by E.A.

Nicholas Ardizzone notes in his catalogue to the Ashmolean Centenary Celebration (item 2) that E.A. shared a studio with his fellow war-artist, Anthony Gross, 'in a room above the Army [Public Relations] magazine Parade'.

C5. 1945 *Party invitation:* [Army] H.Q. PUBLIC RELATIONS. Children's Christmas Party. [Rome], Saturday 6th January 1945.

Single sheet of paper (192 × 158 mm), the verso with the above announcement and details in English of the invitation and programme, with the note *No food will be available for anyone other than the children and their ten Italian attendants.* The recto bears a pen drawing by E.A. of Papà Natale at the feast, with a Christmas tree. A framed panel, hand-lettered by E.A., sets out the invitation in Italian.

In Diary of a War Artist *(item 163 above), under the date 19 December 1944, E.A. notes 'Finish my card for the children's party'. On 6 January 1945 however he left Rome for Florence thus missing the party. Other 'off-the-cuff' jobs which he did over this Christmas period include 'an Xmas airgraph for the 17/21 Lancers' (noted on 10 October) and the cards etc. mentioned above in the note to item 15. None of these has been seen but the Colin Mears Collection at Worthing Museum has a photocopy of a design incorporated in the official Christmas Mail air letter done for 8th Army Public Relations in Rome.*

C6. 1947 *Film brochure:* THE LIFE AND ADVENTURES OF NICHOLAS NICKLEBY by Charles Dickens [vig.] filmed by Ealing Studios, [1947].

Large post 4°. 270 × 210 mm. Pp. [16] stapled in thin card wrappers, the inner rear with imprint: *1947 [Credit] Produced by S. John Woods and pr. by Graphic Reproductions Ltd.* 10 illustrations *in toto* from autolithographs in pen, black crayon and varying combinations of 2 or 3 colours: t.p. vig., frontis., 2 further vigs., a double-page spread and a large tailpiece in text; full-page drawings on front and rear covers, with a further vig. on inner rear.

E.A. also made posters for the film, details of which – with further information – are given in NAP Suite XVI: Cinema Posters. *Brief details may also be found in* Projecting Britain; Ealing Studios Film Posters *ed. by David Wilson (British Film Institute, 1982).*

C7. 1947 *Periodical cover:* BOOKS OF THE MONTH Monthly Book Digest. London. Simpkin, Marshall, December 1947.

Cover design (174 × 143 mm) in line and watercolour by E.A. depicting the interior of a bookshop (one of his favourite subjects).

Published by Simpkin's, the historic book wholesaling house (bombed to bits in the blitz and at this time functioning from an underground garage beside Regent's Park), Books of the Month *was essentially a trade magazine which could be circulated to customers by booksellers with their own names and addresses overprinted.*

C8. 1948 *Christmas card:* ARTS COUNCIL.

White card (220 × 390 mm), single fold with a pen drawing on front and 3 further within, similar in style to the layout for the 1948 Bath Assembly programme (following item).

E.A. was an inveterate designer of Christmas cards, but mostly for the private use of himself and his family. An informal (and hence not very well organised) account of these was given by Edward Booth-Clibborn in My Father and Edward Ardizzone: a Lasting Friendship *(1983) which illustrates some thirty cards which Catherine and Edward Ardizzone sent to their friends from 1934 onwards. The early cards were probably printed in smallish numbers from line blocks, and occasionally they reproduced images related to those in published work. 'Christmas Eve at the Warrington' and* The Local *(1939), for instance, or 'The Saloon Bar at the Prince Alfred', taken directly from, with an acknowledgement to,* Back to the Local *(1949). The run of post-war cards that are now to be fairly regularly encountered were reproductions of autholithographs usually run-off at the Royal College and unsigned copies in good condition are almost certainly from a posthumously published set of some 16 cards produced by the Curwen Studio in 1981*

C9. 1948 *Festival programme:* THE BATH ASSEMBLY. A Festival of the Arts 21st April–1st May 1948.

Paper sheet (213 × 273 mm), folded twice vertically. The letterpress programme is decorated with 5 drawings by E.A. in line and with 2-colour overlays: title design and illustrations for inner panels of 'Opera', 'Play', 'Orchestral Concerts' and the 'Pump Room'.

C10. 1948 *Menu:* DOUBLE CROWN CLUB. Menu for the 92nd Dinner on 14 January.

Single fold (183 × 255 mm). Pen drawing by E.A. on front, printed on pale blue paper.

The Double Crown Club was founded in 1924 by Oliver Simon and Hubert Foss as 'a dining club where people interested in the arts of the book could meet together'. Being 'sceptical as to the ability of … restaurants to supply suitably printed menus' the design of these bills of fare fell to various members and it was ruled that at each dinner the Chairman should criticise the result. E.A.'s drawing shows the staircase at Kettner's where the Club regularly dined at this period. Recognisable members such as Barnett Freedman and Simon himself are depicted. The drawing has been reproduced elsewhere on a number of occasions, including John Dreyfus's article on the Club in Matrix 6 *(see Sources p. 284).*

C11. 1949 *Christmas card:* J.W.T. [i.e. John Walter Thompson agency] Berkeley Square, London.

White card (90 × 350 mm), single fold with 3-colour overlays depicting snowballing in the square.

C12. 1949 *Christmas card:* ENGERT & ROLFE LTD. Barchester Street, London E.14.

White card (285 × 254 mm), single fold with a pen drawing of 'the festive board' on front.

C13. 1949 *Periodical cover:* UNCOMMON PLEASURES The Seventeenth Contact Book. London: Contact Publications Ltd., December 1949.

287 × 215 mm (image 153 × 198 mm). Cover design in line with 3 overlays of a fairground scene; signed 'E.A.' (cropped).

The Contact Books *were edited by A. G. Weidenfeld with Nigel Nicolson as deputy editor (from which the future may be inferred). They were published as substantial 'thematic' magazines at regular (usually bi-monthly) intervals.*

C14. 1950 *Film brochure:* THE MAGNET [cover-title in E.A.'s cursive script below a pen-drawn version of a scene from the film, with a single blue-grey overlay].

Small crown 4°. 237 × 178 mm. Pp. [16] including self-wrappers. White art paper, with a credit-list for the film in E.A.'s hand serving as a t.p. and 6 pen drawings with a single overlay: t.p. drawing, 4 half-page and 1 full-page. The rear wrapper has a wood-engraved cartouche for *Ealing Studios* (by Reynolds Stone?) and the imprint: *Produced by S. John Woods with drawings by E.A. Pr. by the Shenval Press, London and Hertford.*

For details of related material see NAP Suite XVI: Cinema Posters.

C15. [1950?] *Leaflet:* PICTURE LENDING LIBRARY. Association of International Artists.

Paper (202 × 404 mm), single fold, the front with a pen drawing of a lady looking at prints and a gent borrowing one. Signed 'DIZ'.

C16. 1950 *Periodical illus.:* WEATHER NEWS FRONT: a Bimonthly Newsletter on the Weather Written by David Bowen and Illustrated by E.A.

Small Crown 8°. 185 × 122 mm. Pp. [8]. Pen-drawn vig. on wrapper and 2 illustrations by E.A. for no. 1 (January–February) and vig. with 1 illus. for no. 2 (March–April).

C17. 1950 *Menu covers:* OVERTON'S.

Card (320 × 400 mm), single fold. Lithograph worked at the Curwen Press in black crayon and four colours by E.A. then transferred to plates. The front has 2 panels showing diners, the rear shows diners entering and leaving with an advertisement panel. Unsigned.

This menu cover for the restaurant in Victoria 'celebrated for its oysters, lobsters … with a cellar of magnificent wines …', was printed with its reverse side blank so that varying menus could subsequently be printed on it. A version reduced in size to 226 × 318 mm was printed with harsher colouring around 1989. Similar lithographic menu covers were also devised by E.A. in the later 1950s for the associated restaurants Overton's St James's (a wrap-round scene of diners) and Hatchetts, Piccadilly, 'London's Celebrated English Eating House'. For extensive details of these covers and of the restaurants see NAP Suite XVIII.

C18. 1951 *Flyer:* LONDON SEASON OF THE ARTS Festival of Britain. May–June 1951.

Pen-drawn design with overlays, somewhat akin to item C9 above, showing an orchestra, visitors to a gallery, and a balletic opera with sinuous cartouches: *Concerts, Galleries, Drama, Museums, Opera, Ballet.* The design was presumably for all-purpose use during the Season and the copy noted (180 × 115 mm), faced the cast-list for H. M. Tennent's production of 'The Little Hut'.

C19. 1951 *Menu:* SOCIETY OF INDUSTRIAL ARTISTS.

Pen drawing within a double-ruled frame (165 × 295 mm), on the cover of the menu for the 21st Anniversary Dinner of the Society.

— **[1951?]** *Game:* FARMER & PIG: a Chase Game for Two.

Single sheet with a first draft in pen with colour washes by E.A. of a table-game, with rules set out bottom left, suggested to him by a (now unknown) collaborator. The design – entertaining in itself – suggests commercial potential but was never exploited. Its display at the Camberwell exhibition in 1999 evoked much interest. See colour plate III.

C20. 1952 *Invitation:* THE LEICESTER GALLERIES, Leicester Square, London. New Year Exhibition of 19th and 20th Century Artists. Private View Tues. Jan 1st 1952.

Card (125 × 138 mm). Pen drawing with hand-lettering, signed 'DIZ', of the crush at the view.

C21. 1952 *Periodical cover:* IMPRESSIONS The House Organ of the Hazell-Sun Group 2–3 (Autumn 1952).

Crown 4°. 246 × 188 mm. Pen drawing of a compositor with a press in the background, signed 'DIZ', within a central oval on front wrapper. (Front wrapper only seen.)

C22. 1952 *Christmas card*: HAZELL WATSON & VINEY LTD. 52 Long Acre, London WC2.

Cream card (167 × 428 mm), single fold, the front with letterpress titling *The Composing Room at Long Acre* with *Original drawing by E.A.* below and unsigned pen drawing with 3-colour overlay. Greetings on inner recto.

This image is also found as a larger line-block print (190 × 260 mm) probably printed to memorialize the closing of the Long Acre works in 1958. An edition of around 50 copies has been mooted, hand-coloured (perhaps by Raymond Hazell's wife) after a 'model' by E.A.

The day I was bought might have been yesterday.

From *The Tale of an Old Tweed Jacket* ([1952?] item *C23*)

C23. [1952?] *Publicity booklet*: THE TALE OF AN OLD TWEED JACKET [vig.] Specially Written for Moss Bros. of Covent Garden by Eric Keown with illus. by E.A. [Imprint on inner rear wrapper]: Produced for Moss Bros & Co. Ltd. by T. B. Browne Ltd., London W.1.

Demy 8°. 215 × 140 mm. Pp. [2] 3–20, including thin glazed card wrappers. 14 illustrations *in toto* by E.A.: pen and watercolour drawing on front cover, plus 5 of the same printed full-page landscape; t.p. vig. and 6 other pen drawings in text; 1 vig. printed sepia on inner front cover and repeated on rear.

The Tale *is cast in the time-honoured form of the jacket's autobiography, now very redolent of mothballs. Moss Bros (as tailors rather than hirers) figure with commendable brevity, unlike Messrs Blumenthal in the puffs at item C30 below.*

With best Wishes
for Christmas and
The New Year
from
T. S. Eliot

From Faber's 1953 Christmas card (item C24, reduced)

C24. 1953 *Christmas card:* FABER AND FABER, 24 Russell Square, London, 1953.

Card (142 × 362 mm), single fold, depicting 3 bookshop scenes in pen and watercolour on the front and the two inner pages. The first is signed 'DIZ', and the third has a panel superimposed with a typographic greeting.

The copy examined had been signed by T. S. Eliot (see above). E.A. liked drawing bookshop scenes and this design has a close relationship to the panoramic view that featured in Ark *at this time (see Sources p. 278, 'Some Random Thoughts').*

C25. 1954 *Flyer:* THE LONDON MAGAZINE. Introducing a New Literary Journal, ed. by John Lehmann.

Paper (sheet size 200 × 380 mm), folded once vertically, the front with a pen drawing of a man reading at a bookstall, with a yellow overlay. Signed 'DIZ'.

The drawing was also used from February 1954 to March 1961 as a t.p. vig. for the magazine (item C26 below). In his preface to the 1972 Hand-list *John Cotton drew attention to this drawing: 'In three square inches E.A. not only manages to suggest the movement and bustle of a large city, but to capture that magic moment when a new issue of a magazine so catches the imagination that we are oblivious to all around us.'*

C26. 1954 *Title-page vignette:* THE LONDON MAGAZINE ed. by John Lehmann. Pr. in G.B. for the Proprietors of 'The Daily Mirror' Newspapers Ltd. … and distributed by Chatto & Windus.

First published February 1954, with the t.p. vignette noted above (item C25).

During 1954 E.A. had three pen drawings published in the magazine: 'Copper-Quick!', related to the etching NAP 63 (vol. 1, no. 4, May 1954, p.46); 'She may have a lot to forget, poor thing', related to the etching NAP 45 (vol. 1, no. 6, July 1954, p. 74); and 'Private Bar' (vol. 1, no. 7, August 1954, p. 44).

C27. 1954 *Menu:* PARLIAMENTARY PRESS GALLERY LUNCHEON Savoy Hotel. 30 November 1954.

Cream card (170 × 440 mm), single fold, the front a reproduction of the watercolour by E.A. of Churchill speaking at the dispatch box (size of the original – which hangs on the staircase at Chartwell – around 200 × 400 mm). The luncheon was given by the PPG to Sir Winston to mark his 80th birthday, when the portrait was presented to him by E. R. Thompson, Chairman of the lobby journalists.

MS. DRAWINGS: Pages 68–73 of Sketchbook 16 carry preliminary sketches for this work.

The menu itself was printed on paper fastened within the card with a blue ribbon, the whole printed by George Over Ltd, London and Rugby. (Communicated; my informant, Mr Pat Ashton – to whom many thanks – notes that a number of Churchill's front bench are immediately recognisable in the portrait. He also gives the menu itself, which happily includes Le Supreme de Sole Dieppoise.)

C28. 1955 *Brochure:* GAME PIE: a Guinness Indoor Sportfolio [cover title; imprint on inner rear cover]: Designed … by S. H. Benson Ltd. Illustrations by E.A. Pr. by W.S. Cowell Ltd, Ipswich on John Dickinson 'Evensyde' paper, [1955 (date derived from printer's code *GA/21/30/55*)].

Royal 8°. 230 × 160 mm. Pp. [24]. With 12 full-page drawings by E.A. in line and watercolour, plus double-page centre spread, all with inset un-coloured panels with verses, mostly on 'social' games: 'Dominoes', 'Darts', 'Skittles' etc. § Trimmed and stapled into untrimmed paper covers bearing a composite scene by E.A. featuring 7 of the games and his hand-lettered titling.

No. 13 in the bibliography of the Guinness Christmas booklets in The Book of Guinness Advertising *by Brian Sibley (Enfield: Guinness Books, 1985), where the verses are attributed to Stanley Penn and John Trench. E.A.'s association with Guinness also extended to poster designs. 'The Fattest Woman in the World' (1956), done for a series inspired by* The Guinness Book of Records, *is described and illustrated at NAP 85 but no mention occurs there of the famous 'Guinness for Strength' poster of 1954, a watercolour and gouache draft for which was exhibited at the Ashmolean Museum in 2000 (cat. item 21).*

C29. 1955 *Leaflet:* LONDON GROUP PRINTS. Zwemmer Gallery.

Blue paper (sheet size 212 × 286 mm), single fold, the front with a pen drawing printed maroon of a group-member showing a folder to a gentle-man of military bearing. Signed 'DIZ'.

What may be a draft for a poster relating to the Group's Exhibition is in Sketch-book 40.

C30. 1955 *Brochure:* LET'S HAVE A PARTY [below a large vig. by E.A. and above an explanatory puff, all within a framed fleuron border printed pale blue; faced by publishing details]: A 'Fine Drinking' Book Issued by the Houses of Ayala Champagne, Croizet Brandy & Rocher Liqueurs, Sole Concessionaires for the U.K. Blumenthals Ltd. ... London, [1955].

Large crown 8°. 203 × 133 mm. Pp. [1] 2–19 [1]. With 9 pen drawings by E.A.: t.p. vig., 3 headpieces, 3 full-page, 2 tailpieces. § Stapled into paper wrappers.

The booklet was printed at the Curwen Press and acknowledges neither date nor illustrator.

C31. 1956 *Brochure:* THE PICK KNITWEAR STORY 1856–1956 [vig.] by J. P. Pick [Credit] Pr. for J. Pick & Sons Ltd. by C. H. Gee & Co. Ltd. Leicester, [1956].

Demy 8°. 215 × 140 mm. Pp. [6] 5–45 [1]. With 8 pen drawings: t.p. vig. and tailpiece in sanguine, 5 in text with descriptive legends, 1 repeat and 1 new design on card wrappers.

E.A. also provided pen drawings for a series of Pick Knitwear advertisements that appeared in Out of Doors *magazine around 1948. These and drawings in the brochure are based upon a quantity of drafts in* Sketchbook 2.

C32. 1956 *Ceramics:* COUNTRY PLEASURES.

A set of six plates, 250 mm in diameter, each bearing on a decorated rim a lower cartouche labelled in E.A.'s script *Country Pleasures* and an upper one naming the pleasure depicted in the centre of the plate: 'Bathing', 'Boating', 'Courting', 'Drinking', 'Fishing' and 'The Picnic'. Transfers in black and grey from drawings by E.A., some of which have also featured as paintings. Manufactured by the New Chelsea China Co. Ltd.

Six further designs were projected but not made: 'Birds-Nesting', 'Cricket', 'Darts', 'Gossiping', 'The Meet' and 'Point-to-Point'. One or two jeux d'esprit *exist where E.A. and his friend John Verney decorated plain, fired pottery for the fun of it, including a mug with a milking-scene, oval dishes in the style of 'Country Pleasures'; but these were never intended for production.*

'Courting' from the 'Country Pleasures' series (1956 item C32)

C33. 1958 *Menu:* DOUBLE CROWN CLUB 145th Dinner at the Royal Pavilion Brighton 13 June 1958.

Pale brown paper (200 × 292 mm), French-fold, with two pen drawings by E.A.: guests outside the Pavilion (cover) and *The Annual Outing* (inner recto). Colophon on outside verso: *Drawings by E.A. Printed by The Westerham Press.*

The illus. of club members outside the Pavilion was reproduced at the end of E.A.'s article 'The Born Illustrator' in Motif 1 *(November 1958).*

Front cover of a menu for the Omar Khayyám Club,
24 November 1966 (item C35(iii), reduced)

C34. 1959 *Brochure:* PUTTING IT SIMPLY [vig.] a Conversation about Unit Trusts [cover title printed in red and black, imprint on rear cover]: The 'Bank – Insurance' Group … Designed by C. Vernon & Sons Ltd. and pr. … by Metcalfe & Cooper Ltd., [1959].

Non-standard format. 200 × 94 mm. Pp. 8. With 6 pen drawings by E.A., the headpiece on p. 1 also used as title vig. § Stapled into paper covers and brown kraft paper wrappers with flaps. The inner front flap acknowledges *Drawings by E.A.*, the inner rear gives the date *2nd November 1959*.

C35. 1961 *Menu:* OMAR KHAYYÁM CLUB. Menu and List of those Present for the Dinner at Kettner's on March 23rd, 1961.

Card (227 × 406 mm), single fold. Pen drawing by E.A. signed 'DIZ' on front with pale orange overlay, illustrating the stanza 'While the rose blows along the river brink …'.

Three further menus for Club dinners at Kettner's can be recorded, all on card (273 × 404 mm), single fold, with a pen drawing by E.A. on the front:

(i) 28 November 1963. 'And as the cock Crew, those who stood before …'.
(ii) 30 March 1965. 'And we that now make merry in the room …' (single line only).
(iii) 24 November 1966. 'Ah, fill the cup: – What boots it to repeat …' (two lines only). For a reproduction see opposite.

E.A. was installed as President of the Club in 1968.

C36. 1962 *Catalogue:* WINE LIST Second Edition: 1962–1963. Bristol: John Harvey & Sons Limited.

Large post 8°. 208 × 132 mm. Pp. [2] 3–87 [1]. Designed by John Lewis; maps by Sheila Waters; pr. by The Millbrook Press, Southampton. 25 pen drawings by E.A. § Card wrappers panelled in olive green and orange, with 4 of E.A.'s illustrations black on white down the outer margin of the rear wrapper.

Vignette from Harvey's *Wine List* (1962 item C36),
illustrating a quotation from (and depicting) W. M. Thackeray

[1962?] ANOTHER EDITION: as above, but subtitled 'for clubs, colleges, messes and hotels.' Pp. [2] 3–80. Pr. by Partridge & Love Ltd., Wick, Bristol on different paper stocks, the wrappers panelled in turquoise and brown. All E.A.'s drawings are included, but the contents, information and pricing tables are at variance with the general edition (e.g. Vosne Romanée, Tête de Cuvée 1955 changes from 30s. a bottle to 316s. a dozen or 164s. a dozen halves). There is also a mark-up guide.

[1964?] COMPOSITE EDITION: WINE LIST DECORATIONS 1961–1963. Wood-engravings by David Gentleman; decorations by Asgeir Scott; illustrations by E.A.; maps by Sheila Waters. Bristol etc. Royal 8°. 243 × 157 mm. Pp. [6] 7–100 [4]. Printed on varying stocks of paper for the different sections: introduction and maps on pale salmon laid, wood-engravings on an off-white Basingwerk parchment, decorations on pale buff laid, E.A.'s illus. on a creamy cartridge, by the Millbrook Press. Quarter calf stained black, dec. chintz boards, purple endpapers. t.e.g. slip-case. (Devitt, *Ardizzone* 2 (item 156), reports a cheaper binding in full buckram). *This rather pompous affair celebrates the publisher's and designer's taste in graphic art and is devoted primarily to reproducing the illus. from the previous lists without the encumbrance of vinous data and commercial prices. E.A.'s drawings are reproduced one to a page on pages 63–87 and are preceded by an introductory pen drawing, 'A splendid nose', and a page containing 4 vignettes. A prospectus* Announcing a Book of Wine List Decorations *is noted by Devitt (as above, item 154) with the 'fine nose' drawing on the cover. From the introductions to the various sections it would seem that the first edition of these lists was illustrated by Gentleman, the second (which included recipes) by Scott, and hence the third by E.A., not the 'second' as designated.*

1972 SELECTED REPRINTS: Denis Morris's *Daily Telegraph Guide to the Pleasures of Wine* (London & Glasgow: Collins) has 14 of the drawings with their accompanying quotes, acknowledged on p. 187. Published in two bindings: in red linson boards with d.j., and in very dark navy blue padded *faux* morocco, looking rather like a hymn book, with endpapers and edges marbled blue.

The original edition was the third of an annual series of wine lists illustrated by artists chosen by John Lewis (see above). E.A.'s 25 pen drawings are placed above quotations drawn from literary and other works, all aptly arranged to refer to appropriate beverages. The selection of the quotations and the task of reading 'the whole jolly book to find out what the people look like' are the subject of an illuminating conversation between E.A. and Warwick Barraclough printed in Vintage, *a journal published by Harvey's (vol. 2, no. 4, Winter 1962, pp. 18–21), reproducing 9 of E.A.'s pen drawings, one in purple (the cover is, fittingly, a Rowlandson drawing of a bibulous banquet.)[9] In addition to the three later publications mentioned above, six drawings were also used in Wyndham Fletcher's* Port: an Introduction to its History and Delights *(London: Sotheby Parke Bernet, 1978), and one drawing, blown up and with red overlay, was used for the cloth binding of* The Compleat Imbiber 9 *(see item B36).*

C37. 1962 *Brochure:* THE LAYMAN'S GUIDE TO DOCTORS By Paul Jennings [Credit]: with Compliments and Greetings for Christmas and the New Year. C. L. Bencard, [1962 (dated from printer's code *S.962*)] [cover title].

Crown 8°. 226 × 140 mm. Pp. [2] 3–11 [1], including wrappers. With 5 pen drawings (cover vig. and 4 in text). § Pink washed wrappers.

An advertising brochure commending an aspirin tablet, 'Paynocil', with some satiric remarks at the expense of the profession.

9. In *Vintage* (vol. 3, no. 3, Spring 1964, pp. 6–7) E.A. provides three pen drawings for for an article by Robin McDougall, 'Drink Wine in its own Home'.

C38. [1963?] *Christmas card:* HARVEYS OF BRISTOL.

Cream card (145 × 373 mm), single fold, *Printed by Partridge & Love Ltd. Bristol.* The front an illustration in sepia line and watercolour by E.A.: a Victorian lady examining a glass of sherry in Harvey's cellar, with the letterpress legend *If that is Bristol Milk, then this must be the cream.* The inner verso of the card gives the story behind this remark, said to have been made by a French visitor in 1882, and acknowledges *the scene as imagined by E.A., A.R.A.* The inner recto bears a printed greeting.

C39. 1964 *Greetings cards:* UNICEF.

A set of 4 cards (117 × 290 mm), single fold. E.A. depicts in line and watercolour on the front of each: African children with drummers; Arabian children on a flying carpet; English children looking in a toyshop; and Indian children looking at an elephant.

C40. [1965?] *Advertising postcard:* 'THE GASWORKS' 87 Waterford Road. London S.W.6.

Pen drawing (60 × 75 mm), signed 'Drawn by E. Ardizzone', in the left-hand upper corner of a postcard (90 × 140 mm) advertising an eating-house ('Cuisine au Patron') just off the lower King's Road. A map across the bottom of the card, not by E.A., gives directions.

C41. 1965 *Catalogue cover:* THE MAYOR GALLERY. An exhibition of watercolours and drawings by E.A.

Card (185 × 197 mm), the front bearing a pen drawing, signed 'DIZ', of the Gallery's window with Freddy Mayor (an old school-friend of E.A.'s) peeping over the backing-curtain at potential customers.

C42. 1965 *Menu:* DOUBLE CROWN CLUB. Menu for the 180th Dinner on 25 June 1965.

Card (210 × 533 mm), folded twice vertically to give a centre panel 210 mm square. Pp. [1] 2–5 [1]. Three pen drawings by E.A. printed sepia: *The Arrival* on front (see opposite), *The Dinner* (centre) and *The Departure* (verso

The Arrival

From the Double Crown Club menu, 25 June 1965 (item C42, reduced)

of centre) with acknowledgements to E.A., John Bell (designer), Pegasus (material), and Westerham (printers).

For a previous menu with details of the D.C.C. see item C9 above. On p. 2 of the present menu John Bell has composed a double acrostic for the words Double Crown Club and Burlington House.

C43. [1967] *Greetings telegram:* BIRTHDAY GREETINGS TELE-GRAM G.P.O.

Card (214 × 374 mm), single-fold illustrated throughout in red ink line and watercolour and hand-lettered by E.A. The outer pages with a blue wash and a family scene with a postman on the front and a framed greeting on the rear; the inner pages have a pink wash and two festive scenes to the left and a space for the telegram superimposed on present-giving scenes to the right. The telegram card is accompanied by an envelope whose front has a green wash border with pen drawings and lettering in red by E.A.

Several trial designs for the telegram were exhibited at Camberwell in 1999.

C44. 1966 *Masthead vignette:* THE IDLER an Entertainment. Published quarterly at The Old Crown, Wheatley, Oxford. (An Editorial Associates publication).

A tabloid-size quarterly printed on newsprint, the masthead having a vig. by E.A. (42 × 70 mm) showing a fisherman fast asleep under an opened copy of the paper itself (see p. 309). The Editorial Associates were shy of dating their publication but vol. 2. no. 1 (1967?) has an article by Marina Vaizey on 'The Enduring Art of Edward Ardizzone' (see Sources p. 286).

C45. 1969 *Invitation map:* A PARTY at the Royal College of Art 2 January 1969.

Card (203 × 150 mm), single horizontal fold. Outer front a pen-drawn map with directions hand-lettered by E.A.; outer rear the invitation from E.A. and James Reeves in the artist's cursive script. Inner pages blank.

C46. 1969 *Letterhead and script appeal-letter:* ON BEHALF OF THE ARTISTS GENERAL BENEVOLENT INSTITUTION.

Photocopy (as issued?) (330 × 205 mm) of a letter of appeal dated from Elgin Avenue and reproduced throughout in E.A.'s cursive hand with his signature as Steward for the R.A. 1969–1970. At the head is a pen sketch (90 × 150 mm) of a painter working in a garret with a crying child and a child being nursed in the background.

C47. 1971 *Menu:* ROYAL COLLEGE OF ART. Menu for Wine Committee Retrospective on 2 February 1971.

Card (210 × 432 mm), single fold. Pen drawing by E.A. signed 'DIZ': 'A Toast to Robin [Darwin]'.

At some date, probably previous to the above, E.A. also designed a letter-heading for the Royal College of Art Senior Common Room Wine Committee. A line block, printed sepia on pinkish writing paper, sheet size 330 × 185 mm. The masters of wine here represented are Robin Darwin, Robert Gooden, Eddie LaDell, Kenneth Rowntree and E.A. himself.

C48. 1972 *Calendar:* A HORN BOOK CALENDAR 1973 Selected from Illustrations by E.A. Boston, MA: The Horn Book Inc., 1972.

Thin card (166 × 128 mm), 14 leaves fastened with a plaited green silk tie at the head to a thicker card backing. The upper halves of the cover and the cards for the 12 months are decorated with illustrations taken from eight books, acknowledged to E.A. and the U.S. publishers; 7 of the blocks have a green overlay, the rest are plain. The final leaf is printed on both sides with an appreciation of E.A. by Lee Kingman, author, editor and Council Member of The Horn Book, Inc.

Although this item has no new illus. by E.A. it is included here as representing a slightly unusual (but successful) re-use of some of his drawings.

C49. 1979 *Calendar:* CALENDAR for Mackays of Chatham [printers].

Lithographic print (294 × 395 mm) of the 'The Drinkers' set at the head of a standard monthly office calendar. The design also exists as a separate lithographic print (see NAP 49).

C50. 1979 *Invitation card:* EDWARD ARDIZZONE at Illustrators Art 12 November 1979.

Postcard (104 × 117 mm). Pen drawing on front depicting the small and not-very-long-lived gallery of Robin Johnson in D'Arblay Street, with customers leaving and ladies waiting (for what?) on the pavement. Signed 'E.A.' and presumably one of the last drawings that he executed, the lettering on the gallery fascia shows some frailty.

The exhibition was organised to celebrate the publication of Gabriel White's biography and Gabriel made a memorial speech for the artist who had died on 8 November (see Appendix V). In 1981 the Gallery also showed a selection of lithographs, etchings and drawings to coincide with the publication of Visiting Dieppe *(item A11 above).*

Vignettes from *The Strand Magazine* (item D2)

D: DRAWINGS FOR PERIODICALS
AND ADVERTISING

Looking back to my schooldays in the late 1940s I find that (never having encountered Ardizzone's book work) I first became aware of his presence as an illustrator through his appearance in *Radio Times* and later in *Punch*. 'Diz' was not just a memorable signature – as 'Phiz' must have been a hundred years earlier – but it was a guarantee that the drawing above it or around it would have something to say and something to enjoy.

For that reason alone I should have attended far more closely to this section of my survey than I have done. In delving through some of the journals noted below I have not come across a single drawing by 'Diz' that did not have some touch to commend it and the totality of his contributions from the 1930s to the 1950s may be seen as vital both for sustaining his freelance income and creating his reputation as a great graphic artist.

'Totality' however is the drawback. Consistency would have demanded that if I had examined any one of the journals noted below in their entirety I should do so for all of them and I have, I am afraid, flinched at that undertaking. What I have done though is to list the titles of those publications for which E.A. drew with at least some regularity over a given period of time, organising them in chronological order according to his first (or an early) contact with them and annotating my entries with any individual points of interest.

DI. 1932– RADIO TIMES and THE LISTENER.

Founded in 1923, *Radio Times* was at first edited alongside *Titbits* in the offices of George Newnes Ltd. Such was its success that the Corporation brought it under its own wing in 1927 when Eric Maschwitz became editor, to be followed in 1933 by Maurice Gorham, who had previously been responsible for commissioning illustrations for the paper.

Gorham, a childhood friend of E.A., has already figured in this volume (items 9, 26, 32 and 33 above) and the opportunity which he offered for regular work with *Radio Times* was one of the determining factors in the artist's pre-war career. The opening came about when Gorham visited one of E.A.'s one-man shows (perhaps at the Leger Gallery in 1931) and E.A. began to fulfil commissions in 1932. A toned drawing 'In Tonight's Vaudeville' published on 26 February may have been the first.

E.A. was an ideal contributor. In practical terms he had the ability to work to the exact proportions required for the pre-planned placing of the illustrations and to complete the work within the regular three-day deadline. And as an interpreter he fulfilled the demands adumbrated by a later Art Editor, R. D. Usherwood: ... *it may be understood that the highest quality required of an illustrator is intelligence. He must be able to read with understanding and sympathise with his author's intentions ... Many people draw quite beautifully and yet are not equipped to know exactly what they are drawing; there are comparatively few whose hand is guided by understanding of their subject* (from *Drawing for Radio Times*, p. 10).

Throughout the 1930s therefore E.A. is to be found frequently in the weekly numbers, joining a band of regular contributors who were also commissioned to do more extensive work, such as the eight toned drawings 'Back Stage at Covent Garden' (7 June 1935), and full-colour Christmas Number covers (23 December 1932 and 24 December 1937).

Regular commissions of this kind did much to stabilize E.A.'s finances at a time when he was having to make his way as a freelance, but his pleasure in the work and his experience ensured that he would be called upon as a reliable contributor after the war. His work continued to appear until the late 1950s, when *Radio Times* began its terminal decline as an upholder of Reithian ideals. Among special contributions are monochrome pen drawings for a Christmas Number cover (24 December 1948), a four-page inset 'Come Carolling' with a title-piece and 15 drawings (19 December 1958, but also separately issued, printed on thin card) and a 'Spring' cover (18 May 1956). For a vignette from December 1953 see p. 248.

Original drawings have figured in exhibition catalogues such as that of the Scottish Arts Council, and in selling-catalogues of galleries, such as the New Grafton, Sally Hunter and Wolseley Fine Arts, and of booksellers, such as Nial and Margaret Devitt. On the evidence of these and of a note by R. D. Usherwood, E.A. can be seen as making his drawings proportionally exact, but larger than required, feeling that photographic reduction helped to 'tighten' the image.

His connection with *Radio Times* also led the artist into some commissions for its less-heavily-illustrated sister paper *The Listener*. Occasional drawings, including a cover for 26 May 1955, have been noted between 27 June 1940 and 20 December 1962.

D2. 1942–1947 THE STRAND MAGAZINE.

Founded in 1891, the *Strand* was moving towards a graceful end when Ardizzone undertook his first substantial work for it in its October issue of 1946. Published at this stage of its history in crown octavo format (196 × 134 mm), it would have shared the bookstalls with such breezy competitors as *Lilliput* and *Men Only*, but its editor, Macdonald Hastings, sustained a far more ambitious standard for its contents, numbering many leading post-was authors and illustrators among its contributors. (What price Graham Greene illustrated by Brian Robb, or Kingsley Martin assessed by C. E. M. Joad with a caricature in colour by Osbert Lancaster?)

Ardizzone had made one war-time appearance in the magazine, illustrating Thomas Burke's 'The Eternal Cockney' in June 1942, but between October 1946 and December 1947 he was its most prominent contributor. Each month, except July 1947, he produced a cover-picture in pen and watercolour, and at the same time (including July 1947) supplied drawings with one or two colours added for half-tone reproduction to accompany anonymous pieces by Macdonald Hastings. Twelve of these are the ruminations in a bar parlour of the sententious cockney, Mr Quill ('Mr. Quill on Money', 'Mr. Quill on Gratitude', etc.) for which E.A. was an obvious choice of illustrator (see David Garnett's remark quoted on p. 114), but he bowed out of the magazine in December 1947 with his thirteenth contribution, the 'Christmas Pantomime', which has been more fully detailed at item A4 above. The magazine closed in 1950.

During this stint E.A. was himself the subject of the 'Caricature of the Month' feature, introduced by Michael Ayrton and pictured by Osbert Lancaster (see Sources pp. 283).

D3. 1951–1954 LILLIPUT.

Lilliput was founded, as Kaye Webb has said, with 'cheerful independence' as a pocket magazine by Alison Blair and Stefan Lorant in August 1937. They were later joined by Sydney Jacobson, but, unable to finance their own success, they sold up to Edward Hulton in 1939 and the journal became part of the Hulton Press stable, soon to be joined by *Picture Post*.

Its fame is probably founded upon the great cartoonists who drew for it and upon its photographic content, especially the joyous nudes and the 'doubles' which juxtaposed totally unrelated objects and scenes as lookalikes.

Despite its full complement of pictures, *Lilliput* was for many years not so much an illustrator's patch as a decorator's, and cartoonists and artists were not formally acknowledged in the contents list or the text. By 1951 however the style of the magazine was changing, losing something of its sprightliness and attempting a more 'literary' image. Artists were given a by-line and E.A.'s contributions may well have been sought following his work at *Strand*. The first tone and single-wash drawings that I have noted appeared in vol. 29, no. 2 (August–September 1951), where he supplied two pen-drawings for an article by Maurice Richardson. Contributions continued down to 1954 and might be anything from full-page line and wash drawings to pen drawings in line or with a single colour wash added.

D4. 1953–1957 PUNCH.

When Ardizzone began illustrating for *Punch*, the magazine was only just starting to turn restive in the face of post-war changes. Hitherto slow and steady in the changes made to its editorial policies it still kept in touch with its origins through the famous cover by Dicky Doyle which had first been designed for January 1844, three years after *Punch* was founded.

Few magazines can have been so hospitable and so inspiring for so long to a nation's illustrators and the tradition was still in place when E.A. drew a headpiece with initial and two other drawings for 'Crayfish' by G.W. Stonier for the issue of 9 September 1953. At that time Stonier was a busy journalist with a particular liking for the London scene, and during the next three years E.A.'s pen drawings for *Punch* were mostly done for Stonier pieces. (They were more numerous and often more elaborate than the selection that appeared in *Pictures on the Pavement*, item 47 above.)[10]

The artist's skills were not lost on the editor however and between his first drawings and his last in 1957 he produced a number of full-page pen and wash drawings which were reproduced in full colour (e.g. the colour-plate for Stonier's 'Art of the Pub Crawl', 2 November 1953; the cover

10. Ms. drawings for *Punch* are scattered to the winds (those for 'Girls, Girls, Girls' (*Punch* 7 April 1954) surfaced from a private collection at the Ashmolean exhibition in 2000, cat. no. 19). It is agreeable to note however that the drawings for Stonier's article on the London Library, 'Half a Million Books' (6 October 1954) are displayed for the entertainment of members near the Library's administrative offices. A shrunken reproduction appears in Miron Grindea's *The London Library* (Ipswich: The Boydell Press, 1978).

for the Autumn number, 15 September 1954; the cover for the Summer number, 25 May 1955; the cover for the Spring number, 11 April 1956; and a colour-plate of wine-tasters, 9 October 1957). Three of Stonier's pieces with E.A.'s full-dress accompaniments were reprinted in the annual volumes *The Pick of Punch*. These were 'Stranger, Pause' (1954, pp. 115 and 120), 'Southend Fling' (1955, pp. 100–101) and 'The Crystal Palace' (1956, pp. 16–17). The 1954 volume also included E.A.'s headpiece and 3-panel Indian street-scene for P. M. Hubbard's 'Don't Turn Round' (pp. 24–25).

Miscellaneous appearances: The preceding entries outline dates for some of E.A.'s regular appearances in periodicals, and a number of single or occasional appearances are noted in section C above. Evidence has also been found, either in E.A.'s records or in sundry catalogues, of other appearances in journals, and is set down here without any claims for completeness:

1932	Drawings in issue 16 of *New English Weekly* (2 February). See Devitt, *Ardizzone 1* (item 202).
1933	Drawings for the *Daily Herald*.
1934–1935	Drawings for the *Daily Express*.
1939	A drawing in the *London Mercury* no. 234 (April). See Devitt, *Ardizzone 1* (item 200).
1949	One or more drawings for *Leader*.
1950–1952	One or more drawings for *Housewife*.
1955–1959	Occasional appearances in *Collins's Magazine* (e.g. the colour cover for the December 1955 issue) and its successor *Young Elizabethan: the Magazine for Boys and Girls* ed. by Kaye Webb. E.A.'s full-colour cover design for vol. 10, no. 11 (November 1957) was later used in his article for the first *Puffin Annual* (item A31 above). (The magazine later became *Elizabethan*, for which E.A. drew a jolly kitchen scene for the cover of a Christmas number.)
1957	Drawings for a Christmas no. of *The Sketch*.

Advertising: Gabriel White notes in his biography of E.A. that the artist said early on that he would never make a successful commercial artist; and White endorses this reasonably enough by pointing out that his style was 'too anecdotal to drive home a message' and that 'his line suffered from the larger scale necessary for press advertisement'. In consequence, examples of E.A. drawing specifically for an advertising commission are few in number and occur, significantly, early in his career or at the point when he was re-establishing himself after the war:

Early, but untraced: 4 drawings for the slogan 'You'll feel better if you drink more Milk'.

1934   31 proofs have been noted for a series done for Johnnie Walker's with the slogan: 'I said to him – what about a drop of Johnnie Walker'.

1937   Drawings for Rothman's in *Radio Times*.

1938   Drawings from the *Curwen Press Newsletter* (item C1 above) may well have been used by Curwen as advertisements (Devitt, *Ardizzone 1* (item 199) has the drawing of compositors in an advert in *Horizon* for December 1945).

1947   At least one full-colour ad. for P & B Wools.

1948   A drawing for Westminster Bank in *Signature* (new series, no. 6).

1951   A drawing for Associated Electrical Industries.

1956   A sequence of drawings for Pick Knitwear (see item C31 above).

Needless to say, during the thirties E.A. was among the illustrators who caught Jack Beddington's eye in his revolutionary promotional work for Shell. Drawings were done for press advertising with the slogans 'You Can Be Sure of Shell' and 'Times Change So Does Shell'. See also section F below.

Vignette from *The Radio Times*,
18 December 1953 (item D1)

E: MENTIONING THE WAR

A distinction must be made between Ardizzone's life-long career as a free-lance artist and illustrator and the period of his work as an Official War Artist. Everything done within the terms of that appointment was part of the government enterprise to record 'the war through artists' eyes' and copyright was and remains the property of the Crown. A central repository for E.A.'s sketches, drawings and paintings is the Imperial War Museum, whence material can be dispersed to other public institutions, and the holdings are listed on pp. 2–15 of the Museum's World War 2 catalogue. They have also been the subject of a closely-detailed and heavily-illustrated doctoral dissertation by the artist's younger son, Nicholas (*Edward Ardizzone 1900–1979: Commissioned Work of the Second World War*, 1997) . This is as yet unpublished but may be consulted under the usual regulations at the Museum. A general account of the work of official war artists is given in *The War Artists* by Meiron and Susie Harries (London: Michael Joseph in association with the Imperial War Museum and the Tate Gallery, 1983).

Although the bulk of E.A.'s official work is made up of individual drawings, some of these have found their way into published books. *Baggage to the Enemy* and *The Battle of France* (items 14 and 12) are cases in point, but the dust-jacket only of the *Diary of a War Artist* (item 163) is copyright to the Crown.

In addition to the use of war drawings as illustrations integral to a given text, a number of occasions arise when they appear in books as reproductions of 'war art', much as any painter's work may find itself included in a book on a particular subject: *Edward Lear's Corfu*, for instance. Nevertheless, because of the special purpose behind the appointment of Official War Artists and the use of their work for information and (in the best sense) propaganda it seems appropriate here to give a number of entries for occasions and publications in which E.A.'s art may have had a significant representation.

E1. 1940 The first War Artists exhibition was held at the National Gallery in July and included paintings by E.A. who had joined the scheme in February. Among reviews of the show were the following:

Herbert Read. Pictures of the War. *The Listener.* 4 July 1940.
Eric Newton. [Review]. *Sunday Times.* 7 July 1940.
H. K. Official War Artists. *Jewish Chronicle.* 19 July 1940
Douglas Cooper. War Artists' Exhibition at the National Gallery.
    Burlington Magazine. Vol. 70, no. 451, October 1940.

See also item 13 above for Cooper and Freeman's Road to Bordeaux.

Three further summer exhibitions were held at the National Gallery in 1941, 1942 and 1943, and the following associated books were published:

E2. 1941 BRITAIN AT WAR Ed. by Monroe Wheeler. Text by T. S. Eliot, Herbert Read, E. J. Carter and Carlos Dyer. New York: The Museum of Modern Art.

Crown 4°. 98 pp. An illustrated handbook accompanying an exhibition at MOMA in May 1941, with a 'Catalog of Paintings and Drawings' on pp. 95–97. 12 watercolours by E.A. were included of which 'Priest Begging for a Lift' and 'A Pub in Silvertown' were illustrated in monochrome. T. S. Eliot's contribution was a poem 'Defense of the Islands' first published as a broadside in an edition of around 50 copies (Gallup E26).

E3. 1942 WAR PICTURES AT THE NATIONAL GALLERY. Printed for the Trustees by the Curwen Press.

Small crown 8°. [32] pp. 28 plates of which 5 were in colour. E.A. was featured with 'Camouflaged soldiers' in monochrome and 'Basement Ward, Royal Herbert Hospital' in colour.

1944 *New edition:* retaining 16 of the plates, including 'Camouflaged Soldiers', and adding 13 new ones, including E.A.'s 'Bivouac in the Evening' in colour. His work shown in this exhibition was the subject of a 2-page illustrated article 'War Artist in the Front Line' in the *Illustrated* magazine for 4 March 1944.

E4. 1942 BLITZ with an Introduction by J. B. Morton. London, New York, Toronto: Oxford University Press, 1942. (War Pictures by British Artists no. 2).

Crown 8°. 64 pp., including 48 pp. of monochrome half-tone reproductions. Pr. by Harrison & Sons Ltd. Printers to H. M. the King. Crown copyright reserved. § Thin card covers, blank; wrapper in 2 colours.

Includes reproductions of 8 pen and wash drawings by 'Captain Edward Ardizzone' who is noted, with Captain Anthony Gross, as holding 'a salaried post under the War Office'. Fourteen reproductions were similarly printed in Army, *with an intro. by Colin Coote (no. 4 in the series, 1942); thirteen in* Soldiers, *with an intro. by William Coldstream (no. 3 in the Second Series, 1943), and one in* Air Raids, *with an intro. by Stephen Spender (no. 4 in the same, 1943).*

E5. 1945 WAR THROUGH ARTISTS' EYES, paintings and drawings by British War Artists. Selected and introduced by Eric Newton. London: John Murray, 1945.

Crown 4°. 96 pp., of which 86 are plates displaying 121 examples in monochrome and colour. Eight are by E.A. of which two are in colour.

— **1947** TOLLER REPORTS. See item A5 above.

Barnett

Thumbnail portrait of Barnett Freedman from
Baggage to the Enemy (1941 item 14)

EX LIBRIS   HUMPHREY LOFTUS BROWN

Illustration from item 2 adapted as a bookplate

F: A NOTE ON PRINTS, POSTERS AND BOOKPLATES

In between Ardizzone's drawing for reproduction and his work as a painter there lies the rather indeterminate range of activity that he undertook as a printmaker. This is work that he was engaged in intermittently from almost the start of his career to around 1968 and it consists primarily of runs of lithographic prints with some etchings (a process which he did not much care for). The scale and the complex detailing of his prints – allied to his occasional commissions as a poster-artist – are the subject of a book by his younger son, Nicholas Ardizzone, where a near-complete roster of work with full details is to be found: *Edward Ardizzone's World: the Etchings and Lithographs* (see Sources p. 283). As noted at that point, where Nicholas Ardizzone's listings impinge on entries in this commentary they are acknowledged with *NAP* references.

Perhaps the description of 'Evening in Maida Vale' (*NAP 56*), should include a comment on the different treatment of the subject noted here at C3, while two other posters should be mentioned: a boating scene (395 × 530 mm), lacking title, imprint and date; the 'Guinness for Strength' poster noted above at C28 (1954); and a poster produced to publicize Catholic Book Week in the United States (communicated). The reservation with regard to the 'atelier mark', on p. 20 above, should be noted here since it also occurs on some prints.

With regard to bookplates, these 'were never an important part of Ardizzone's work' according to Colin White in his account of them in the *Bookplate Journal* in 1996 (see Sources p. 286). He lists some thirteen known plates in his very helpful study, which also includes one of the best short assessments of E.A.'s capacity and technique as a draughtsman. Of these thirteen plates however only six were specifically drawn as such, those for: The Detection Club, Moor House School, Anthony and Francesca White, David Ardizzone (draft in Sketchbook 48, f. 24), Drusilla and Colin White, and Derek Clifford. The last design was adopted (without permission) by Hilary Rittner.[11]

11. The design for Catherine Ardizzone's bookplate (White A6) is not original but is reworked from a decorated initial in item 47 above.

Some doubt must linger over whether a plate for the Youth Libraries Group was designed as such or for the cover of item B19 above, but the remaining examples fall into Colin White's category of 'adaptive' plates, being based on drawings originated for another purpose. Two of these are reprints of a drawing in *The Library* (see item 2 above and page [252]), one is a second use of the Moor House School plate, and one, for the Edward Ardizzone prize at Ipswich School, was adapted, with permission, from a drawing in *The Young Ardizzone* (item 151 above).

Victoria & Albert Museum

G: A NOTE ON 'ADOPTIONS'

The clarity and complete professionalism of Ardizzone's graphic work make it very attractive to many groups, such as publishers, printers, gallery-owners, literary societies and librarians, who seek images for decorative or publicity purposes. Occasionally in the above sections such use has been noted, one of the most frequently adopted drawings being that of the child in 'the little bookroom'. The following list of examples makes no pretence either to being complete or offering the earliest known appearances within each category, but it may help to show how readily E.A.'s graphic work was adopted to various other purposes.

POSTCARDS

1938	'Scenes at the Curwen Press' (see item C1 above).
1942	Adaptation of war art, such as 'Dispatch Riders' (monochrome) and 'Basement Ward at the Royal Herbert Hospital' (colour), both published by the National Gallery.
[c.1970]	Three postcards published by Walkerprint, reproducing photographs of E.A.'s altarpiece in the Carmelite Church, Whitefriars, Farnham, Kent.
1980	'Interior of a Paris Restaurant', issued by the National Gallery.
2000	'Drinkers' from the Wolseley Fine Art exhibition.
2000	'Bathers' from the Ashmolean exhibition.

ADVERTISEMENTS

1945	For the Curwen Press, illustration from *Signature* in *Horizon* no. 72, December.
1947	For *Alphabet and Image* no. 5, September 1947. (Not seen).
1980	For Harvey's, Shippers of Fine Wines, illustration from *Wine List Decorations* (item C36) in *The Times* 20 June, p. 22.
1983	For J. Clarke-Hall Ltd (booksellers), illustration from *Tim All Alone* (item 55) in *Antiquarian Book Monthly Review* no. 114, November.

Opposite: Drawing for a Christmas card 'adopted' for an invitation to an exhibition launch at the Victoria and Albert Museum (see p. 257)

LEAFLETS, ETC.

1951   *BBC Transcription Service*. Mayor of Casterbridge drawing from *Radio Times* (see item D1).

1960   *Books for Boys and Girls: Supplement 1953–1958* ed. by Jean Thomson. Toronto: Public Library. Drawing from *The Wandering Moon* (item 61) as the frontispiece.

1964   *Reader's Guide to Children's Books* compiled by Elizabeth Bewick. London: County Libraries Group of the Library Association. Vignette from the dust-jacket of *Intent Upon Reading* (item B30) on the cover.

1970   *Australian Children's Books: a Select List*. Fourth edition. Victoria: Children's Book Council of Victoria. Untraced drawing (attributed wrongly to *The Little Bookroom*) signed 'Diz' on the wrapper and t.p.

[*c.* 1970] *Cambridge Resources for English Teaching: Word Card 8*. Two illustrations from *Stig of the Dump* (item 104).

1972   *Children & Books: a Guide to Information* ed. by Brian Alderson. London: Times Newspapers Ltd. Drawing from *The Wandering Moon* as a tailpiece.

1999   *Journal* of the Royal Society of Arts, no. 214. Early drawing from *Radio Times* (see item D1) of children listening to the wireless in an article on 'The Art and Alchemy of Traditional Storytelling'.

BOOK-RELATED WORK

[*c.* 1955] *Three Hundred Years of Paper Making*. Eynsford, Kent: Arnold and Foster. A paper specimen book, printed at the Curwen Press and including reproductions of work by Reynolds Stone, Edward Bawden, E.A. and others. Specimen [6] is a reprint of the lithographic frontispiece to *The Tale of Ali Baba* (1949 item 29) as an example of work 'Drawn Offset in five workings on Hand Made Toned Laid Record and Repair paper …'.

1961   *Paper for Books: a Comprehensive Survey*. Revised edition. London: Robert Horne and Company Ltd. Reprints the t.p. illustration from *A Stickful of Nonpareil* (item 54) to show the quality of Huntsman Standard White Cartridge paper. Devitt 1, no. 240, lists a drawing from *Travels with a Donkey* (item 139) used on a paper sample printed by Mackay of Chatham for Grosvenor Chater and Company, around 1967.

1967   *Dent and Phoenix Junior Books* [catalogue]. With a colour illustration from *The Stuffed Dog* (item 138) on the cover. One of the numerous examples of E.A.'s work being used by his publishers on their seasonal catalogues.

1981   *The Child and the Book* by Nicholas Tucker. Cambridge: C.U.P. With the title-page drawing from *The Little Bookroom* (item 45) on the d.j.

INVITATIONS

1970   Illustration from *The Young Ardizzone* (item 151) for a party to celebrate its publication.

1973   Drawing for a Christmas card from around 1950 used for an exhibition launch at the Victoria and Albert Museum.

1974   Three illustrations from *Diary of a War Artist* (item 163) for a reception.

1974   Two illustrations from *Baggage to the Enemy* (item 14) for an Imperial War Museum exhibition reception.

1979   Drawing for an undated Christmas card used for a preview party for a Scottish Arts Council exhibition.

1980   Watercolour (also used as a postcard) for the opening of a Mayor Gallery exhibition.

1980   Watercolour for an invitation to a private view of the Scottish Arts Council exhibition on its transfer to the Imperial War Museum.

2000   Drawing from *Tim's Friend Towser* (item 100) for an invitation to the opening of, and publicity for, 'Colin's Gift', the exhibition at Worthing Museum celebrating the gift of Ardizzone material from the collection of the late Colin Mears.

MISCELLANEOUS

2001   *Lettercards:* the Royal Academy of Arts published at least one with a reproduction of a watercolour from *Tim's Friend Towser* (item 100).

2001   *Menu:* four assorted pen drawings used on a menu for a dinner meeting of the Wynkyn de Worde Society on 15 May, which was addressed by Nicholas Ardizzone.

APPENDIX I

ON THE ILLUSTRATING OF BOOKS
BY EDWARD ARDIZZONE

This article on his craft was first published by the Private Libraries Association in its journal P.L.A. Quarterly *(vol. 1, no. 3, July 1957, pp. 26–30). It was a version of his ideas about illustrating which later appeared in a reworked form as 'The Born Illustrator' (see Sources p. 279). A few literals in the original text have been silently corrected.*

I write this with some hesitation. I am a professional illustrator and therefore have little time to gather and, dare I confess it, little interest in the sort of information and knowledge that the critic, art historian, or bibliophile, has to have to write comprehensively on such a subject.

My work is all engrossing. Other people's work, except for that of a few artists I admire, passes me by. I don't look out for it. Therefore who am I to discuss this or that trend, to compare one artist to another, to fulminate on such subjects as the influence of the Banhams on book design in the 20's? I have no erudition.

As I *can't* be learned all that is left to me then is to write about a few things appertaining to my craft and give you a few of my ideas about it, simple ones I fear, which have come to me in the course of 30 years or more of practising it.

Now the art of illustration is an odd one. Odd because all the great illustrators seem to have had one very curious thing in common. They did not like to draw from life.

Cruikshank was furious with Maclise for making a caricature of him sketching. 'This is something I have never done in my life,' he said, and then pointing to his temple, 'It all comes from here.' Rumour, however, has it that he made sketches on his thumbnail.

Daumier said he could not draw from life. In fact nobody knows where he learnt to draw.

Doré's drawings on the spot were extremely summary, mere aids to memory, and so one could multiply this list down even to minor men.

Among the great, Keene was an exception. He was a very great artist, but I am going to stick my neck out by saying that he was too much of a realist to make the perfect book illustrator. In fact, of course, he illustrated few books and those only in his early days. The bulk of his published work was confined to *Punch*.

Keene's work in *Punch* was known and loved by the impressionists, who, after all, were the true realists. Pissarro had *Punch* sent to him in France so that he could cut out the Keene drawings. Van Gogh copied Keene. But in spite of this, Keene as a book illustrator would have been on the wrong side of the fence. Actuality concerned him, but actuality, the true look of things, is not necessarily the same as the authors' image of them and it is that image that the illustrator must grasp. Keene's talent was not a literary one.

For many years I bowed my head in homage to Keene, but I still vividly remember the moment when I realised I could qualify my admiration. It was a moment of some liberation.

However, my attitude to Keene will be more fully explained when I go on to discuss the born illustrator and what I consider his job should be.

The born illustrator does not work from life. His knowledge as he will say, comes from the head. Words of course create images for him, or rather his creative imagination is aroused by words rather than by the thing seen. He has a sympathetic understanding of the author's ideas. In fact he is the perfect reader. He works fast, the very nature of his work often making this a necessity. Doré made 16 drawings every day before lunch.

The training of the born illustrator, if any, is academic in the true sense, which is the learning of the right way to draw things rather than the particular way to draw a particular thing. All his life he collects symbols for forms. In fact he compiles in his head a dictionary of those symbols to which he can have recourse. The larger the dictionary the more efficient he becomes.

Japanese art is, or has been, a highly academic one, and in this connection I remember hearing of a Japanese drawing book giving 60 ways to draw a bridge.

What a boon such a book would be to the illustrator! If only there were other books like this giving 60 ways to draw a man or a woman, or a dog or a tree and so on, and we could learn these ways. We would then be free from the trammels of life, free to create at will at the author's behest.

However, there is one qualification, and a very important one, which I must make. It is that the illustrator, having learnt to draw the symbols for things, must still have recourse to life using his eye and his memory to augment and sweeten his knowledge. Life gives him his pictorial ideas. It increases his repertoire and raises it above a repetition of old work carefully learned.

In this context let me quote from Leonardo's treatise on painting. Leonardo is discussing the training of a student and this is what he says:

'The young man should first learn perspective then the proportions of all objects. Next copy work after the hand of a good master to gain the habit of drawing parts of the body well; and then work from nature to confirm the lessons learned.'

Is not the pattern the same? You copy first, you learn your symbols for things and then with knowledge turn to nature.

When I said that life gave the illustrator his ideas, I should have rather said that living does, for in fact, to put it colloquially, the illustrator is always on the job. Illustration, like any other art, is not just a job but a way of life.

The born illustrator's method of drawing is usually what I call the empirical one, a matter of trial and error. For example, should he want to draw something and is not entirely certain how to do so, instead of finding the object and drawing directly from life, he is more likely to practice drawing it, doing it over and over again, until it looks right on paper. This gives his drawing that personal quality which is usually his.

I must now write of what I believe is the illustrator's job.

However, before I do so, let me say at once, that what I am about to write comprises only my personal ideas on the subject. I lay no claim to their being the whole truth, but no whole truth can be written about any art. What I will write can be disagreed with, dismissed, or argued over with valid reason. All I can hope for is that one small facet of the truth, which has a million sides anyhow, will emerge.

So, having covered myself with this preamble, let me say that, to my mind, it is, first and foremost, the illustrator's job to evoke a visual background which the reader can people with the author's characters. This visual background or world that he creates must be analogous to the author's.

Just as the author's world, if he is a novelist, is not reality but a semblance of it, so must the illustrator's world not be reality but a semblance of it created specially to fit the author's.

Characters should be suggested in their settings rather than too fully described. Large close-ups of faces can be disturbing. To my mind, the best view of the Hero or Heroine is the back view.

The truth is that it is not the illustrator's job to supplant the reader's imagination but rather to help it, and to give it ground to work on. It follows, I think, that dramatic scenes are best avoided. It is the view from the window, the picnic in the fields, the mystery of the empty room, rather than sudden death or violent action that should be the illustrator's subjects. In any case violence is usually better described in words, and it is not the illustrator's business to dot the i's and cross the t's of the author.

To say in other words what I have said before, I like to think of the illustrator as a kind of stage designer, and, as such, designing the settings for the author's play of character, thereby doing something that the author cannot do in words and also, in a sense, adding another dimension to the book.

As we all know the art of illustration differs from the other visual arts in that the public rarely sees the artist's original work. They see it only through the medium of reproduction.

But what few people realise is that this medium can alter and falsify to an extent which is hardly credible to the uninitiated. Few realise, too, that, from the original drawing to the reproduction of it, there is nearly always a loss in artistic quality. Many will unthinkingly accept what they see on the printed page as a true copy of the artist's work and will judge him by that.

In fact, of course, reproductions do vary widely from their originals, and this is particularly so in cheap and moderately priced books.

The biggest difference is naturally in the more complicated field of colour half tone reproduction and the reason for this is basic. Colour in half tone printing is arrived at by the super imposing of dots of primary colour in oily inks. This can never do more than approximate to the artist's water colour washes made of ready mixed colours and laid on to the paper with a brush.

In the usual 3 and 4 colour half tone processes certain greys, greens and violets cannot be produced at all.

Even in the simplest process of all, the black and white line block, the print can be very different from the original. For example, the artist uses pen and ink on paper. Now when the ink begins to run dry in the nib the resulting mark on the paper will be slightly greyer or paler than the preceding ones. But it is this greying of the ink, though often hardly perceptible, which adds an atmosphere quality to the drawing. This quality can never be picked up by the process employed. Also, separate lines will tend to thicken and hatched areas will either look starved and scratchy or become areas of solid black owing to the vagaries of the machine minder and the machine.

In truth, no illustrator of experience hopes for a facsimile of his work, all that he wants is a pleasant interpretation of it by blockmaker and printer. Alas, few in the trade understand this and most content themselves with producing only a bad copy. Indeed, few in the trade have the artistic sensitivity to interpret successfully, though of course there are some splendid exceptions.

So please, when you pick up a book and look at the illustrations and find fault with some of them, don't at once and without thought, blame the artist. It may be, and often is, the fault of the printer.

APPENDIX II
TWO NOTES ON TECHNIQUE

Ardizzone several times set down simple practical statements about his illustrative methods. We here reprint notes about his pen drawing, written for Robin Jacques's Illustrators at Work *(1963), and an article on his use of Kodatrace in making a number of full-colour picture books written for* The Penrose Annual *(vol. 46, 1952).*

From *Illustrators at Work:*

EQUIPMENT: Heavy hot press paper; a hard pencil; a pen holding a nib called 'Mitchell's post office pen No. 0784', and any good indian ink.

METHOD: I first make a fairly elaborate drawing in tone with my hard pencil. The point of using a hard pencil being that the resulting drawing is grey and will not get in the way of the ink drawing which follows.

Then using the back of my nib I make a fairly light and hesitant line around the main forms. This is like making a new drawing, as one does not exactly copy the pencil underneath but re-draws and extemporizes as one goes along.

The next stage is to block in the main areas of shadow with an even horizontal hatch and rub out the underlying pencil. One then has a slight but complete little picture in light and shade.

The third stage is to elaborate the drawing, carrying it into the shadows, and to augment the shadows by cross-hatching.

Finally, by heavier cross-hatching particularly in foregrounds, one suggests the local colour, and by accenting the outlines here and there one gives an added sense of depth.

I always try to avoid finishing any one part of the drawing at the expense of the rest but always try to build it up in stages, just as if one was painting a picture.

If I make a mistake I never use process white but scrape out the offending area with a knife and re-draw. Hence the necessity of using good paper.

From *The Penrose Annual:*

A SIMPLE TECHNIQUE IN LINE
AND COLOUR WASH

Line and wash is one of the most delightful mediums for the artist to work in. It is a traditional medium combining the beauty of swift flowing line with clear soft colour and is particularly suited to illustrative work.

Unfortunately, this medium as we all know, is impossible to reproduce, even moderately well, by the usual halftone process, except at the expense of much handwork on the plate and, therefore, at a cost which makes it quite prohibitive to-day.

If one wants a good reproduction, that is one in which the line has the clean and spontaneous quality of the original and the colour is bright and clear, then it is necessary that the line should be separated from the colour.

But here, alas, is the rub. It is difficult for the man who commissions the drawing, be he publisher or art editor, when presented by the artist not with a completed work, but with a line drawing on one sheet of paper and some colour on another, to visualise the result when the two are combined. To do so requires some small amount of imagination, a quality not always to be found.

To separate the line is also an added difficulty for the artist, whose job in all conscience is difficult enough. Those last minute touches to a drawing, the accenting of the line here and there to give the drawing depth and brilliance, that 'working over' which all artists do to perfect their work, have to some extent to be foregone.

A solution to this problem, though not a complete one, is the use of a transparent overlay on which to draw the black line. This is a method which I, as an illustrator, have used for my recent children's books, and it works more or less as follows:

I make on a sheet of good paper my design in pencil and colour and add two register marks. Over this I lay the transparency and freely draw the line, not forgetting to trace these register marks. This done I remove the transparency, rub out the surplus pencil, and touch up the colour. I then put back the transparency and add to the line; from now on I work alternatively on the line and colour till the required effect has been achieved.

The result of this is that when complete and the transparency is laid over the colour one has a very fair idea of what the finished job should look like. I have also been able to work on the drawing, adding those finishing touches mentioned before which are so necessary to the vitality of a drawing.

There are, however, some snags. All transparent films are not suitable. I well remember the first time I attempted this method as it ended in disaster. I had used 'Cellophane' and it shrank. I now use Kodatrace, which is not only fairly stable, but has a matt side which takes ink easily. It has unfortunately one drawback, though not a very serious one, that is it is a little blue in colour and therefore slightly falsifies the colour of the work beneath it.

Another drawback in the use of a transparency, and one that has to be allowed for by the artist, is that the line, being raised above the colour underneath, stands out in a sharper contrast to the colour than if drawn direct onto the paper.

The printers tell me that the reproduction of work separated in this way is simple. The Kodatrace is put to camera for line and the wash drawing reproduced by three-colour halftone.

I believe, if one could find a thinner and more stable transparent material and an ink which flows well but is more opaque than Indian ink, that the line on its transparency could be used as a photographic positive and put down direct to the printing plate, thereby cutting out the camera stage and reducing even more the cost of reproduction if it is to be the same size as the original.

The use of three-colour halftone instead of the more usual four seems to entail some loss in the rendering of the greys; but this, however, is more than offset by the clean sharp line and the clarity of the colours which are not degraded by the inevitable screen of small black dots when the fourth colour, a black, is used.

Again, if the artist can collaborate with the printers and plate makers as I did over my last book *Tim and Charlotte*, the result can be a delightful interpretation of the original colour, and something far more pleasing to look at than the bad approximation achieved by the usual methods.

Of course this method, as I have said before, is not a complete answer to the problem – this would be a new and better form of reproduction.

Shifts like this always entail some loss and the loss, as usual, is borne by the artist.

Agreed, it is imperative that the artist should collaborate with the printer in order that the result should be better and cost less; but in doing so he increases the difficulty of his work, and, when the job is over, he is left with no completed originals, and originals, if the artist is a good one, have value.

Admittedly, the most important thing about illustrations is that, when reproduced, they should look well and have some beauty in their own right. If this can only be achieved by sacrificing the originals then it is a necessary sacrifice, but one that seems a pity.

It is to be wondered what one's attitude would be if, when looking at the original work of some past illustrator, one saw, instead of a fine drawing, only some line on Kodatrace and a little colour on paper.

APPENDIX III

PEACOCK PIE

Most of the poems in *Peacock Pie* were written between Walter de la Mare's release from servitude to Anglo-American Oil in 1908 and the book's publication by Constable in June 1913. There were 82 of them, arranged in eight sections, and the work was printed as a prestige job: a square octavo (196 × 140 mm) on heavy laid paper with a pronounced tooth on the wire side so that plenty of 'bonk' was needed to get a good impression. There were no illustrations and the book was bound in blue glazed cloth gilt. Stereotype plates were made of this text-setting, and with the third impression of February 1916 the format was altered to demy octavo (222 × 140 mm) of which there were ten reprintings on an unimpressive antique wove paper in a drab greeny-grey paper board binding before the run continued with eleven further impressions of a reset edition down to 1935.

As Theresa Whistler notes in her biography of de la Mare, *Imagination of the Heart* (1993), the poet was keen for his book to be illustrated by Lovat Fraser whom he had met and liked in 1912. Fraser forthwith set about making what he called 'embellishments' for the poems but the publisher then decided that these would be too expensive to reproduce. In consequence, the first edition to have illustrations was that with a colour frontispiece and nine line drawings by W. Heath Robinson which Constable published, undated, in 1916 – another prestige job in an unpropitious time, a foolscap quarto (212 × 166 mm) in dark green linen boards with gilt titling and the title-page design blocked on the front in white and gold.

Not until eight years after this did Constable introduce an edition with Lovat Fraser's embellishments, posthumously published, since Fraser had died in 1921 of injuries sustained during his war service. De la Mare composed a preparatory note to the volume recalling his and Fraser's delight in the work: 'I can remember ... as vividly as if it were yesterday, talking to him as he sat at his board with his brush and his bright inks, and watching [the pictures] leap into life on the paper.'

By this time *Peacock Pie* had achieved something of the status of a classic and Constable issued the text and its sixteen inserted colour plates in both a trade edition in blue cloth gilt (a book almost never seen in a dust-jacket) and a collector's edition in white cloth in a slip-case, limited to 500 copies signed by the author. This edition clearly relates back to what must have been an ur-*Peacock Pie*, since Fraser had done pictures for four poems that must have been dropped before the 1913 publication came out. Of necessity therefore these four poems were re-instated, along with six others, to make what was later (in 1969) called 'the definitive edition'.

Definitive or not, Constable's next venture into an illustrated version reverted to the 82-poem grouping 'with eighty-one [actually sixty-five plus repeats] little pictures in colour by Jocelyn Crowe' – another demy octavo edition, published in 1936 and subsisting alongside the early plain-text edition which was still in print. That however was the end of the line for the Constable sequence. In 1929, de la Mare's son Richard had become a director of Faber & Faber and he gradually brought under their imprint books by his father published earlier, as well as taking on new ones, starting with the 1929 edition of *Stories from the Bible*.

The first Faber edition of *Peacock Pie* was the war-time large crown octavo 'with decorations by F. R. Emett', his typical spindleshank drawings here confined to framed designs for the title-page and the eight pages reserved for the section-titles. It was a modest but satisfying piece of work which was not superseded but was joined, after the war, by Ardizzone's more extensive exercise in interpretation, where, for the first time, the (always rather arbitrary) eight-part division of the book was abandoned and the original sequence of the 82 poems was slightly adjusted, apparently to give a more natural flow to the succession of subjects. That order has been retained with interpolations for the 'definitive' edition in hardback and paperback (1969 and 1988) and for the one subsequent edition of consequence to be re-illustrated, that 'with pictures by Louise Brierley' published in 1989. (An abridged edition, illustrated with twenty-three pencil drawings by Barbara Cooney had been published in New York in 1961.)

This brief history of de la Mare's text should be sufficient to justify claims for the affection in which the book has been held from its first appearance. Affection however is not a guarantee of adequate presentation and *Peacock Pie* has proved a persistent challenge to publishers and designers alike.

In some ways that first edition of 1913, on its generous pages and without illustrative distractions, is an ideal one. It allows de la Mare's poems to speak for themselves and its get-up harmonizes with the backward-looking and nostalgic elements of its poetry. For *Peacock Pie* is essentially a threnody in which a fascinating tension exists between the felicity of much of its writing and the veiled regrets of much of its substance. This is not immediately apparent because of the diversity of de la Mare's subjects and verse forms. Nursery rhymes, ballads and Victorian lyricism find echoes in poems that range from the inconsequential charm of 'The Huntsmen' or 'The Bandog', through the narratives of 'Off the Ground' or 'The Thief at Robin's Castle' to the very de la Mare-ish numinosity of the famous 'Some One' and the reverberant poem from which the collection takes its title.

The air of regret that permeates even so simple a lyric as 'Bread and Cherries' makes *Peacock Pie* a severe test for its illustrators who are liable to read the book at the superficial level of its narrative or ghostly events. Lovat Fraser's embellishments may indeed be 'vivid pictures' as the poet described them but their hefty intrusion on leaves of art-paper does not have anything of the cogency that a few of his 'Flying Fame' quasi-wood-cuts might have had (and their effect is also occasionally further subverted by their placement – 'The King of England' lies eleven pages beyond his verses, and 'A Sea-Legged Sailor' thirty).

Heath Robinson's substantial performance is more successful in a scattergun way. With his skill as a draughtsman, his eye for comedy, and such room to exercise it, he could hardly help but find dozens of images that fit particular lines in particular poems – especially the character-studies. Where he falls short though is in the accuracy and consistency of his imagery, linked to his highly variable use of page-space (for instance, some of his 33 full-page drawings are foregrounded, some are scenes-in-depth, some are framed, some are vignetted) and the variable quality of the whole undercuts de la Mare's carefully organised transitions of mood. By contrast, Jocelyn Crowe's pretty little three-tone designs may be placed consistently at the bottom of pages, but are divorced from any emotional or comedic attachment to the words they are meant to be illustrating. There is more than a hint of the dire influence of *When We Were Very Young* here.

Against so much in all those pre-war illustrations that is misconceived, uncertain or over-coarse, and against Louise Brierley's recent interpretations, which are self-indulgent to the point of eccentricity, the pen-drawn illustrations of Ardizzone are a model of how illustration can function in support of the most demanding of texts. In his notes 'On the Illustrating of Books', reprinted above as Appendix I, he writes that 'it is not the illustrator's job to supplant the reader's imagination but rather to help it, and to give it ground to work on'. This is exactly what happens in *Peacock*

Pie. He has read the poems with absorption, has recognised the coherent music of the verse and has set his drawings to its tune so that they enhance the imaginative potential. The characterisations and scene-paintings are muted, compared, say, with Heath Robinson, but they all belong to de la Mare's world. Comedy, 'weather', mystery are all present where they need to be but they are indeed helping their sources and not supplanting them. There is, I believe, no better example in all Edward Ardizzone's book illustrations of sympathy and artistry combined.

Editions of *Peacock Pie*: a summary:

1913 *Peacock Pie: a Book of Rhymes* by Walter de la Mare. 'He told me his dreams ...' Isaac Watts. London: Constable and Company Ltd.

Square crown 8°. viii 122 pp. unillustrated. Blue cloth gilt. D.j. pale blue sugar paper with dark blue lettering. The first edition, text stereotyped and reprinted to 1925 when it was reset and further reprinted to 1935.

[1916] *Peacock Pie* ... with illustrations by W. Heath Robinson. Constable.

Foolscap 4°. viii 180 pp. + inset frontis. (96 illus. in all, including 33 on a full-page and 46 at the head of poems). Dark green linen gilt. Dark green d.j. following cover design. (Beare no. 89). *An American edition printed in Britain was published in New York by Henry Holt in 1917. This continued to be published (but printed in the U.S.) at least until October 1941 when its cloth-board cover sported the peacock design that had been used in Jocelyn Crowe's edition, and when its t.p. and section-titles were given hand-colouring, apparently by the publisher.*

[1924] *Peacock Pie* ... with embellishments by C. Lovat Fraser. London, Bombay, Sydney: Constable.

Royal 8°. xii 128 pp. + frontis. and 15 further insets. Blue cloth gilt. D.j. not seen. *Undated, but a short note by the author is dated 1924. Also issued in a signed edition limited to 500 copies, in white cloth with a slip-case.*

1924 *U.S. edition:* New York: Henry Holt.

1936 *Peacock Pie* ... with eighty-one little pictures in colour by Jocelyn Crowe. Constable.

Demy 8°. viii 112 pp. With 81 illus. in 3 tones, placed below the text throughout and including 16 repeats of small emblems. Blue cloth gilt. D.j. grey paper with blue lettering and decoration.

1936 *U.S. edition:* New York: Henry Holt. Printed in G.B.

1941 *Peacock Pie* ... with illus. by F. R. Emett [attrib. only in imprint and on d.j. flap] London: Faber & Faber Ltd.

Large crown 8°. 128 pp. With 9 full-page pen drawings (t.p. and 8 section-titles). Straw-coloured cloth boards, green lettering. D.j. in 3 colours by Emett.

1946 First Ardizzone edition. See item 15 above for a full history.

1961 Edition illus. by Barbara Cooney. New York: Knopf.

1989 Edition illus. by Louise Brierley. London, Boston: Faber & Faber.

'Three jolly Farmers' from *Peacock Pie* (1946 item 15, reduced)

APPENDIX IV

THE CASE OF PETER PAN

Peter Pan is evanescent in more ways than one. Where *Peacock Pie* presents the illustrator with an established text requiring a delicate response, *Peter Pan* has no determinate identity as either character or book. He first materializes in a curious farrago called *The Little White Bird* which Barrie published for adult readers in 1902. Production of the play followed at the end of 1904, its success leading to the excerpting of a section from *The Little White Bird* as the gift-book *Peter Pan in Kensington Gardens* (illustrated by Arthur Rackham) in 1906. No play text was published until 1928 however, and what readers got first was an authorised retelling of the story drawn from the play-script by Daniel O'Connor: *The Peter Pan Picture Book* (illustrated by Alice Woodward) in 1907 and second a prose story by Barrie himself, *Peter and Wendy* (illustrated by Francis D. Bedford) in 1911. These two texts are the foundation of many varied tellings of the story for children down to the present time, most notably that of 1925 'for children from 9 to 12' by May Byron which *in toto*, or in various abridgements, was the text primarily used by that ubiquitous illustrator Mabel Lucie Attwell.

With Eleanor Graham's volume (item 92 above) a further substantial attempt at a retelling was made, but as with the other adaptors, she realised that 'preserving Barrie' was a vital part of her job so that she ended up with what she called (in the *Note* to the U.S. edition) 'a piece of scrupulous and careful editing, not a free retelling'. In the event, although she interestingly blends in some elements from *Kensington Gardens*, she really produces a scrupulous dilution of Barrie's inimitable *Peter and Wendy*, many of her cuts and interpolated explanations detracting from the headlong rhetoric of Barrie the impresario.

The peculiarities of *Peter Pan* as an unstable text present difficulties in deciding what one might wish children to read (assuming any child today is up to coping with Barrie's, rather than May Byron's or Walt Disney's, voice). Arguably the play, in any production that uses the authentic script, is the 'ideal copy' of the story, while the prose narratives that modify the text do its primal form one sort of injustice or another. The ambivalence of Barrie's attitude to both his story and his audience is an inescapable *donné* and the dilutions that occur in O'Connor, or Byron, or in the Disney adaptation, or in Eleanor Graham's version lead inevitably to strictures over their betraying 'the essential Barrie' to a greater or lesser extent.

Such a view of textual imperfections can carry over to illustrative ones for, as with the text, the 'ideal illustration' is the play in performance, to be judged on the skill of the director and designer in interpreting Barrie's often perverse script. By extension, an ideal for printed illustrations would be to reflect scenes events and gestures that may be significant in the drama without dominating what Barrie has to say, or the playfulness that he exercises in varied fashion throughout. Thus it comes about that the requirements imposed on the illustrator here run parallel to what Ardizzone has elsewhere seen as his prime function: *I like to think of the illustrator as a kind of stage designer, and, as such, designing the settings for the author's play of character, thereby doing something that the author cannot do in words and also, in a sense, adding another dimension to the book.* ('On the Illustrating of Books', see Appendix I above).

A comparison of his pen drawings for the Graham text with the work of other monochrome draughtsmen demonstrates how well, in practice, he measures up to his own idea of this theatrical dimension. The elaborate colour-plate or largely colour-printed editions from such as Rackham, Woodward, Hudson, Blampied and, in early manifestations, Mabel Lucie Attwell rule themselves out since they are attempts at a visual takeover *tout court* – and certainly in the case of Attwell hopelessly misconceived anyway. (Bedford's rococo plates for the octavo *Peter and Wendy* of 1911 were themselves done up in pea-green for a quarto gift-book edition.)

In placing Ardizzone alongside the not-always less pretentious production jobs of such black-and-white practitioners as Nora Unwin (1951), Richard Kennedy (1967), Shirley Hughes (1976), Trina Schart Hyman (1980), Robin Lawrie (1988) and Jan Ormerod (1988) it is worth abstracting certain elements in *Peter Pan* which every illustrator has to confront and making comparisons: the portrayal of central characters, Peter, Wendy and Hook; the problematic domestic arrangements of the Darling household, not forgetting the nursemaid; the flying children; the poisoning of the near-invisible Tink. Those illustrators who draw big and engage in fancy graphics (the over-emphatic Unwin and Hyman, the wayward mingling of colour-plates, silhouettes and quasi-etchings by Jan Ormerod) fail the test here, while a specialist in vignettes like Shirley Hughes comes much closer to the Ardizzone idea, knitting the visual much more closely in to the verbal. Exceptionally, Richard Kennedy – whose illustrations were commissioned for a small format Puffin Story Book – brings such verve to his great tumble of eccentrically-placed drawings that he matches the knock-down panache of Barrie's 1911 text.

Where Ardizzone stands among all these competitors must inevitably be a matter of opinion, as must the adequacy of the version that he was given to illustrate. But – leaving aside his unremarkable colour-plates, which were an afterthought anyway – not a single drawing in the Brockhampton/ Scribner edition can be faulted either for its choice of subject or for its execution in the progress of the story's drama. The theatre-manager on his graphic stage practises what he has preached.

Note: Essential reading for anyone seeking guidance on the complexities of Barrie's work is the introduction by Peter Hollindale to his edition of *Peter Pan in Kensington Gardens* with *Peter and Wendy* (Oxford University Press, 1991; World's Classics series). A survey of illustrated editions of *Peter Pan* 'focusing on Barrie's 1911 text' by Chris Routh appears as 'Peter Pictured' in *The Neverland: Two Flights over the Territory* ([Hoddesdon, Herts]: Children's Books History Society, 1995; Occasional Paper II).

English editions of the largely monochrome-illustrated editions mentioned above are: *Peter Pan* illus. Nora S. Unwin (Hodder & Stoughton, 1951); *Peter Pan* illus. Richard Kennedy (Puffin Books, 1967; Brockhampton Press, 1971); *J. M. Barrie's Peter Pan and Wendy* retold by May Byron ... illus. Shirley Hughes (Hodder etc., 1976); *Peter Pan* illus. Trina Schart Hyman (Hodder etc. 1980); *Peter Pan* with decorations by Robin Lawrie (Collins, 1988); and *Peter Pan* illus. by Jan Ormerod (Viking Kestrel, 1988).

APPENDIX V

GABRIEL WHITE'S MEMORIAL ADDRESS

The following address was given by Gabriel White at the Illustrators Art Gallery on 13 November 1979 at the launch of his book *Edward Ardizzone: Artist and Illustrator*. E.A. had died the week before, on 8 November 1979. The text is reprinted from *Signal* (no. 31, January 1980, pp. 8–10).

On such an occasion it is right that someone should speak and one had hoped that it could be Ted himself. What a pleasant little speech it would have been, as his speeches always were. Now that this cannot be, it seems to me hardly necessary that anyone should take his place. He is so much present here in spirit, both in the individual memories of all of us who knew him and in the drawings and prints with which we are surrounded. No artist I know so evokes his personality in his works. Some critic has remarked on the little feet he gave all his figures. He had small feet himself and was proud of them.

I would like to congratulate Robin Johnson on the little exhibition he has got together. You have Ted from the beginning of his career to the end; in fact, the invitation cards of which you can see the original must have been one of his last drawings. It is hard to think of Ted as he was only a year or two before he made the earliest drawings we have here, 'funny little drawings' he described them himself, made for the Radio Times. He has only just ceased to be a thin, gangly young man, painfully shy and with a stammer. His family had a story of him that when it first moved to London from Bath, he was sent off by his sister Betty to pay a call on someone to whom they had an introduction. Resistant and very unwillingly he went. He then regarded himself as woman-ridden, living with a mother and two sisters. When he got to the house and had rung the bell, his hostess was told to her amazement, 'I, I, am Betty's sister.'

However all that disappeared very shortly afterwards. He became the plump character we all knew him – self-assured and confident, he spoke with ease and charm. His was a transparent personality – nothing was concealed. As someone described him, 'he was like a piece of Brighton rock, Ted all through.'

276

I think we can say he had a happy life. Though he had his share of misfortune, sickness that we can all expect and perhaps some may feel more than his share, he was happy in spite of them. And I think this happiness was due to the fact he never stopped working. He was like that Japanese artist, whose name I have forgotten, who was mad about drawing. In the days when tablecloths and table napkins were more common than they are now, he would cover them with drawings in an evening's session. It is a pity that some did not survive; luxuriously mounted and framed by Robert Sielle they would fetch a high price.

I have said that his was a happy life but there was one moment when it was not. In 1978 he had his harmful fall, he lost both his son Philip and his grand-daughter Hannah, and within a few weeks his old friend James Reeves. Last summer the shock of all these misfortunes struck him. He had reached what one of his favourite authors had described as the slough of despond. He could draw no more and he gave up two commissions. But he was not to end in that mood. Five or six weeks ago his spirits revived, he was keen to start drawing again and he took on a new book. A wonderful serenity came upon him. Though he might still be in pain, he was happy in spirit.

I would like to give you a last glimpse of him. Some of you have heard this little story and must forgive me if they have to hear it again. It is characteristic and a happy note on which to leave him. His niece Charlotte went to see him a few days ago; walking into the studio she found him absorbed in the Bodley Head book [Gabriel's biography]. When she announced her arrival he looked up and said 'You have caught me at it ... I think I have made it. I need not do another drawing again.' I am sure you will agree with me that he had made it. He saw his life work as a whole and he was satisfied with it. What greater happiness can one wish any artist?

SOURCES, REFERENCES, ETC.

The place of publication is London unless otherwise stated. More extensive biographical and bibliographical minutiae may be found in Nicholas Ardizzone's *Edward Ardizzone's World* (see p. 283 below).

I: ESSAYS AND OTHER PIECES BY E.A.

About Tim and Lucy. *The Horn Book Magazine* (Boston). No. 14, March 1938, pp. 88–90. Reprinted in *A Horn Book Sampler*, ed. by N.R. Fryatt. Boston: Horn Book, [1959], pp. 1–3.

Brian Robb. *Signature.* New series 11, 1950, pp. 37–45. *E.A. on one of his great (and still too-little revered) contemporaries, with brief but penetrating notes on Robb's illus. for* The Golden Asse, Baron Munchausen *and* Tristram Shandy.

An Autobiographical Note. *Junior Bookshelf* (Huddersfield). No. 14, 1950, pp. 39–45. Reprinted in *Authors and Illustrators of Children's Books*, ed. by Miriam Hoffman and Eva Samuels. New York: Bowker, 1972, pp. 1–5.

A Simple Technique in Line and Colour Wash. *The Penrose Annual.* Vol. 46, 1952, pp. 66–67, with a 4-page insert from *Tim and Charlotte. Reprinted here in Appendix II. The* Annual *also has an inserted leaflet announcing the BBC Transcriptions Service recording of* The Mayor of Casterbridge *with an E.A. vig. on the front.*

How the Tim Books were Created. *Radio Times.* 9 July 1954, p. 19. *A first draft of this article is in Sketchbook 16.*

Some Random Thoughts on the Art of Illustration. *Ark: the Journal of the Royal College of Art.* No. 11, Summer 1954, pp. 8–11. *The illustrations include a panoramic bookshop scene similar to that found in item C24 above.*

A Comment on the above Articles. *Society of Industrial Artists Journal.* No. 41, October 1954, pp. 6–7. *Commenting on pieces by Robert Lusty and David Bland about the commissioning of 'Commercial Artists'.*

278

On the Illustrating of Books. *P.L.A. Quarterly.* Vol. 1, no. 3, July 1957, pp. 26–30. *Reprinted here as Appendix I. The essay was also published as a prettily-produced book, limited to 200 copies in patterned paper boards, by the Weatherbird Press, Pasadena, CA, 1986.*

The Born Illustrator. *Motif: a Journal of the Visual Arts.* No. 1, November 1958, pp. 37–44. Reprinted in *Folio.* January–March 1962, pp. 1–10; and in *Signal: Approaches to Children's Literature.* No. 3, September 1970, pp. 73–80. *A 'Reply' by Lynton Lamb, 'The True Illustrator', was published in* Motif *no. 2 (February 1959, pp. 70–76). In* Motif *no. 5 (Autumn 1960, pp. 4–5) E.A. featured as one of the 'Six Portraits' pictured with a brief text by Richard Gauyatt.*

Creation of a Picture Book. *Top of the News: the Quarterly Journal of the Association for Library Service to Children ... of the American Library Association.* Vol. XVI, no. 2, December 1959, pp. 40–46. Reprinted in *Junior Bookshelf.* No. 25, 1961, pp. 325–335; and in *Only Connect: Readings on Children's Literature,* ed. Sheila Egoff *et al.* Toronto and New York: Oxford University Press, 1969, pp. 347–356.

In the Lamont Room: Book Illustration. *Books: the Journal of the National Book League.* No. 329, May–June 1960, pp. 94–95. *A record of a discussion evening with James Reeves and E.A.; he notes how his own picture books begin and then 'gather accretions' through family storytelling with 'the little horrors'.*

Paying the Artist. *The Author.* Vol. 78, no. 4, Winter 1967, p. 181. *A comment on a publisher's statement that £95, as an outright payment, was the going rate for an illustrator to design a book-jacket and the equivalent of 11 full-page black and white drawings for a children's book. E.A. commends a proposed 'Refresher Scheme' which would bring illustrators a further payment if the book were successful.*

Tape casettes: One or two privately recorded tapes exist of E.A.'s castaway reflections on 'Desert Island Discs', Saturday 5 August 1972.

Interview: Emma Fisher and Justin Wintle (eds). *The Pied Pipers: Interviews with the Influential Creators of Children's Literature.* New York and London: Paddington Press, 1974. *E.A. is interviewed by Emma Fisher on pp. 35–48.*

On Illustrating Miss Farjeon's Work. *Chosen for Children: an Account of the Books Awarded the Carnegie Medal 1936–1975,* ed. by Marcus Crouch and Alec Ellis. The Library Association, 1977, pp. 79–80.

Interview: David Driver (ed.). *The Art of Radio Times: the First Sixty Years.* Intro. by Asa Briggs. BBC, 1981. *E.A. is a featured illustrator with questions and answers and illustrations on pp. 60–64.*

II: EXHIBITION CATALOGUES AND REVIEWS, AND BOOKSELLERS' CATALOGUES CENTRED UPON E.A.'S WORK

D. W. Last. Edward Ardizzone: a First One-Man Exhibition at the Leger Galleries. *The Studio.* No. 461, August 1931, pp. 136–137. *Short review of the 40 water-colours and oils on show.*

Adrian Bury. Oil Paintings and Watercolours by Edward Ardizzone. *Saturday Review.* 15 August 1931. *Review of the Leger Galleries exhibition.*

Edward Ardizzone at the Nicholson Gallery. *New Statesman.* 1 April 1939. *Anonymous review.*

Book Illustration in England 1949–1954. The Arts Council of Great Britain, 1954. *Items 1–6 only by E.A., comprising three books, six pen drawings from* The Warden, *and two pen and wash drawings from* Tim and Charlotte *with Kodatrace overlays.*

Edward Ardizzone: England by the Sea. Mayor Gallery. November 1970.

Gabriel White. *Edward Ardizzone: a Retrospective Exhibition.* Victoria & Albert Museum. 15 December 1973–13 January 1974.

Edward Ardizzone: Drawings and Doodles. New Grafton Gallery. 13 March–9 April 1975. *70 items.*

Words Etcetera (Julian and Edith Nangle). Catalogue 16. *Edward Ardizzone: Literary Periodicals: First Editions.* September 1977. *Pages 14–21 (items 358–501).*

[Andrew Murray]. *Edward Ardizzone.* Edinburgh: The Scottish Arts Council, 1979. *Subsequently toured to Aberdeen, Stirling, Stromness, Manchester* and the *Imperial War Museum, London. Probably the most important exhibition so far assembled. The 163 catalogue entries include many with multiple contents. Several items in this present list have been quoted directly from the catalogue's bibliography.*

Edward Ardizzone 1900–1979. New Grafton Gallery. 19 February–18 March 1979. *79 items.*

Phillips, Son & Neale. *Edward Ardizzone: a Collection of Autographed Illustrated Books … to be Sold by Auction.* 1 December 1980. *156 items.*

Ardizzone by the Sea. Middlesbrough Art Gallery Touring Exhibition, 1982. *Held at Middlesbrough, York and Durham. 74 items including watercolours, illustrations and prints.*

Edward Ardizzone with his Friends and Relations. Sally Hunter and Patrick Searle Fine Art. 2–19 December 1986. *84 items by E.A. including Christmas card designs and drawings for* Radio Times.

H. R. W. Taylor. *Books and Magazines illustrated by Edward Ardizzone.* Felixstowe, Winter 1990. *165 items.*

Vera Coleman. *Edward Ardizzone and Ronald Searle.* November 1990. *66 items by E.A.*

Chris Beetles Ltd. *The Illustrators: the British Art of Illustration 1800–1990* [at the Beetles gallery]. 28 November–14 December 1990, with a separate price list. *E.A. items 17–25. This was the first of a series of annual exhibition sale catalogues put out by Chris Beetles Ltd with extensive descriptions and illustrations. E.A. figures in the subsequent catalogues as follows: 1991 items 361–374A; 1992 items 328–359; 1993 items 452–476; 1997 15 scattered items; and 1999 items 468–485.*

Nial Devitt Books. *Ardizzone Catalogue 1.* April 1991. *36 pp. (including wrappers), 256 items.*
    Catalogue 2. 1993. iv, 28 pp. (plus wrappers), 171 items.
    Catalogue 3. 1994. [2], 30 pp. (plus wrappers, in 2 variant designs), with 4 pp. supplement of original drawings, 226 items in all.

Edward Ardizzone: Drawings and Paintings. Michael Parkin Gallery. 15 October–1 November 1991. *69 items including watercolours, illustrations and prints.*

Edward Ardizzone. Sally Hunter Fine Art. 30 November–20 December 1994. *116 items, with nos 78–114 being originals or proofs of illustrations.*

Running Away to Sea: Work by Edward Ardizzone ... (1900–1979). Camberwell College of Arts. 26 October–10 November 1999. *A three-fold leaflet is the main record of this important exhibition, organized by Nicholas Ardizzone and Francis Tinsley: 'the first of a number of events ... to celebrate the centenary of E.A.'s birth'. Alongside an extensive display bringing out the relationship between E.A.'s original drawings and paintings and their graphic reproduction there was the first public exhibition of his magnificent murals commissioned for the First Class nursery of the P & O ship* Canberra.

Edward Ardizzone ... A Centenary Exhibition: Painting, Sculpture, Illustrations, Drawings, Watercolours and Prints. Intro. by Nicholas Ardizzone. Wolseley Fine Arts. 2–26 February 2000. *Nicholas Ardizzone's book* Edward Ardizzone's World *also served as a guide to an exhibition of prints that travelled to many venues 2000–2002.*

Nicholas Ardizzone. *Edward Ardizzone RA 1900–1979: a Centenary Celebration.* Introduction by Timothy Wilson, with a memoir by Christianna Clemence. Oxford: Ashmolean Museum, 2000. *48 items. The exhibition ran from 19 September to 19 November 2000.*

Ardizzoddities. Harrogate, 28 October 2000. *12 annotated items. Produced by the Provincial Booksellers Fairs Association and the Children's Book History Society for a book fair.*

III: BOOKS AND ARTICLES RELATING, WITH VARYING DIRECTNESS, TO E.A.'S WORK

Brian Alderson. *Edward Ardizzone: a Preliminary Hand-list of his Illustrated Books 1929–1970.* Published as an offprint from *The Private Library.* Second series, vol. 5, no. 1, Spring 1972. Refered to here as the '*Hand-list*'.

Brian Alderson. *Sing a Song for Sixpence: the English Picture-Book Tradition and Randolph Caldecott.* Cambridge University Press and the British Library, 1986.

Nicholas Ardizzone. *Edward Ardizzone's World: the Etchings and Lithographs: an Introduction and Catalogue Raisonné*. Introduction by Christopher White, preface by Paul Coldwell. Unicorn Press and Wolseley Fine Arts, 2000. *The list of numbered prints has been referred to here with 'NAP' numbers.*

Michael Ayrton. The Modern 'Phiz'. *The Strand Magazine*. Vol. 113, nos 677–678, May–June 1947, pp. 78–83. *In the series 'Uncommon People Pictured by Osbert Lancaster'. See item D2 above.*

Edward Booth-Clibborn. *My Father and Edward Ardizzone: a Lasting Friendship*. Illus. with Ardizzone Christmas cards. Patrick Hardy Books, 1983.

Aidan Chambers. Ardizzone at Seventy. *T.E.S. Review*. 16 October 1970, p. 19. *One of the first of a group of newspaper and journal articles celebrating the artist's seventieth birthday and also noticing publication of* The Young Ardizzone. *Other articles include:*
   Philip Oakes. The Lively Art of Ardizzone. *The Sunday Times*. 28 June 1970.
   Pooter [Alex Hamilton]. *The Times*. 15 October 1970.
   Nicholas Tucker. *Children's Literature in Education*. No. 3, November 1970, pp. 21–29.
   Marcus Crouch. *T.L.S.* 11 December 1970, pp. 1446–1447.

Christianna Clemence. A Memoir of My Father. *Ardizzone Catalogue 2*. Leamington Spa: Nial Devitt Books, 1993, pp. iii–iv. *See p. 281. A different account from that published in the Ashmolean* Centenary Celebration *(see p. 282).*

Derek Clifford. Edward Ardizzone C.B.E., R.A. *The Old Water-Colour Society's Club*. 55th annual vol., ed. by Adrian Bury. London: The Bankside Gallery, 1980, pp. 19–20.

Anne Commire (ed.). *Something About the Author: Facts and Pictures about Authors and Illustrators of Books for Young People*. Vol. 1. Detroit: Gale Research, 1973. *An on-going series. This first volume contained an entry on E.A. on pp. 10–12 and his complimentary copy had a manuscript note with it from the editor: 'Great honor! You are the first one in the whole thing'. Later the piece was expanded for a fuller article in vol. 28, pp. 25–38. Gale Research specialize in multivolume compendia of this kind and E.A. also features in the series excerpting reviews:* Children's Literature Review. *Vol. 3, 1978, pp. 1–9.*

John Dreyfus. The Curwen Press Collection in Cambridge University Library. *Matrix*. No. 5, Winter 1985, pp. 23–32. *With 29 pages of plates and explanations and an 8-page inset of types and borders.*

John Dreyfus. The Early Years of the Double Crown Club 1929–1949. *Matrix*. No. 6, Winter 1986, pp. 38–49. *With 14 pages of inset plates and explanations.*

John Dreyfus. *A History of the Nonesuch Press.* With a 'Descriptive Catalogue' by David McKitterick *et al.* Nonesuch Press, 1981.

Peter Eads. *H. E. Bates: a Bibliograhical* [sic] *Study.* Winchester: St Paul's Bibliographies, 1990.

Pat Gilmour. *Artists at Curwen: a Celebration of the Gift of Artists' Prints from the Curwen Studio.* Tate Gallery, 1977.

Hand-list *see* Alderson.

Denis Hart. Life in a Frame, Character in a Line. *The Daily Telegraph Magazine.* No. 612, 3 September 1976.

Charles Hennessy. Recent Graphic Work by Edward Ardizzone. *Image.* Spring 1951, pp. 45–64.

Fred H. Higginson. *A Bibliography of the Writings of Robert Graves.* 2nd ed. revised by W.P. Williams. Winchester: Saint Paul's Bibliographies, 1987.

Edward Hodnett. *Five Centuries of English Book Illustration.* Scolar Press, 1988. *E.A. is discussed on pp. 240–243 in an article which, unusually, gives critical attention to his work on 'classic' texts rather than on children's books.*

Grace Hogarth. The Artist and his Editor. *Illustrators of Children's Books 1957–1966.* Pp. 36–53 (see Mahony below).

Grace Hogarth. Children's Publishing in the 1930s: Memoirs of an American in London. *Signal.* No. 61, January 1990, pp. 51–63.

Grace Hogarth. Remembering Eleanor Farjeon. *Signal.* No. 35, May 1981, pp. 76–81.

June Hopper. Edward Ardizzone. *Book and Magazine Collector.* No. 137, August 1995, pp. 34–48. *A so-called bibliography and price-guide of dubious accuracy.*

Alan Horne. *The Dictionary of 20th Century British Book Illustrators.* Woodbridge: Antique Collectors Club, 1994, pp. 75–76.

Robin Jacques. *Illustrators at Work.* Studio Books, 1963. (A Studio Handbook). *Practicalities of black-and-white work, with a statement by E.A. on his methods (pp. 32–33), reprinted here in Appendix II.*

Lynton Lamb. *Drawing for Illustration.* Oxford University Press, 1962.

John Lewis. *A Handbook of Type and Illustration: with Notes on Certain Graphic Processes* ... Faber & Faber, 1956. *E.A. is discussed under the rubrics 'Line Drawing' (pp. 67–72) and 'Water-Colour Drawing' (pp. 109–112). For reproductions of his three stages of drawing see pp. 97–98.*

Bertha E. Mahony *et al. Illustrators of Children's Books 1744–1945.* Boston: The Horn Book, Inc., 1947. *Essays, followed by 'brief biographies of living illustrators' and bibliographies of their works. Ten-year supplements were published: (a) 1946–1956 compiled by Bertha Mahony Miller et al.; (b) 1957–1966 compiled by Lee Kingman et al.; (c) 1967–1976 compiled by Lee Kingman, Grace Allen Hogarth and Harriet Quimby, with a cumulative index to all the vols.*

NAP *see* Nicholas Ardizzone.

Paul W. Nash. *Folio 50: a Bibliography of The Folio Society 1947–1996* ... Folio Press and the British Library, 1997.

J. M. Richards. Edward Ardizzone. *Signature.* No. 14, May 1940, pp. 22–28.

James Reeves. Edward Ardizzone. *Twentieth Century Children's Writers.* Ed. by D. L. Kirkpatrick. Macmillan, 1978. *A short encomium, retained in later revised editions of this reference book.*

Maurice Richards. S.I.A. Profile: Edward Ardizzone *S.I.A. Journal* [Society of Industrial Artists]. No. 82, December 1959, p. 4.

John Ryder. *Artists of a Certain Line: a Selection of Illustrators for Children's Books.* Bodley Head, 1960. *E.A. is noted on pp. 44–45.*

Maurice Sendak. *Caldecott & Co.: Notes on Books and Pictures*. New York: Farrar, Straus and Giroux (Michael di Capua Books); London: The Bodley Head, 1988. *Notes on E.A. reprinted from reviews on pp. 119–121 and 133–137.*

Oliver Simon. *Printer and Playground: an Autobiography*. Faber & Faber, 1956. *Reproduces an illustrated letter by E.A. as an 'epilogue'. The volume includes an index to* Signature *1935–1940.*

Judy Taylor (ed.). *Edward Ardizzone: Sketches for Friends*. John Murray, 2000. *A selection drawn from many of his treasured illustrated letters, including some of the 'Snodgrass correspondence'. A translation into Japanese by Kimoko Abe was published in Tokyo by Koguma Publishing in 2001.*

R. D. Usherwood. *Drawing for Radio Times*. Bodley Head, 1961. *Shortish notes on 48 illustrators who worked for the author who was Art Editor from 1950 to 1960. E.A. is featured (mostly by pictures) on pp. 12–15.*

Marina Vaizey. The Enduring Art of Edward Ardizzone. *The Idler: an Entertainment*. Vol. 2, no. 1, [1967?], pp. 1–2. *See item C44 above.*

John Verney. Meeting Captain Ardizzone. *The Compleat Imbiber*. No. 3, 1960, pp. 151–158. *Reprinted in* A John Verney Collection. *Alistair Press, 1989.*

Antony White. Personal Memories of Edward Ardizzone. *The Ashmolean*. No. 38, Spring 2000, pp. 18–21. *Preceding the centenary exhibition that was held at the Museum in Oxford from 19 September–19 November 2000 (see section II above for the catalogue).*

Colin White. The Bookplates of Edward Ardizzone. *The Bookplate Journal*. Vol. 14, no. 1, March 1996, pp. 10–28.

Gabriel White. *Edward Ardizzone: Artist and Illustrator*. Bodley Head, 1979. *A picture postcard of a restaurant scene taken from the book was issued by the publishers at the time of publication. At the book's launch at Robin Johnson's Illustrators Art Gallery (item C50 above) Gabriel White made a memorial speech for the artist who had died a week earlier. This was reprinted in* Signal *(no. 31, January 1980, pp. 8–10) and is reprinted here as Appendix V.*

INDEX

The following index includes the names of all the authors, editors, translators, publishers, printers and others involved with the books and ephemera described in this bibliography (with the natural exception of E.A. himself). The titles of books, periodicals and series are also included, along with the names of the categories used in section C (and to a lesser degree throughout the bibliography) and any significant names mentioned in the notes to each entry. Titles are given in *italic* type, with the omission of initial articles. References to item numbers are in **bold** type; all other references are to page numbers, those in *italics* being to illustrations and facsimiles.

ADDENDA

60 *Sugar for the Horse.*

1957 PAPERBACK EDITION: Penguin Books. 120 pp. Not seen.

1959 COUNTRY BOOK CLUB EDITION: London: Country Book Club. Not seen.

114 *Three Tall Tales.*

MS ARTWORK: Nial Devitt Books Cat. 53/1 includes the pen drawings for six spreads on each of which E.A. has (unusually) inscribed the whole of Reeves's text, presumably to assist him in visualising the layout.

Vignette from *The Idler* (1966 item C22)